Pricing in Big Business — A Case
Approach   A D Kaplan
          Joel Dirlam
R into K   Robert F Lanzilotti.

see p 83.
  p 85 + very good.

COMPETITION IN THE ALUMINUM INDUSTRY

1945 – 1958

This is the sixth in a series of studies on competition and monopoly in American industry financed by a grant from the Merrill Foundation for the Advancement of Financial Knowledge. The series has been planned to include a number of studies focusing on the effectiveness of competition in particular industrial markets accompanied by certain investigations into the effect on competition of various elements of market structure and business practice common to many industries. Although each volume is an independent study representing only the views of its author, all are expected to contribute to the central objective of the whole project: an evaluation of monopoly policy in the United States.

COMPETITION IN THE ALUMINUM INDUSTRY

1945–1958

Merton J. Peck

HARVARD UNIVERSITY PRESS

Cambridge, Massachusetts

1961

PREFACE

The aluminum industry occupies an important place in the teaching of both industrial organization and antitrust law. Its importance in these respects is due primarily to the existence of Donald Wallace's *Market Control in the Aluminum Industry* (1937), which is the model for subsequent studies by economists of competition in various industries, and to the opinions of Judges Hand and Knox, which are landmarks in the development of antitrust law. Yet examination of the aluminum industry has stopped short of considering the economic results that these decisions helped bring about. This volume is intended to fill the gap by describing the nature of competition in the postwar aluminum industry. The changes in the structure of the industry were brought about not only through formal antitrust litigation but also through acts of administrative agencies and investigations by Congressional committees. Indeed, we shall argue that the "informal antitrust" represented by nonjudicial action has had a greater economic effect than have the decisions of the courts.

The aluminum industry is frequently thought of as consisting only of the big primary producers, Alcoa, Reynolds, and Kaiser. In fact, however, the industry also includes other types of firms: the independent fabricators, distributors, and producers of secondary (scrap) aluminum. This study includes an examination of all these types of firms. The emphasis is on the relation between the primary producers and the less well-known sectors of the industry, for it is largely the existence of the primary producers that determines the pattern of competition and that creates the difficult questions of public policy.

This study is limited to the years 1945 to 1958. Current events are ill-suited for a book format, and Congressional investigations, the source of much of the data, lag behind the latest happenings. As a result, this study does not discuss the recovery from the 1958 period of slack demand, the efforts of Reynolds Metals to obtain control of the British Aluminium Company, Ltd.,[1] or the antitrust action brought in 1959 against the Aluminum Company of America, a civil complaint under Section 7 of the Clayton Act to prevent Alcoa's acquisition of an independent fabricator.[2]

As with most studies in industrial organization at Harvard, this volume benefited from the guidance of Professor Edward S. Mason. The first version was undertaken as a doctoral thesis under his direction. The subsequent revision benefited extensively from the editorial and substantive comments of Professor Carl Kaysen, also of Harvard. To them my debt is considerable.

The manuscript was typed by Sybil Williamson, Helen Gower, Barbara Johnson, Deborah Berkman, and Janice Cronk. I thank them here for executing this sometimes frustrating task.

MERTON J. PECK

August 1960

[1] "How Reynolds Brought Off Its British Coup," *Fortune,* 59:112 (June 1959), This English firm is not to be confused with Aluminium Limited, in Canada.
[2] *Antitrust Bulletin,* 5:101 (January–February 1960).

CONTENTS

OLDE STYLE

CONTENTS

TABLES

FIGURES

COMPETITION IN THE ALUMINUM INDUSTRY

1945 – 1958

I

INTRODUCTION

THE aluminum industry is distinguished by a lengthy history of government actions which transformed a single-seller monopoly into its present oligopolistic structure.[1] Yet the issue of competition in the aluminum industry is not settled. Some argue that these government actions have hindered the realization of the efficiencies of size and diminished the incentives for expansion. Others argue that effective competition in the aluminum industry has yet to be achieved.

The latter view appears to have predominated in the policies of government agencies in such matters as stockpiling, tax amortization, and materials controls, and in the tenor of various Congressional investigations. In this respect, the aluminum industry is in the limbo position peculiar to such industries as automobiles and steel. It is considered as neither sufficiently monopolistic for antitrust action nor sufficiently competitive for a hands-off policy to be workable. Recent political practice may have added a new form of public control for such industries — regulation through public opinion, the vague consequences of Congressional displeasure, and the policies of miscellaneous executive agencies.[2]

In a society conditioned to a government of laws, such "informal antitrust" is viewed with uneasiness. This study attempts to answer,

[1] The single-seller period is the subject of Donald Wallace's classic industry study, *Market Control in the Aluminum Industry* (Cambridge: Harvard University Press, 1937).

[2] J. K. Galbraith, *American Capitalism: The Concept of Countervailing Power* (Boston: Houghton Mifflin, 1952), suggests that the market power of the buyers serves to offset or check the power of the sellers. Adolf Berle, *The 20th Century Capitalist Revolution* (New York: Harcourt, Brace, 1954), offers a corporate morality to restrain the market power position of the corporations. Each of these views can be considered as attempts to provide a public policy for these intermediate cases of market power. Similarly, the current investigations into "administered prices" by the Senate Subcommittee on Monopoly can be viewed as an effort to establish policy for these intermediate cases of market power.

at least for the aluminum industry, the following questions. Is the industry already sufficiently competitive that laissez-faire is the proper policy? Or is this a real-life example of the dilemma often stated in the literature of antitrust — a situation in which the costs of further antitrust action are excessive and yet the industry is not sufficiently competitive by the standards implicit in the Sherman Act? If so, what are the proper public policies?

Obviously these questions involve in large part political philosophy. Economic analysis, which is the focus of this study, should, however, at least clarify the costs and consequences of the various alternatives.

These are the larger issues of public policy. The aluminum industry also exemplifies a narrower issue of public policy, the conflict between small and big business over the extent of vertical integration. All the primary producers are integrated forward into the fabrication of such products as sheet, foil, and rod and bar. The primary producers supply ingot to the nonintegrated fabricators of these same products, so that the primary producers are in competition with their customers. Not unexpectedly, such arrangements create friction between the customers and their supplier-competitors. Economic analysis here should identify the sources of conflicts and the alternatives in their resolution.

The Theoretical Structure of the Investigation

The underlying theoretical framework of this study is the familiar approach of distinguishing between market structure and market behavior. Market structure includes the following factors:[3] (1) the number and size distribution of both the sellers and the buyers; (2) the characteristics of demand, including not only the price elasticity, but the type of consumers and products; (3) the characteristics of costs; (4) the rate and direction of change in sciences underlying the technology of the industry; (5) the geographical pattern of demand and supply; (6) the legal setting — and in particular, the patent system, government regulation, and taxation; (7) the conditions for the entry of new firms; and (8) the internal organization of the sellers and buyers.

[3] For a discussion of the market structure–market behavior approach see Edward S. Mason, "Price and Production Policies of Large-Scale Enterprise, *American Economic Review* 29:61–74 (Supplement, March 1939); and "The Current State of the Monopoly Problem," *Harvard Law Review* 62:1265–1285 (June 1949).

These factors of market structure are assumed to interact to produce a pattern of market behavior consisting of the following five elements: (1) the level and structure of prices in relation to costs; (2) the cyclical variation of output; (3) the degree of product differentiation; (4) the rate of technological change; and (5) the rate of growth of new capacity in relation to the rate of demand. This formulation is intended to serve the public policy requirement for an economic analysis that provides a set of conditional forecasts about how market behavior can be altered through variations in the market structure by government action.

The organization of this study follows in crude fashion this theoretical approach. Chapter II, in summarizing the historical background of the antitrust litigation, states the number and size distribution of the sellers. Similarly, Chapter III examines the structural factors created by the nature of the demand for aluminum. But, from that point on, the distinction between structure and behavior breaks down. In discussing pricing, output variation, marketing, entry, investment, and technological change, the subjects of Chapters IV to XI, the structural and behavioral factors become intermixed. In part this is a consequence of our empirical evidence which often bears simultaneously on both questions of structure and behavior. In part this is because the theory does not articulate a sharp distinction between the two, particularly for the dynamic process in which the behavior of one period shapes the structure of the next period.

At a more abstract level, the confusions between market structure and behavior may arise because the components of a market structure listed above are excessive. It can be shown that all these elements of a market structure are derived from three factors: the technology, the preferences of consumers, and the preferences of the entrepreneurs.[4] Economists have devoted considerable effort to the development of the model of pure competition from simple assumptions about the nature of these three factors. Yet the same approach to oligopoly has failed, for apparently similar technologies and preferences appear to yield highly diverse patterns of market behavior. Consequently, the definition of market structure has been enlarged to include various institutional factors. Hence, Mason's

---

[4] See William Fellner, *Competition Among the Few* (New York: Knopf, 1949), ch. I.

oft-quoted remark, "The theory of oligopoly has aptly been described as a ticket of admission to institutional economics."[5]

The analysis here supports in part the older neoclassical position, for much of the market behavior of the aluminum industry can be explained by the demand and the cost characteristics alone. But an after-the-fact explanation is hardly a prediction, and these demand and cost conditions could have generated numerous patterns of market behavior. Other crucial determinants of market behavior are the attitudes of the sellers towards uncertainty and long-run profit-maximization, the peculiar historical circumstances creating the postwar aluminum industry, and the continuing government policies towards the industry. These other factors cannot be fully incorporated into systematic models.[6]

The empirical materials for the study are drawn largely from public documents. These provide extremely detailed information on the aluminum industry, for few other industries have had as many or as extensive judicial and Congressional investigations. Such documents contain extensive testimony by the executives of the primary producers, the owners of independent fabricating firms and the officials of government agencies. Even though such evidence is limited by the public relations prudence of the witnesses, as well as its courtroom setting, it offers some of the advantages afforded by interview. Complete access to the records of the firms involved obviously would have been preferable and might have permitted the substitution of evidence for conjecture in many parts of this study.[7]

---

[5] Mason, "Price and Production Policies," pp. 64–65. Dean Mason goes on to say, "It is to be regretted more theorists have not availed themselves of this privilege."

[6] Perhaps the theoretical solution lies along lines suggested by the newer models of economic development. The problems in the analysis of economic development are analogous to those of market organization. The basic factors of neoclassical economics, natural resources, technical knowledge, and population are insufficient to explain or predict the patterns of economic development even at the abstract level customary in economics, just as the narrow models of price theory fail to explain and predict market behavior. Newer models of economic development attempt to include time and history explicitly, and since the current industry studies suggest that unique historical events can be built into the structure of an industry, these development models may have interesting possibilities for price theory. Yet such economic dynamics are a long way from operationalism even at the aggregate level. It may then be even more premature to apply such an approach to the problems of markets where the data to specify parameters are even more inaccessible.

[7] It is by no means obvious that access to the executives through interviews will be free from public relation prudence, or that in terms of publishable materials much will be made available that is not in the public domain.

THE HISTORICAL BACKGROUND OF THE INDUSTRY

J UDGE Learned Hand's 1945 opinion found the Aluminum Company of America guilty of monopolization and in so doing enunciated what was to some commentators a "new" Sherman Act. The general implications of this opinion have been extensively discussed elsewhere. The emphasis here is upon the economic effects of Hand's decision and of subsequent government actions for the American aluminum industry. As a background for such a study, this chapter recounts briefly the history of the antitrust litigation and the character of the technology of the industry.[1]

The Technology and Terminology of the Aluminum Industry[2]

The aluminum industry can be divided into the five stages of production portrayed in Fig. 1. Each stage involves a distinct technology and a separate geographical location so that the industry is

[1] This history is more fully discussed in the opinions of Judge Hand, United States v. Aluminum Company of America, 148 F. 2nd, 416 (2d cir. 1945), and Judge Knox, United States v. Aluminum Company of America, 91 F. Supp. 333 (S.D.N.Y., 1950) and in Harold Stein, "The Disposal of Aluminum Plants," in Harold Stein, ed., *Public Administration and Policy Development* (New York: Harcourt, Brace, 1952). For a detailed prewar history, see Donald Wallace, *Market Control in the Aluminum Industry* (Cambridge: Harvard University Press, 1937). This study is much in debt to Professor Wallace's work. The model of oligopoly developed in this book is an extension of Wallace's views, and the investigation of such topics as economies of scale, the nature of demand, and the difference between monopoly and oligopoly confirms, in large part, Wallace's observations.

[2] This description of the aluminum industry is based upon chapters IV, V, and VI in U. S. Business and Defense Services Administration, *Aluminum: Material Survey* (Washington, 1956).

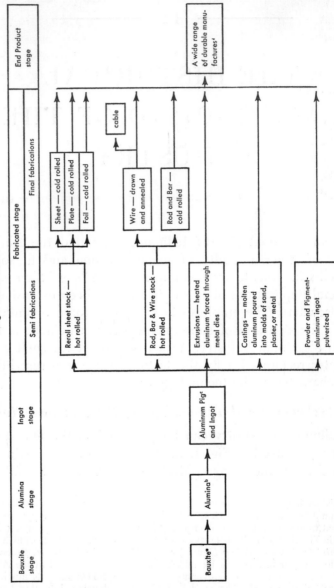

FIGURE I

THE PRODUCTION PROCESSES IN THE ALUMINUM INDUSTRY

Stages of Production

a Bauxite ore — usually open strip mined from a large range of alumina-bearing ores.
b Alumina — extracted from bauxite ores by various chemical processes.
c Aluminum pig and ingot — reduced from alumina by an electrolytic process which separates the oxygen and aluminum composing alumina. Aluminum ingot is further treated while molten to reduce impurities, whereas this step is omitted for aluminum pig. Aluminum is alloyed with lead, chromium, boron, and other metals. The physical characteristics of almost every existing metal can be duplicated by one of the 200 alloys in commercial use.
d Examples are building materials, automobile and aircraft components, and household appliances.

defined for the most part by its ownership pattern rather than by its technology. The bauxite is mined largely in the Caribbean area and is processed into alumina near the Gulf Coast ports, the alumina is reduced to aluminum ingot at plants near the cheap hydropower of the Northwest and Tennessee Valley, and the ingot is fabricated near the eastern markets. Even though this geographical pattern is changing, the location of alumina, aluminum, and fabricating plants at the same site, as in the new facilities in the Ohio valley, does not mean a physical integration of the various stages of production.

The technologies of the first three stages — bauxite mining, alumina manufacture, and aluminum reduction — are unique to the aluminum industry and the several vertically integrated producers of aluminum ingot (the primary producers) are the only suppliers. In contrast, the technologies in fabrication are similar to those for other metals. The vertically integrated facilities of the primary producers account for three quarters of the fabricated output. Independent fabricators, who buy their ingot from the primary producers, account for the remainder.

There are three further complications. First, sheet, rod, and bar require two distinct substages of production: hot rolling to produce reroll stock and cold rolling to produce the finished fabrication. Independent fabricators often buy semifabrications from the primary producers for final fabrication. Extrusions and castings have but one clearly defined stage in fabrication and consequently the independent fabricators buy aluminum ingot.

Second, foil and aluminum cable are customarily classified as fabricated products, even though they require no further manufacturing before their final use. In contrast, the other fabrications are bought by a diverse group of manufacturers for incorporation into almost every type of durable product. (This final product is usually termed an end-product.) The primary aluminum producers manufacture end-products, but only 15 percent of the primary aluminum output is so consumed.

Third, secondary or scrap aluminum is produced by approximately fifty smelters who buy both new scrap (the clippings, chips, and borings generated in end-product manufacture and in fabrication) and old scrap (discarded aluminum aircraft components, pots and pans, and so forth) for smelting. In the postwar period, secondary aluminum output was approximately one-quarter of the aluminum output made from bauxite (that is, primary aluminum). Secondary aluminum is the near technical equivalent of primary aluminum for many applications, so that it is a close but inferior substitute for primary aluminum.

The Transition from Monopoly to Oligopoly

Until 1940, the Aluminum Company of America (Alcoa) was the sole American producer of primary aluminum.[3] The company was the founder of the aluminum industry, holding the patents of Arthur Hall, the inventor of a commercially feasible electrolytic process for converting alumina into aluminum. After a brief period as the Pittsburgh Reduction Company, the company acquired its present name as well as the Mellon family as a principal stockholder. By 1909, when the Hall patent expired, aluminum had developed from material for costume jewelry to an industrial metal for cooking utensils, transmission cable, and various automotive parts. During World War I there was a 50 percent expansion in reduction capacity, for lightweight aluminum was uniquely suited for the manufacture of aircraft engines. The demand for aluminum as well as the capacity of the industry continued to increase throughout the 1920's at an annual rate of about 10 percent. The depression created a hiatus in the growth of the industry, but beginning in 1938 aluminum consumption resumed its increase, largely because of the expansion of the production of military aircraft.

During the early years there were abortive attempts to compete with Alcoa. The Southern Aluminum Company, formed in 1912 by French aluminum interests, began the construction of a hydropower plant and a reduction plant in North Carolina. World War I prevented the French promoters from obtaining additional capital at home and in 1915 these plants, still unfinished, were sold to Alcoa. In the early 1920's the Uihlein family, owners of the prohibition-bound Schlitz Brewing Company, acquired mining rights for bauxite deposits in the Guianas with the intention of producing aluminum. These rights were later sold to Alcoa. Alcoa also acquired the facilities of a third would-be entrant, J. B. Duke of tobacco-fortune fame. In 1920 he and Sir William Price, an English financier, acquired power sites in Canada for the production of nitrogen. Shortly thereafter, George Haskell, president of the Bausch Machine Tool Company, an independent die caster of aluminum, approached Mr. Duke with the proposition that this hydropower

[3] This section is based largely upon Wallace, *Aluminum Industry*.

capacity be used to produce aluminum. Mr. Duke was sufficiently interested to spend $180,000 on the exploration for bauxite and to incorporate the Quebec Aluminum Company. In 1922 Alcoa approached Duke with an offer to buy the electric power for aluminum production. This was initially declined, but two years later a representative of Mr. Duke contacted Alcoa to see if the offer were still open. In the negotiations which followed, Mr. Duke exchanged his unfinished power facilities for a substantial block of Alcoa stock.

From 1925 to 1928 Alcoa completed these power plants and constructed considerable reduction capacity in Canada. These properties, together with Alcoa holdings in Europe, were assigned to Aluminium Limited (commonly called Limited), a new company created through the distribution of stock to Alcoa shareholders. Henceforth, these two companies were legally independent, although the same eleven stock holders held about half the common stock in each company until the remedy in the antitrust case.

In 1937 the Department of Justice filed a complaint charging Alcoa with monopolization. In the renewed antitrust activity of the Thurman Arnold era, Alcoa was a likely candidate for antitrust prosecution. There were sufficient practices of doubtful legality for a conventional Sherman Act case, while proceeding against the sole producers in a major industry afforded the possibility of a reversal of the U. S. Steel dictum that size alone was no offense.

In 1940 District Judge Caffery acquitted Alcoa of all charges.[4] He found the alleged competitive abuses involved events long past or unsubstantiated by the record. Furthermore, he rejected the government argument "that the power to fix prices and keep others out of the market irrespective of intent is monopolization" with the observation that "as far as I can discover, the Supreme Court had never given the slightest support to such an interpretation." [5]

The Supreme Court was soon to define monopolization in largely this way, that is, as the power to fix prices and the power to exclude. This pronouncement, however, did not come initially from the Supreme Court itself. The Supreme Court could not muster a quorum for the Alcoa case for several Justices disqualified themselves because of a previous connection with the litigation, a by-product of President Roosevelt's practice of promoting attorney generals to the

[4] United States v. The Aluminum Company of America, 44 F. Supp. 97 (S.D.N.Y., 1940).
[5] Id. at 152.

Supreme Court. At its next session, Congress passed legislation authorizing the Circuit Court of Appeals in whose jurisdiction the case originated to act as the Supreme Court whenever the Supreme Court lacked a quorum. That the Second Circuit Court of Appeals acted as the Supreme Court does not jeopardize the authority of the Alcoa opinion, for the Supreme Court has subsequently quoted the Circuit Court's opinion as a precedent.

The opinion of the Circuit Court, as set forth by Judge Hand in 1945, defined the offense of monopolization as the power to exclude and the power to fix prices.[6] Either of these powers exercised through contracts between firms had long been illegal per se. According to Judge Hand: "It would be absurd to condemn such contracts unconditionally and not extend the condemnation to monopolies; for such contracts are only steps towards that entire control monopoly confers, they are really partial monopolies." [7]

Intent, previously an important element of monopolization, need no longer be shown by the defendant's overt actions in such matters as price cutting or the buying out of competitors. Instead, it was argued that "no monopolist monopolizes unconsciously of what he is doing." Only if a monopoly were thrust upon a firm would it be legal and the "thrust upon" exception was limited to monopolies created either by the demise of competitors through events unconnected with the behavior of the monopolist, or through the existence of economies of scale permitting only one efficient firm in the industry. Alcoa, according to Judge Hand, fitted neither of these narrow exceptions.

Alcoa, as the sole domestic producer of primary aluminum ingot, obviously had considerable power over the price of aluminum ingot. Imports were the only other source for primary aluminum, and these were but 10 percent of the total consumption of primary aluminum. Thus Alcoa controlled 90 percent of the output of primary aluminum. In a much-quoted dictum, Judge Hand said, "That percentage [90 percent] is enough to constitute a monpoly; it is doubtful whether sixty or sixty-four percent would be enough; certainly thirty-three percent is not." [8]

However, secondary aluminum was a technically adequate substitute for primary ingot, and if this metal were included as part of

[6] 148 F. 2nd, 416.
[7] Id. at 445.
[8] Id. at 424.

the market, Alcoa's share became close to two-thirds of the market. Judge Hand argued that, since secondary (scrap) aluminum could only be made from the primary metal, Alcoa, through its control of the primary aluminum, could also control the supply of the secondary. Such an argument presupposes a mode of long-range business planning that seldom occurs in business. It further assumes that Alcoa could control the time span of obsolescence, even though this is the result of numerous individual decisions on scrappage. Still, secondary aluminum, despite its technical similarity, is not an adequate economic substitute for primary aluminum. Its supply is extremely inelastic (at some point supply does not increase with further price increases). Therefore, increases in the supply of secondary metal are not forthcoming in periods of high demand to limit increases in the price of primary aluminum. Furthermore, the primary producers are sufficiently sizable purchasers of secondary aluminum so that their own purchasing activities are an important determinant of the current price of secondary aluminum.

Judge Hand also found that Alcoa had created a price squeeze for the independent sheet fabricators through lowering its list price of aluminum sheet while holding constant its list price of ingot. This narrowed the margin between the two prices to less than the cost of fabrication. Since the independent fabricators had to meet Alcoa's sheet price while paying Alcoa's ingot price, it was difficult for them to compete with Alcoa. The District Court was instructed to enjoin such a practice.

But Judge Hand ordered any major remedy postponed until the end of the war, largely because of changes in the industry since the commencement of the litigation. In 1942 the government had begun the construction of aluminum capacity to support defense requirements for 50,000 planes a year. By 1944 these government plants, owned by the Defense Plant Corporation, a subsidiary of the Reconstruction Finance Corporation, constituted approximately one-half of the nation's reduction capacity. Alcoa operated four-fifths of the government's capacity under a management contract, with the remainder divided between the Olin Corporation and the Reynolds Metals Company. The year prior to Judge Hand's decision, Congress had passed the Surplus Property Act directing the sale of these and other government plants so as "to discourage monopolistic practices." With half the capacity of the industry subject to the disposal program, the scope of the judicial remedy depended upon the outcome of the distribution of the government plants.

The establishment of competitors to Alcoa through the sale of government facilities involved several difficulties. Alcoa argued that it should participate in the disposal program in view of its wartime service, its established record of efficiency, and the price it could offer the government for these plants. One of the two plans considered by the Surplus Property Board, the agency created to carry out the Surplus Property Act, was that proposed by businessman Gordon W. Reed. This plan envisaged the disposal of half of the government's capacity to Alcoa so that Alcoa would have three-quarters of the industry's capacity. Such a plan was a literal interpretation of Hand's dictum that in establishing the power to control price "it is doubtful whether sixty per cent [of the market] would be enough," and Reed argued that even reducing Alcoa's share from 90 percent to 75 percent would create competition. The alternative plan, that of government economist Sam Moment, envisaged the creation of two new primary producers and the exclusion of Alcoa from the disposal program.[9]

Despite its conviction as a monopolist, Alcoa had a strong bargaining position for its claim on a share of the government facilities. Alcoa held leases on the government plants extending until 1947 or 1948, and it held several patents necessary for their operation. There was local Congressional pressure to operate the plants without interruption in order to insure continuous employment, an objective best accomplished by their sale to Alcoa, the present operator. Finally, there was a scarcity of other qualified applicants. Even Reynolds, the other leading contender for the plants, initially asked for a guarantee by the government to purchase any unsold aluminum from these plants during the first years of their operation. Some Congressmen strongly supported Alcoa's objection to any subsidization of new producers.

Stuart Symington, then the administrator of the Surplus Property Board, was the central figure in this dispute. After some vacillation, he decided to exclude Alcoa from the disposal program. Shortly thereafter, the Surplus Property Board cancelled Alcoa's leases under a provision in the management contract permitting cancellation whenever production was less than 40 percent of the capacity. Such cancellation was a calculated risk since the provision's wording

[9] The two programs are described in Stein, "Aluminum Plants," p. 315.

was ambiguous, but Alcoa, perhaps from public relations considerations, did not contest the issue in the courts.[10] The patent issue was resolved by a negotiated settlement in which Alcoa offered licenses at nominal royalties in return for the recognition of the validity of its patent rights.[11]

These actions cleared the way for the creation of new firms. There were, however, only two government-owned alumina plants, which obviously limited the number of new alumina producers to two. It was further decided by the Surplus Property Board that the new entrants should be as vertically integrated as Alcoa, that is, from alumina to fabricating, and as near to Alcoa's size as possible. In this way the new entrants were considered to have the best chance to emerge as effective competitors to Alcoa. There was, of course, the possibility the courts might later direct a vertical or horizontal dissolution of Alcoa, but this event, it was argued, could not be presumed by a disposal agency. Reynolds and Kaiser received leases for alumina, aluminum, and fabricating plants, thus creating a postwar aluminum industry of three vertically integrated primary producers.

In 1947, Alcoa petitioned the District Court for a ruling that Alcoa no longer monopolized the market for primary aluminum. The government moved to dismiss Alcoa's petition. On the appeal of these motions, the Circuit Court directed the District Court to join the issues in an examination of the need for further remedies, whereupon there was a protracted trial before Judge Knox.

On July 6, 1950, Judge Knox delivered his opinion. He held that the divestiture of Alcoa's properties to create a fourth producer, as urged by the government, was not necessary for effective competition.[12] Instead, he ordered the eleven individuals who held the major share of the stock of both Limited and Alcoa to sell their interest in one or the other of the companies, the elimination of the grant-back provision in Alcoa's licenses to Kaiser and Reynolds,

---

[10] It was unclear whether this provision referred to output below 40 percent of the over-all capacity of Alcoa or the capacity of individual plants.

[11] The Government contended that in building patented processes into government plants, Alcoa had given the rights to these processes to the government.

[12] U. S. v. Aluminum Company of America, 91 F. Supp. 333. Alcoa's escape from divestiture has a certain irony. Even with the establishment of Reynolds and Kaiser, Judge Knox underlined "the impressive industrial power of Alcoa." Had Alcoa been successful in its 1945 efforts to be included as a major participant in the disposal program, it would probably have been divested of more than the assets it would have acquired.

and the retention of the Court's jurisdiction over Alcoa for five years in order to determine if Reynolds and Kaiser would emerge as effective competitors. At the end of this time, the government might reopen the issues.

The government did so, asking for judicial jurisdiction over Alcoa for an additional five years, arguing that the price controls, the purchase guarantees, and the material controls which accompanied the Korean War made the years 1950 to 1955 atypical. Hence, the relative success of Reynolds and Kaiser was not indicative of the normal competitive structure of the aluminum industry. There was again an extensive hearing, this time before District Judge Cashin. Delivering his opinion in June 1957, he said the "economic hothouse" of the Korean War favored Alcoa equally with Reynolds and Kaiser so that at least their relative standing should not be termed artificial. He also pointed out that the next five years might be equally atypical and so no more indicative of the so-called "normal" competitive situation. Thus there would be no limit to the court's supervision of the aluminum industry. With these arguments Judge Cashin dismissed the government's petition.[13] Thus ended the Alcoa case, spanning twenty years and ninety-two volumes of testimony and exhibits.

The Ownership and Management of the Primary Aluminum Producers[14]

In an era of wide dispersion of the stock ownership of large corporations and the consequent divorcement of management and ownership, the aluminum industry is atypical in the extent to which the major shareholders are active in the management of the corporations. In the case of Alcoa, the eleven stockholders owning close to a majority of the stock include the families of the original investors and management — the Hunts, the Mellons, and the Davises.[15] Most of these families are still represented on the board of directors. The election of I. W. Wilson as president, the first

[13] United States v. Aluminum Company of America, 153 F. Supp. 132. (S.D.N.Y., 1957).

[14] This section is based upon the articles in the business press, the annual reports of the various companies and The First Boston Corporation, *Aluminum: The Industry and the Four North American Producers* (New York: The First Boston Corporation, 1951).

[15] Judge Knox required these families plus the Dukes to sell their stock in either Limited or Alcoa. Since blocks of stocks are substantial, those sales will tend to create widespread public ownership in the future.

without large ownership interests, perhaps signified the transition to management control which has eventually occurred in most large American firms. Mr. Wilson personified another characteristic of Alcoa's management, an emphasis on internal recruitment, for his service with Alcoa dates back to 1914. The other officers have similarly long records of service.

Aluminium Limited is a Canadian corporation formed from Alcoa properties, as described above. The ownership of the company is at present uncertain, for a substantial block of stock is held by trustees, an outcome of the court order to insure the separate ownership of Limited and Alcoa. These trustees are eventually to sell the stock in the open market. Limited's directors, management, and ownership have been largely American, although in the past few years the company has added an increasing number of British and Canadian executives and directors. Limited, itself, is largely a holding company. A wholly owned subsidiary, Aluminum Company of Canada, owns and operates 97 percent of Limited's ingot reduction capacity, while partially and wholly owned subsidiaries in each of its major markets own and operate the fabricating facilities.

Reynolds Metals, one of two beneficiaries of the disposal of the government plants, was founded by R. S. Reynolds.[16] Mr. Reynolds began his business career in 1903 when he joined his uncle's tobacco firm, the R. J. Reynolds Tobacco Company. In 1912, both uncle and nephew married, and the younger Reynolds decided he wanted a business "of and for his own." [17] After World War I, the R. J. Reynolds Company and the British-American Tobacco Company jointly founded the United States Foil Company for the manufacture of tin foil for use in cigarette packaging. R. S. Reynolds became the company's first president, and in 1926 he bought the stock held by the two tobacco companies and changed the company's name to the Reynolds Metals Company. At about the same time, the product was changed from tin to aluminum foil. The company was highly profitable throughout the 1930's, for cigarette consumption was little affected by the depression, while aluminum foil came to be used in packaging of other products. These profits were used for the expansion of foil capacity and for the acquisition of companies making thermostats, radiators, and ice cream products.

[16] The best account of the origins of Reynolds Metals is Robert Sheehan, "Look at the Reynolds Boys Now," *Fortune,* vol. 48, no. 2: p. 110 (August 1953).
[17] Sheehan, "Reynolds Boys," p. 172.

From 1938 on, the increase in the production of aluminum foil was limited by the shortage of aluminum ingot. In 1939, reportedly as the result of a European trip, Mr. Reynolds proposed the doubling of the domestic aluminum capacity in order to support a greatly enlarged aircraft industry for national defense. The advocacy of an expansion of the aluminum industry brought him in contact with Senator Lister Hill of Alabama, who, in turn, introduced him to officials of the RFC. In 1940, the RFC loaned Reynolds $16,000,000 for the construction of an aluminum-reduction works in Alabama at a site later named Listerhill. After Pearl Harbor, the RFC loaned Reynolds another 36 million dollars to construct a second reduction plant and an aluminum-sheet plant. Reynolds also operated some of the government plants under management contracts and was the first serious contender other than Alcoa for the ownership of the government plants.

Kaiser Metals also originated in the activities of its namesake.[18] Henry J. Kaiser began his business career as a highway contractor and in the 1930's became the general contractor for various federal dams built in the West. Mr. Kaiser expanded his interests to include first a cement plant and, in 1940, one of the largest of the wartime shipbuilding operations. Both these ventures were largely financed by the RFC. Government policy issues were a crucial consideration in the granting of these loans; in the case of the cement plant, the promotion of competition, and in the case of shipbuilding, the fulfilling of defense requirements.

In 1942, Mr. Kaiser founded Permanente Metals (later renamed The Kaiser Aluminum and Chemical Corporation) to operate government-owned magnesium plants under management contracts. These plants were closed after the war. This organization actively sought the ownership of the government aluminum plants shortly after Reynolds had begun its negotiations with the government.

The origins of the two companies have much in common. Both were created by a single individual, with all the daring and aggressiveness of a classic nineteenth-century entrepreneur. As an article in *Fortune* stated, "It is possible mere managers might not have the will and daring to buck Alcoa." Perhaps a peculiar twentieth-century phenomenon, however, is that each man was aided at crucial points in his career by the RFC. Finally, both companies are

[18] Again, *Fortune* provides the best account of Kaiser Metals. See, "The Arrival of Henry Kaiser," *Fortune* vol. 44, no. 1: p. 68 (July 1951).

still owner-controlled. Henry Kaiser is the chairman of the board, and his son is the president of Kaiser Metals. Until his death in 1958, R. S. Reynolds was the board chairman; his eldest son, the president; and the three other sons, vice presidents of Reynolds Metals. Although the stock of both companies is listed on the New York Stock Exchange, the founding families remain the major owners.

There are now three additional primary aluminum producers who entered the industry since 1954. These firms are described in Chapter X.

The Resources of the Primary Producers

The American and Canadian aluminum industry jointly account for two-thirds of the world's aluminum capacity. In 1960 Limited is estimated to have an annual reduction capacity of about 1100 thousand tons compared to 1000 thousand tons for Alcoa, the next largest producer.[19] Since the war, Limited has exported about three-quarters of its ingot output, largely to the United Kingdom, other parts of Western Europe, and the United States.

Limited is apparently also the lowest-cost producer of aluminum in North America. In 1949, Limited's mill cost was 8.66 cents per pound of ingot compared to 10.5 to 11.6 cents for the three American firms.[20] Limited's cost advantage may have declined since then, but the greater availability of good hydropower sites combined with a smaller demand for electricity for other uses means lower costs in Canada than the United States.[21] Limited has concentrated its recent expansion at Kitimat in British Columbia, one of the world's largest hydropower developments. In contrast, the American producers have utilized higher-cost steam-generated power to supply their newer plants. Limited sells largely ingot in the United States, for the high tariff on aluminum fabrications discourages the import of fabricated products.[22]

[19] These estimates are based upon data in Economic Commission for Europe, Steel Committee, *Competition between Steel and Aluminum* (Geneva, 1954), and in [The United States Aluminum Producers], *World Trade and the Aluminum Industry* (New York: United States Aluminum Producers, 1958).

[20] 91 F. Supp. 333 at 375 and Record, United States v. Aluminum Company of America, 91 F. Supp. 333 (S.D.N.Y., 1950), Government Exhibit 233, henceforth cited as *Remedy Record*. Mill cost excludes transportation of the pig, selling expenses, general overhead, and interest on investment, but includes depreciation, transportation of the raw materials, labor, power, and raw materials.

[21] *Modern Metals*, vol. 10, no. 5: p. 38 (June 1954).

[22] The First Boston Corporation, *Aluminum Industry*, p. 59.

Table 1 indicates the distribution of reduction capacity among the American producers. In 1949, Alcoa not only was considerably

TABLE 1. Distribution of aluminum reduction capacity, 1948 and 1958

Company	1948 capacity (thousands of tons)	Percent of total	1958 capacity[a] (thousands of tons)	Percent of total
Alcoa	369	51	1000	35
Reynolds	225	31	701	27
Kaiser	133	18	610	23
Anaconda	0	0	60	3
Harvey	0	0	54	3
Ormet	0	0	180	9
Total	727	100	2605	100

[a] Capacity completed or under construction by mid-1959.

Source: 1948, United States v. Aluminum Company of America, 91 F. Supp. 333 (S.D.N.Y., 1950) at 368; 1958, [The United States Aluminum Producers], *World Trade and the Aluminum Industry* (New York, 1958), pp. 42–43.

larger than Reynolds and Kaiser, but it had approximately a 10 percent cost advantage and considerably greater financial resources. But, just as the relative size of Alcoa is now nearer the other two, Alcoa's cost and financial advantages have also declined. Nevertheless, in terms of all these factors, Alcoa remains the industry's senior citizen.

Alcoa, Reynolds, and Kaiser are among the largest firms in the American economy. In *Fortune's* 1958 directory of the five hundred largest industrial firms as measured by sales, Alcoa ranked forty-sixth, with sales of $753,000,000 and net assets of $1,300,000,000; Reynolds ranked eighty-seventh, with sales of $445,000,000 and assets of $853,000,000; and Kaiser ranked ninety-fifth with sales of $408,000,000 and assets of $754,000,000.[23] Limited is probably larger than Alcoa in terms of total sales, but its accounting data does not fully consolidate the sales of partially owned subsidiaries. The annual report, however, shows assets of $1,200,000,000, the same order of magnitude as Alcoa.[24]

The generosity of the government was an important factor in these companies' ability to achieve this impressive size. Kaiser paid $43,500,000 for government plants with a construction cost of

[23] "The Fortune Directory. The 500 Largest Corporations," *Fortune*, vol. 60, no. 2, part II (August 1959).

[24] Aluminium Limited, *Annual Report*, 1957 (New York, 1958).

$127,000,000 and with an even greater reproduction cost. Of this payment, $3,500,000 was in cash, with the balance as a long-term note. Reynolds fared even better, paying $57,600,000 for plants with an original cost of $174,000,000. Of the purchase price, $3,000,000 was paid in cash.[25] Limited's expansion during World War II was financed largely through a long-term loan from the British Ministry of Supply and through advance payments for aluminum by the RFC.[26] Alcoa did not share so directly in the government aid, but at least through accelerated amortization in World War II, the company doubled its ownership of reduction capacity from 1941 to 1946 and still accumulated $32,000,000 in cash and marketable securities.[27]

The World Aluminum Market and the Domestic Aluminum Industry

The American and the world market, largely that of Western Europe, are two distinct markets with different prices prevailing in each market. Canada represents still a third market. (The prices in these three markets are shown in Table 2.) Yet the American tariff on aluminum ingot is currently only 1.5 cents per pound and the transportation costs are relatively nominal. Hence, there is a limit to the price differences that can exist without creating trans-shipment of metal between these markets. Furthermore, there is an "administrative" linkage in the sense that Limited's timing of price changes for the world market tends to coincide with those announced for Canada. To the extent that the Canadian price moves with the world price (largely based upon the United Kingdom price), then the world price places limits on the price that can be charged in the American market.

For most of the postwar years, however, aluminum has been in sufficiently short supply to permit American producers to take pricing actions independently of the developments in the world market. American exports of primary aluminum have been only 0.5 percent of the total output, and while imports have been 10 to 20 percent of the primary aluminum consumption, over 90 percent

---

[25] Loeb, Carl M., Rhoades and Company, *Aluminum: An Analysis of the Industry in the United States, Aluminum Company of America, Reynolds Metals Company, Kaiser Aluminum & Chemical Corporation, Aluminium Limited* (Canada); New York: Loeb, Rhoades, 1950), pp. 63–65.

[26] Charlotte Muller, *Light Metals Monopoly* (New York: Columbia University Press, 1946), pp. 88–95.

[27] *Remedy Record*, Government Exhibit 165.

TABLE 2. Aluminum price changes in the United States,
United Kingdom, and Canada

Price (cents per pound)	United States[a]	United Kingdom[b]	Canada[c]
15.00	In effect since about 1942	Oct. 9, 1950	In effect since about 1942
15.50		Jan. 1, 1951	Dec. 13, 1948
16.00	June 28, 1948		
17.00	Oct. 11, 1948		Sept. 28, 1948
17.50	May 22, 1950		
18.00			Oct. 23, 1951
19.00	Sept. 23, 1950		Feb. 16, 1953
19.50		Average for 1952 and 1954	
19.60		Average for 1953	
19.75			Jan. 3, 1953
20.00	Aug. 4, 1952		
20.38		Jan. 1, 1955	
20.50	Jan. 23, 1953		April 4, 1955
21.00	July 15, 1953		July 1, 1955
21.25			Jan. 1, 1956
21.50	Aug. 1, 1955		
22.38		Jan. 1, 1956	
23.50	Aug. 1, 1956		March 1, 1956
23.63		April 1, 1956	
24.50			Aug. 14, 1956
24.63		Aug. 1956	
25.00	March 24, 1956		
26.00	Aug. 10, 1956		

[a] In the United States the date of price change is that for Alcoa.
[b] In Great Britain the British Ministry of Supply fixed the selling price until June 30, 1953. Prices are converted to American dollars by the official exchange rule.
[c] Canadian prices are in American dollars.
Source: *Year Book of the American Bureau of Metal Statistics* (New York: American Bureau of Metal Statistics, 1958).

of these are from Limited.[28] (Limited always sells in the United States at the domestic price.)

The 1957 recession altered this situation in several ways. Producers like those in Formosa, which had previously produced only for the domestic market, began to export to Limited's traditional markets. Similarly, the American producers began to export to Western Europe, while Western European fabricators began to sell in the eastern United States, despite the high tariff barriers on fabricated products. And the Russians began to export aluminum. It is difficult to say whether these events, described more fully in

[28] Data from *Aluminum: Material Survey*, p. VIII 30.

Chapter V, indicate that a highly integrated world market may have developed. But, for the years 1946 to 1957, market behavior in the American aluminum industry can be examined with little reference to developments abroad.

THE DEMAND FOR
ALUMINUM

MUCH of the writing on the subject of oligopoly has concentrated upon the rivalry between business firms and has ignored the economic environment in which such rivalry occurs. But the demand and cost conditions are as much responsible for the observed behavior in oligopolistic industries as are the purely oligopolistic interactions. Indeed, one of the recurring themes of this study is the interplay between the economic setting of an oligopolistic industry and the kind of oligopolistic behavior that occurs. Chapters V and VI examine the impact of the cost structure for aluminum reduction and fabrication upon market behavior.

This chapter examines the four characteristics of the demand for aluminum which have important consequences for the business strategies pursued by sellers of primary aluminum.

First, apart from the changes in sales attributable to the variations in the current volume of industrial production and the fluctuations in the inventories held by buyers, aluminum consumption varies because of manufacturers' shifts from one industrial material to another. Such transfers usually require the modification of either the product or the production process, which, in turn, usually requires capital expenditures. Consequently, the switch from one metal to another is an investment decision entailing the uncertainty and the irreversibility characteristic of these decisions. The switch between metals is not greatly influenced by short-run variations in the relative prices of the metals. Therefore, the short-run demand for aluminum is price inelastic.[1]

---

[1] Elasticity of demand is defined as the percentage change in quantity which would result from a 1-percent change in price. An elastic demand (value greater than —1.0)

Second, aluminum is bought as an industrial input by the cost-conscious, professional purchasing agents of manufacturing firms. At the same time, there is a technically and economically feasible substitute for most applications. Hence, the long-run demand for aluminum will be relatively price elastic.

Third, adopting a new application for aluminum involves considerable uncertainty about the consumer acceptance of the product redesigned to use aluminum and the costs of the modifications in the production process. To overcome these uncertainties, a much lower price is required to create new applications than to retain buyers already familiar with aluminum. As a result, the long-run demand curve for aluminum has a "kink" with demand relatively more price elastic for new applications of aluminum and relatively more inelastic for the established uses. Note that the direction of the "kink" is the opposite from that in the theory of oligopolistic pricing. It is more elastic at prices below the kink and less elastic above the kink.

Finally, price stability per se increases aluminum consumption by reducing the uncertainties in a purchase decision with an investment character.

The Interviews with Buyers

These four characteristics are not directly discernible from a statistical study of the demand for aluminum. They are, however, apparent in the replies of buyers of aluminum in a market survey conducted by Professors Engle, Gregory, and Mossé.[2] This study, even though an excellent example of market research, has limitations for the testing of these four propositions. Interviewing, the basic source of data, is an unreliable method of establishing business behavior, and furthermore, the interviews were not designed to test the propositions set forth here. The open-ended nature of the interviews precluded quantitative summarization. Finally, the survey was made in 1944 when the conditions in the industry were different from those prevailing in the 1950's.

---

is one for which a given price change will cause a more than proportional change in quantity. An inelastic demand is one for which a given price change will cause a less than proportional change in quantity. Hence, with an elastic demand low prices will expand revenues; with an inelastic demand they will not. See Kenneth Boulding, *Economic Analysis* (New York: Harper, 1948), pp. 128–139.

[2] Nathaniel H. Engle, Homer E. Gregory, and Robert Mossé, *Aluminum: An Industrial Marketing Survey* (Chicago: Richard D. Irwin, 1945), see particularly Part III.

Nevertheless, the survey indicates that the respondents ranked price as an important determinant of the decision to buy aluminum. The general tenor of the comments on price is indicated by the following examples: "Aluminum will be used if its price is brought down to a level competitive with cast iron" (California appliance manufacturer).[3] "Aluminum at ten cents a pound will cut heavily into our use of steel" (Ohio duplicating machine manufacturer).[4] "Our consumption of aluminum depends on the relative price of aluminum and copper" (electrical equipment manufacturer).[5] "Our company has not used aluminum much in the past because of the high price" (purchasing agent of a food mixer manufacturer).[6]

These statements make no distinction between the short-run and the long-run response to price. The existence of substantial transfer costs in the switch from one metal to another indicate that the buyers will respond only to long-run price changes. Although no dollar estimates of these transfer costs are available, the comments of the interviewees indicate their importance: "The cost of redesigning and tooling must be considered" (machinery manufacturer).[7] "Why should we incur the additional cost of retooling and revamping our organization to use aluminum?" (electrical control manufacturer).[8] "A shift from aluminum to steel would doubtless entail equipment changes, personnel shifts and the redesign of the product" (appliance manufacturer).[9]

Not only do these transfer costs delay the response to price changes, but there are uncertainties about their magnitude because of the adoption of an untried process or product. Only actual experience demonstrates the amount of the total transition costs. Once an adoption of aluminum has been made, these uncertainties disappear. Such a situation creates an irreversible demand function, that is, one in which the quantity sold at any price is greater than that sold before the initial adoption. (This is more accurately a shift in the demand curve to the right than a change in its slope.) In contrast, inertia and transfer costs operate for shifts both toward and away from aluminum.

This implies that firms learn from their own experience and

[3] *Ibid.*, p. 314.
[4] *Ibid.*, p. 333.
[5] *Ibid.*, p. 328.
[6] *Ibid.*, p. 326.
[7] *Ibid.*, p. 335.
[8] *Ibid.*, p. 320.
[9] *Ibid.*, p. 344.

such learning is sufficiently costly that special inducements are required. One example illustrates why this is so. Certain specific machine-tool operations involve 71 percent less operator and machine time for turning, 61 percent less time in milling, and 33 percent less in drilling when aluminum replaces iron.[10] But whether these figures apply to the operations of an individual firm can be established only by examining its operating experience. The acceptability to the consumer of new products of aluminum can also be known only by experience.

One close substitute for the firm's own experience is the experience of other manufacturers with similar applications of aluminum. This learning from other firms is termed here the demonstration effect. At the outset of any type of aluminum application, adoption is limited to the leaders in technological change. As these leaders come in contact with other firms and prove their success with aluminum to the industry at large, a rapid rate of adoption of aluminum follows.[11] As we shall see in Chapter VIII, another close substitute for the firm's own experience is the efforts of the primary producers to aid and educate potential users. At this point, however, we shall concentrate upon the autonomous and self-perpetuating character of the demonstration effect.

The demonstration effect is, of course, a theory of innovation. As such it is not novel. Professor Schumpeter visualized the innovation process as divided between a primary wave of leaders (the "true innovators") and a secondary wave of followers.[12] Professor Healy in a study of technological change in railroading divides the history of any one technical change into a period of experimentation by a few, experimentation by many and adoption by a few, and, finally, industry-wide adoption.[13] The demonstration effect, however, adds the additional proposition that the adoption process depends criti-

---

[10] "Saving Machining Costs with Aluminum Castings," *Modern Metals,* vol. 10, no. 9 (October, 1954), pp. 68–69.

[11] This demonstration effect is a further extension of Professor Duesenberry's analysis of the dynamics of consumer demand. However, psychological and sociological factors are of more importance for consumers' than for producers' goods. See James Duesenberry, *Income, Saving and the Theory of Consumer Behavior* (Cambidge: Harvard University Press, 1949).

[12] Joseph Schumpeter, *The Theory of Economic Development* (Cambridge: Harvard University Press, 1934), chap. III.

[13] Kent Healy, "Regularization of Capital Investment in Railroads," in National Bureau of Economic Research, *Regularization of Business Investment, A conference of The National Bureau Committee for Economic Research* (Special Conference Series No. 4; Princeton: Princeton University Press, 1954), pp. 147–212.

cally on the actual observation and imitation of the success of the leaders with the new innovation.

The demonstration effect is a plausible hypothesis in both decision-making and real-cost terms. As an investment decision, the adoption of aluminum depends on the comparison of the expected cost savings with the transfer costs. Both the cost savings and the transfer costs can be estimated only within fairly wide ranges. The risks inherent in this uncertainty are further increased because aluminum utilization is generally an all-or-none decision. For example, it is often expensive to manufacture aluminum and steel windows on the same assembly line or make identical components of the same automobile model simultaneously from aluminum and steel.[14] Therefore a firm cannot hedge through a partial adoption of aluminum.

In such a situation, different firms develop different cost estimates and have different responses to the uncertainties inherent in such estimates. The leaders, having a higher estimate of the cost-benefit ratio or a greater willingness to bear risks, adopt a given application. Success in such adoptions leads other firms to a revaluation of the risks and uncertainties, since there is no more effective teaching device than the successful example, and every adoption yields more reliable information on the cost-benefit ratio. Competition furnishes additional force to the demonstration effect, for it punishes a failure to follow a successful innovator. In addition, cost savings are available to the followers, for a new application of aluminum involves costs for experimentation in the development of products and processes. For the followers, these costs are reduced to the extent that the follower can by-pass or shorten the experimental process

[14] The experiences of two companies with the simultaneous production of steel and aluminum are described by Professor Corey as follows: "It is of interest to note that the two companies each found the manufacture of aluminum windows to be basically incompatible with the manufacture of windows of steel. Steel bar was given, and could take, rough handling in warehousing and during the fabrication process. Aluminum required some degree of care to avoid surface scratches and denting of extruded sections. In addition, although aluminum windows were put together by the same methods used for steel windows, some of the techniques and equipment required for fabricating each differed. Furthermore, men trained to weld steel manually had difficulty in applying their skills to aluminum welding. One of the companies, on experiencing the difficulties of putting the manufacture of the two products in the same shop, set up a separate operation at a different location to manufacture aluminum windows." E. Raymond Corey, *The Development of Markets for New Materials* (Boston: Division of Research, Graduate School of Business, Harvard University, 1956) pp. 37–38.

by utilizing the experience of other firms. In addition, of course, the marketing efforts of the primary aluminum producers are directed at accelerating the demonstration effect.

In interviews with buyers of aluminum, made for the survey mentioned earlier, there was repeated mention of the need for technical information about the utilization of aluminum: "More technical data is needed on various alloys" (vice president of a major producer of trucks);[15] "More information is needed on welding techniques" (president of a medium-size manufacturer).[16] Specific mention occurs of the need for more experience in actual applications: "Aluminum can be used whenever copper or brass is used, yet more experience is needed with the actual use of aluminum in flexible cords" (chief engineer of a large Chicago manufacturer of electrical wire).[17] Such an emphasis upon the need for technical information provides an indirect confirmation of the demonstration effect.

The automotive utilization of aluminum provides a more aggregative confirmation of the demonstration effect. In 1956 the average amount of aluminum per car was 35 pounds. Yet several higher-price models were substantially above the industry average, ranging up to 100 pounds per car, with the highest-priced Cadillac, the Eldorado, at 192 pounds. Since the innovations occurring in the higher-priced cars are subsequently adopted in the lower-priced cars, this provides a basis for the prediction of the growth curve as shown in Fig. 2.

This curve reflects the practice in the automobile industry of introducing innovations at the top of the price class. Nevertheless, fragmentary data indicates the existence of the same exponential growth pattern in other applications. The test of the demonstration effect, however, lies in whether postulating such a concept adds to the explanation of market behavior in subsequent chapters.

The last proposition, the value of price stability per se in promoting the demand for aluminum, is substantiated by two statements. The president of Alcoa stated, "We attempt to hold the price as steady as we can because we believe that it will insure the maximum development of the aluminum industry,"[18] while a buyer

[15] Engle, *Aluminum: An Industrial Marketing Survey*, p. 278.
[16] *Ibid.*, p. 326.
[17] *Ibid.*, p. 323.
[18] Testimony of I. W. Wilson, House Committee on the Judiciary, Subcommittee on Monopoly Power, *Hearings: Study of Monopoly Power, Serial No. 1, Part I, Aluminum*, 82nd Cong., 1st Sess., 1951, p. 632.

of metals stated, "Aluminum's remarkable record of price stability is an added incentive of incalculable value." [19] This is limited proof. But it is clear that frequent variations in the price of materials raises pricing problems for manufacturers and fabricators. In many industries, there is considerable uncertainty about whether a price

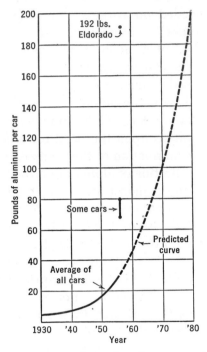

Fig. 2. Actual and predicted consumption of aluminum in automobiles as of 1956.

Source: A. L. Boegehold, "Why Tomorrow's Cars Will Use More Light Metals," *Modern Metals*, 12:72 (Nov. 1956).

change will be followed by competitors. Furthermore, price changes must often be justified to the final buyers, and some items are sold under long-term contracts. Price stability, in turn, requires the cost stability that can be provided by a stable materials price. The extent to which aluminum can provide more price stability than other metals encourages its use. Therefore the demand for aluminum is not only a function of the level of its price, but also of the stability of its price.

[19] F. L. Church, "The Crisis in Metals." *Modern Metals*, vol. 9, no. 4 (May 1953), p. 72. Statement of Mr. During of Precision Castings.

The Statistical Study of the Demand for Aluminum

This qualitative information describes only the general nature of the demand function. For example, the existence of transfer costs indicates the demand function is more elastic in the long run than in the short run. But a quantitative study is required to say whether the long-run demand function is, in fact, elastic.

Estimating the elasticity of demand has usually been plagued by the identification problem. If a market is always in equilibrium, the only observable price-quantity pairs are at the intersection of the supply and demand curves. The observations will not necessarily trace out either the demand or supply curve, but rather shifts in both functions.[20] One solution for this problem occurs in agricultural products, where the time lag in production insures that the output for any one year is determined by exogenous variables such as past years' prices and the weather. The price-quantity observations then trace out a demand curve.

A somewhat similar simplifying assumption may be made for industrial products, according to an argument developed by Franklin Fisher.[21] The sellers set prices in response to long-run demand and cost conditions, and at each price will supply the quantity demanded. Hence, the various price-quantities pairs reflect the demand function, for the supply is exogenously determined. As a subsequent chapter will show, this assumption applies to the aluminum industry.

Professor Fisher fitted a multiple regression to data for the years 1919–1939 less the years 1922–1924 and 1938. From 1922 to 1924 there were marked shifts in the consumption of aluminum by the automobile industry. In 1938, there may have been recession-induced inventory accumulations and for that year data are unavailable for correction in the output statistics. Fisher's dependent variable is the consumption of aluminum ingot, Q_t, defined as the output of primary aluminum corrected for stockpiling (that is, changes in producer's inventory), and the independent variables are the price, P_t, defined as the real price of aluminum ingot (that is, the money price of 99 percent aluminum ingot divided by Bureau of Labor Statistics Price Index of Metals and Metals Products), and an income variable, Y_t,

---

[20] The classic article on the identification problem is Elmer Working, "What Do Statistical 'Demand Curves' Show?" *Quarterly Journal of Economics*, 41:212 (1929).

[21] Franklin M. Fisher, "The Demand for Aluminum Ingot in the United States 1925–1940," in *A Priori Information and Time Series Analysis* (Amsterdam: North Holland, 1961).

defined as the Federal Reserve Board Index of Manufacturing output. Aluminum is consumed largely in manufacturing operations, and the inclusion of this third variable accounts for the changes in consumption attributable to changes in the current level of economic activity.

The form of the regression equation is a first difference of the logarithms to eliminate the trends in the various time series and to make the function exponential as most demand curves are assumed to be. Mr. Fisher's results are as follows:[22]

$$\Delta \log Q_t = 0.0325 + 0.950 \; \Delta \log Y_t - 0.428 \; \Delta \log P_t$$
$$ (0.161) (0.608)$$
$$R^2 = 0.904.$$

The price elasticity is not statistically significant, but according to Mr. Fisher, "These results are probably as good as could be expected; first, in view of the paucity of observations and relatively small fluctuations in the money price during the period . . . and, second, in view of the fact that the effect of price on the demand for aluminum is relatively long run. The estimate of short-run price elasticity, for what it is worth, appears to be somewhere in the neighborhood of $-.43$."[23] Although these statistical results are somewhat disappointing, they do indicate a short-run price inelasticity, a conclusion supported by the qualitative information on the nature of aluminum purchases.

In view of our preceding discussion, the estimate of the long-run demand for aluminum is based upon the assumption that the expansion of the market for aluminum indicates the long-run elasticity of demand. Furthermore, an irreversible or "kinked" long-run demand curve is assumed to exist, with the long-run price elasticity much greater as aluminum consumption expands beyond its current volume. It is this "expansion" price elasticity that is particularly relevant to the market behavior of the postwar years.

This hypothesis can be tested by a multiple regression of the following variables: consumption, Q_t and Y_t, defined as in Mr. Fisher's study, price, P_t, defined as the money price of aluminum, for only those years in which aluminum consumption exceeds its

[22] Fisher, "The Demand for Aluminum Ingot." The presentation of this one summary equation hardly does justice to Mr. Fisher's craftsmanship. The testing of successive possibilities and the careful use of outside information make this study a model for both the fields of econometrics and of industrial organization.
[23] Fisher, "The Demand for Aluminum Ingot."

previous highest level.[24] The assumption here is that the expansion of aluminum consumption is attributable both to the general expansion of the economy (represented by the income variable) and to the adoption of new applications, partially in response to price decreases. The multiple regression is intended to sort out these two effects. The difficulty is that there are other factors, namely technical change and increased knowledge, "the demonstration effect," but these long-run factors are at least minimized by working with year-to-year changes. A more serious difficulty is the lagged response over several years of quantity to price. The lagging of quantity by one year, however, produced about the same results.

The results of this multiple regression, again using first differences of the logarithms, are as follows:[25]

$$\log \Delta Q_t = 0.001133 + 1.14559 \Delta \log Y_t -$$
$$(0.60825)$$
$$1.15108 \Delta \log P_t$$
$$(0.56248)$$
$$R^2 = 0.77410.$$

All the coefficients are statistically significant. The long-run price elasticity is -1.15, meaning that, for a 1-percent change in price, unit sales change inversely by 1.15 percent. The demand is price elastic, though it exceeds unity only by a relatively small margin.

It is clear, however, that it is the relative rather than the absolute price of aluminum that determines its substitution for other metals. For the analysis of market behavior, the cross-elasticity of demand is of more importance than the absolute price elasticity. Steel is the closest substitute for aluminum in most applications.[26] The preceding equation was recomputed with P_t defined as the price of

---

[24] The device of previous peak years is used in an analogous fashion by Professor Duesenberry to establish the short-run and long-run consumptive function. Duesenberry, *Income, Saving and the Theory of Consumer Behavior*, chap. V.

[25] The data was obtained from James E. Rosenzweig, *The Demand for Aluminum: A Case Study in Long-Range Forecasting* (Urbana: Bureau of Economic and Business Research, College of Commerce and Business Administration, University of Illinois, Business Study No. 10, 1957), Appendix.

[26] Steel is estimated to be "competitive" with aluminum in uses which account for half the current level of aluminum output. See The Economic Commission for Europe, Steel Committee, *Competition between Steel and Aluminum* (Geneva: United Nations, 1954), pp. 61–62. Copper has been considered the principal substitute for aluminum, but as the relative importance of cable consumption in total aluminum demand has decreased, steel rather than copper has become the principal substitute.

aluminum in terms of the price of steel.[27] The results were as follows:

$$\log \Delta Q_t = 0.11364 + 0.85014 \, \Delta \log Y_t -$$
$$(0.53566)$$
$$2.06703 \, \Delta \log P_t$$
$$(0.11266)$$

$$R^2 = 0.8706.$$

This is a notably high cross-elasticity of demand. A 1-percent change in price is accompanied by an inverse change of 2.07 percent in the quantity sold.

These statistical results are properly open to criticism as involving a limited sample and arbitrary assumptions, and, more fundamentally, as failing to reflect adequately the complex dynamics and lags in the demand for aluminum. They are not a conclusive demonstration of the elasticity of demand for aluminum, but in conjunction with the other evidence, they do support a finding of price inelasticity of demand in the short run and a relatively high price cross-elasticity of demand in the long run.

Estimates of the Long-run Price Elasticity from Survey Data

Further confirmation of a high cross-elasticity between the prices of aluminum and other metals is provided by the results of a 1944 survey of aluminum buyers by Professors Engle, Gregory, and Mossé. One hundred thirty-five manufacturers were interviewed about the expected change in their consumption of aluminum if the price of aluminum were reduced by one-third.[28] Implicitly, the question referred to long-run consumption decisions. A further implicit assumption was that the price of other metals would be unchanged. These responses were cross-checked by a larger mail questionnaire.

From this survey it is possible to compute for each industry an index of the quantity that would be bought with a one-third reduction in the relative price of aluminum (Table 3). Each industry was then assigned a weight based upon its percentage share of total aluminum consumption in 1952. The product of columns 3 and 4

---

[27] Relative prices were adjusted to reflect the fact that two pounds of aluminum are required to replace one pound of steel. This is based on the relative strength of the two materials and varies around this 2:1 ratio depending on the particular application. For a discussion, see Rosenzweig, *The Demand for Aluminum*, p. 20.

[28] These companies consumed 51,000,000 of the 413,000,000 pounds of 1940 production. Unfortunately there is no evidence about the representativeness of the sample. Engle, *Aluminum: An Industrial Marketing Survey*, p. 254.

TABLE 3. Computation of price elasticity for aluminum

(1) Consuming industry	(2) Index based on percentage of civilian aluminum consumption in 1952	(3) Index of change with one-third price reduction	(4) Index of aluminum consumption after price reduction (2) × (3)
Construction			
Electric power	9.9	1.20	10.9
Industrial maintenance	1.3	1.00ᵃ	1.3
Other construction	1.9	1.00ᵃ	1.9
Building materials	18.2	2.00	36.4
Transportation			
Aircraft, civilian	0.6	1.00	0.6
Railroad	0.9	1.00	0.9
Motor vehicles	11.8	1.50	17.7
Shipbuilding	0.2	1.00¹	0.2
Machinery and equipment excluding electrical	13.2	1.67	22.1
Electrical and communication equipment			
Electrical equipment	4.7	1.34	6.3
Electronics	1.9	2.00	2.8
Communication equipment	0.5	2.00	1.0
Consumer durables	14.2	1.34	21.3
Packaging	4.9	1.00	4.9
Motion pictures and photographic equipment	0.5	1.00¹	0.5
Chemicals	0.6	1.00	0.6
Destructive use	7.3	1.00	7.3
Other	7.4	1.70	12.6
Total	100.0		160.3

ᵃ No data available, assumed to be unchanged in order to produce a conservative estimate of the elasticity of demand.

Sources: Column 2: Percentage Distribution of Civilian Consuming Industries for 1952, from U. S. Bureau of Census, *Shipments of Aluminum Products by Industry Group,* 1950–1953 (Facts for Industry Series BDAF–122–03: Washington, 1954); column 4: Nathaniel H. Engle, Homer E. Gregory, and Robert Mossé, *Aluminum: An Industrial Marketing Survey* (Chicago: Richard D. Irwin, 1945), pp. 252–258.

indicates the total change in aluminum consumption with a one-third price reduction. Dividing the percentage change in quantity by the percentage change in price yields a relative price elasticity of −1.818. This result further supports the proposition that the long-run demand for aluminum is relatively price elastic.

The changing pattern of aluminum consumption by industries, together with the price elasticities estimated from the survey responses, are shown in Table 4. The sectors with the higher price

TABLE 4. The changing pattern of aluminum consumption. Percent of total consumption by various uses, 1930–1948, compared with their price elasticities

Industry	Percent of total consumption			Elasticity[a]
	1930	1938	1948	
Building construction	3	8	18	—3.00
Nonferrous foundries and metalworking	4	4	25	—3.00
Machinery and electrical appliances	8	15	13	—1.14
Cooking utensils	16	14	9	—1.00
Transportation	38	29	13	—0.44
Electric wire and cable	16	10	6	—0.40
Other	11	20	16	
Total	100	100	100	

[a] As of 1944, based on Table 3.

Sources: Aluminum consumption: 1930, Donald Wallace, *Market Control in the Aluminum Industry* (Cambridge, Massachusetts: Harvard University Press, 1937), p. 64; 1938 and 1948, Carl M. Loeb, Rhoades and Company, *Aluminum: An Analysis of the Industry in the United States* (New York, 1950), p. 19. Elasticities computed from data in Nathaniel H. Engle, Homer E. Gregory, and Robert Mossé, *Aluminum: An Industrial Marketing Survey* (Chicago: Richard D. Irwin, 1945), pp. 253–259.

elasticity show a much higher rate of growth of consumption. Yet it is important to distinguish between the two types of consuming industries which have high price elasticities. In one category are those representing new applications of aluminum in which a substantial price advantage over the presently used material is required to overcome the resistance to innovation. In another category are industries in which the high price elasticity is due to the existence of substitutes. Only in the latter case is the high price elasticity reversible.

The data here do not permit making such a distinction. The greater importance of such sectors as building materials, in which substitutes are numerous, suggests that the over-all demand for aluminum has become more price elastic in the traditional "reversible" meaning of the term. If this is the case, the long-run price elasticity of demand constitutes restraint on the power of sellers to increase prices. In any event, as the subsequent chapters indicate, the high price elasticity for the expansion of aluminum consumption, together with the short-run price inelasticity, are important factors in the explanation of the behavior of prices of aluminum products.

THE PRICING OF INGOT

Even though there are numerous prices in the aluminum industry, the price of primary aluminum ingot or pig is, by common consent, considered the price of aluminum. (Since there was a constant one cent difference until 1953 between the two prices, the choice of product is a matter of stylistic preference.) This is not because these prices account for most of the transactions. Indeed, the prices of ingot and pig are in large part accounting entries, for approximately two-thirds of the ingot output is consumed in the fabricating plants of the primary producers. Rather, the importance of changes in pig and ingot prices is that such price variations are often accompanied by identical changes in the list prices of various fabricated products. A further analytical advantage in examining ingot and pig prices is that the primary producers are the only sellers. Therefore the behavior of these prices represents a problem in oligopolistic pricing uncomplicated by the existence of a small-business fringe.

A Model of Oligopoly

The model developed here is largely a reformulation of the existing literature in terms of a set of assumptions specifically applicable to the aluminum industry.

The first of these assumptions is that there is a high price cross-elasticity of demand between the products of the oligopolists. A high price cross-elasticity of demand defines a condition in which small differences in the prices of two or more sellers have a significant influence upon their relative physical volume of sales. This is likely to be so for undifferentiated products such as aluminum. If rival sellers charge different prices, a substantial number of buyers will shift their patronage to the lower-price seller and eventually a higher-price seller will be bankrupt. It is not necessary to consider such draconian prospects to conclude that with a high price cross-elasticity of demand no seller will charge a higher price than another. As long as the firms attach considerable importance to maintaining their market shares, either as an administrative approximation to profit maximization or as an independent measure of business success, there will be price uniformity in an oligopolistic market with a high cross-elasticity of demand.

The second assumption is that the sellers have different views about the most desirable level for the market price. Indeed, considering the host of reasons why there should be such differences (differing cost structure, differing estimates of the elasticity of demand, differing financial requirements, or differing concerns about government or union relations) it would be strange if firms had identical views about the most desirable market price.

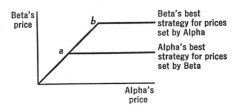

Fig. 3. Strategy curves of duopolists.

With these two assumptions, the argument follows from Fig. 3, portraying the optimum strategies of two duopolists, Alpha and Beta. (Duopoly exists as a topic in economic analysis because graphs can be best drawn in two dimensions. The argument for two sellers can be generalized to three or more firms.) Alpha is the firm preferring the lower price equality (that is, the low-price preference firm) and Beta the firm preferring the higher price. Beta's strategy curve depicts the following logic. Up to point *b*, the market price most preferred by Beta, Beta will match any price set by Alpha (as indicated by Beta's 45° line), for a higher price will reduce Beta's market share and a lower price will simply be matched by Alpha and result in a price pair even farther from *b*. Beyond point *b*, however, Beta will keep his price constant, for a higher price, even if matched by Alpha, would result in a higher market price than Beta desires.

The argument for Alpha is symmetrical to that for Beta. Up to point *a* (the market price preferred by Alpha), Alpha will match any price set by Beta (as indicated by the 45° slope), since at a lower price Beta will match Alpha's price and so result in a price equality even farther from *a*. On the other hand, maintaining a price higher than Beta's results in a loss of Alpha's market share, given the high price cross-elasticity of demand.

Thus changes in the equal-price pairs up to point *a* result in increases in utility for both parties, since both move toward their individually preferred market prices. For the price to move to *a*, however, the leader must be assured of followership. Otherwise, a "kinked demand"–curve stalemate may develop, that is, Alpha may not increase his price because of the uncertainty of followership by Beta, and Beta would not increase his price because of the uncertainty of followership by Alpha. The paradoxical result, then, is that each firm prefers a higher price and takes no action because of a failure in communication.

This outcome is unlikely. There is no incentive for either party to adopt a poker face; instead, it is to the advantage of both to remove the doubts precluding a price increase. The most direct method is through public statements by executives that the current market price is too low. (At times, this has been a recurring feature of stockholders' meetings in the steel industry.) A more expensive method is for one firm to announce a price increase and to assume the risk that the other will follow. Granted that excessive price experimentation could create sufficient ill-will to jeopardize a firm's market share, a few such actions can demonstrate that a firm might welcome a price increase. Finally, the history of price behavior usually eliminates uncertainty about followership. Relative price preferences are a stable phenomenon dependent upon such long-run factors as demand, cost conditions, and managerial policy. If Beta has always followed Alpha in the past, Alpha will infer Beta has the higher-price preference and will continue to follow Alpha's price leadership. For these reasons, a kinked-demand stalemate can be ruled out.

Instead, one of the parties will initiate price increases which will be followed up to point *a*. At *a*, Alpha will not initiate further price increases, since his preferred market price has been realized. If Beta should take the initiative, Alpha will not match the price increase, for this will create a higher market price than Alpha desires, while given the high cross-elasticity of demand Beta cannot maintain a higher price without Alpha's followership. Hence, the market price will be at a, that is, the market price desired by that oligopolist with the preference for the lowest market price.

Only the most general limits can be specified for this market price. It cannot be less in the long run than the costs of the low-price preference firm nor can it be higher than the next lowest market price preferred by another oligopolist. (At that point the first firm by definition is no longer the firm with the lowest price preference.) Within these wide limits the level of the market price becomes a problem of the theory of the firm rather than of the theory of oligopoly.

It is possible to specify more exactly the mechanism of price leadership. Should Alpha decide that the market price should be increased, he can simply change his price and Beta will match it, for this outcome results in a price closer to Beta's preference. Should Alpha decide the market price should be decreased, the high price cross-elasticity of demand insures Beta's followership. Since Alpha's decisions effectively set the market price, this firm will be the price leader. Beta gains nothing by assuming the price leadership since Alpha will not follow upward unless his price preference has changed, while price decreases only create a market price even farther from Beta's preference of the market price.

This model does not yield the contract-curve solution stressed in much of the current literature. A contract curve defines the price pairs for which both parties are gainers relative to any other price pair. In the outcome here, both parties would be gainers if Beta could compensate Alpha to set a market price nearer Beta's preference. According to the standard argument, if both parties are gainers, "it would be irrational for the parties to come to any combination of prices which does not lie on the contract curve." [1] As an empirical matter, such a complex bargain usually requires an overt agreement, which our model rules out. Barring the unlikely occurrence of identical preferences in market price, this would preclude a contract-curve solution as well as the joint maximization of profits (a special case of the contract-curve solution). [2]

---

[1] Alexander Henderson, "The Theory of Duopoly," *The Quarterly Journal of Economics,* 68:569 (November 1958). This is an excellent survey of the literature of duopoly.

[2] Joint profit maximization with qualifications has become almost the standard oligopoly solution. See William Fellner, *Competition among the Few* (New York: Knopf, 1949).

The collusive interpretation of duopoly implicit in the contract-curve solution fails to discriminate between the desirability of various duopolistic (and by implication, oligopolistic) markets except to condemn them all as tacitly collusive. Furthermore, a contract-curve solution does not underline the gap separating a cartel, in which Beta could trade some sort of new market division or even a part of its profits to Alpha for a higher price, and a standard duopoly in which such agreements are impossible. And in the latter case the market price is lower, thus supporting the presumption underlying the prohibition of interfirm agreements which is the least controversial aspect of the antitrust laws.

Furthermore, the model set forth here supports several propositions in the literature of industrial organization. For example, market power has come to be defined as the freedom of a firm from market restraints. The range between Beta's preferred market price and Alpha's costs defines a range of discretion analogous to market power. It is generally agreed that market power decreases as the number of sellers increases. Given the large number of factors — relative costs, expectations, managerial attitudes — that create a price preference, the probability of a price preference close to that of the price leader increases with the number of sellers, and this in turn would decrease the freedom in pricing exercised by the leader. It is also generally agreed that market power depends upon the quality of competitors as well as on their number. A single competitor with a price preference near that of the leader's could constitute a greater reduction in the leader's pricing freedom than several competitors with price preferences substantially higher than that of the leader. Finally, price preferences are a managerial attitude, thus conforming to the repeated observation that the competitiveness of an industry or a nation is in large part dependent on the mores of the business community.

This version of oligopoly, of course, excludes some situations. It says nothing about predatory behavior in which one firm seeks to maximize the other firms' losses in order to drive them from the market. This outcome is largely a historical curiosity because of the present-day concern with public relations and the current vigor of the antitrust laws. Nor is this model applicable to situations in which the price preferences of the firms are nearly identical, for here joint profit maximization may be a more likely outcome. If the price preferences are constantly changing, the consequent uncertainty might make the kinked demand–curve stalemate occur. Likewise, as the number of firms increases, the uncertainty concerning price preferences may again bring about a kinked-demand stalemate. If one oligopolist is markedly larger than the others, price leadership may be associated with the largest firm. Here some theory of partial monopoly may be more applicable. Finally, there are situations of quasi-oligopoly where the number of rivals is neither so few that the recognition of mutual interdependence is a foregone conclusion nor so numerous that it is clear there will be no recognition of mutual interdependence. As to which of these situations most frequently occurs, the most that is claimed is that the situation described by the model set forth here may be common. More to the point, these other outcomes are not relevant to the aluminum industry.

Our model does not include the mechanism by which market shares change. Since the prices are uniform among the sellers, shifts in market shares are created by various forms of nonprice competition — variation in product quality, advertising, and marketing effort. This is because the matching response by competitors in nonprice competion is more delayed and more difficult than in price competition and so such competition may not be self-defeating. The forms and extent of nonprice competition in the aluminum industry are described in subsequent chapters. The complexities of nonprice competition are such as to preclude simple generalizations that could be meaningfully added to this model.

For the purposes of this chapter, a more pressing addition to the model is the possibility of extra-market pressures exerted by the high-price preference firms upon the low-price preference firm to increase the price. Such pressures may be exerted in actions before a tariff commission, a regulatory agency, or a legislative chamber. Given the current pervasive role of the government, it is not surprising that the government should be enlisted as an ally in market rivalry. Furthermore, the American political ideology and political processes favors the new or the small firm, the likely possessors of the higher price preferences, so the role of the government is likely to be that of assistance to the higher-price preference firms.

At this point, however, the argument transcends the logic of a model and becomes a matter for empirical investigation. This model of duopoly is intended only as a hypothesis which, whatever its general applicability, explains price-making in the aluminum industry.

Price Leadership in the Aluminum Industry

Table 5 depicts the pattern of price leadership in the aluminum industry. Alcoa was the price leader in nine price changes, with Reynolds and Kaiser following in a few days. Reynolds led one price change and Kaiser three, but at least two of these price changes can be accounted for by special circumstances. The one leaderless change, that of August 4, 1952, reflects simultaneous approval of the applications for a price increase by the Office of Price Stablization.

Ignoring for the moment the exceptions, this kind of evidence corresponds to the preceding model of duopoly. There is a price leader, Alcoa, that can be assigned the role of the low-price preference firm. For much of the period 1946 to 1958, Alcoa has the attributes which such a role requires; the lowest cost of production, and, as the established firm, the least need to demonstrate a dividend and earning record in order to secure a financial reputation. Furthermore, Alcoa as a convicted monopolist is most likely to be concerned with the public relations aspects of price increases. Finally, both Reynolds and Kaiser had explicitly stated before various congressional committees and tariff commissions that the price of aluminum was too low, further confirming their role as the higher-price preference firms.[3] (Assignment to a high- or low-price preference role is not necessarily associated with public virtue. Rather, it simply reflects differing financial needs and marketing policies of the various firms.)

As Table 5 further indicates, the price uniformity required by the model generally prevails. The rationale for price uniformity

[3] An example is the following testimony on the price of aluminum by Mr. Reynolds, Jr., president of Reynolds Metals: ". . . if you want my opinion on price, I think the price [for aluminum] is too low. . . . You know perfectly well we could not sell at a higher price than other producers. You might temporarily, but you would lose all of your customers. . . . I think the price should be higher. . . . I do not know what it should be, but it should be more than it is." House Select Committee on Small Business, Subcommittee No. 3, *Hearings, Aluminum Industry*, Part I, 84th Cong., 1st Sess., 1955, pp. 243–244. Cited hereafter as *Small Business Hearings, 1955*. Similarly, Mr. Rhoades, vice president of Kaiser, stated, ". . . we have had the price of pig under study for some time. We had had two reports made by outside people with respect to the price relationship of pig, because it has been our feeling that the price of pig has been too low." *Small Business Hearings, 1955*, p. 314.

Table 5. The pattern of price leadership and followership
in the price of 99–percent pig aluminum

Price (cents per pound)	Date of price change (price leader italicized)		
	Alcoa	Kaiser	Reynolds
14.0	In effect since June, 1944		
15.0	*June 28, 1948*		
16.0	Oct. 11, 1948	*July 7, 1948*	July 15, 1948
16.5	*May 22, 1950*	May 25, 1950	May 23, 1950
18.0	*Sept. 25, 1950*	Sept. 28, 1950	Sept. 29, 1950
19.0	Aug. 4, 1952	Aug. 4, 1952	Aug. 4, 1952
19.5	Jan. 23, 1953	*Jan. 22, 1953*	Jan. 23, 1953
20.0	*July 15, 1953*	July 20, 1953	July 20, 1953
20.5	*Aug. 5, 1954*	Aug. 6, 1954	Aug. 6, 1954
21.5	Jan. 13, 1955	Jan. 12, 1955	*Jan. 10, 1955*
22.5	*Aug. 1, 1955*	Aug. 2, 1955	Aug. 6, 1955
24.0	March 29, 1956	*March 26, 1956*	March 27, 1956
25.0	*Aug. 10, 1956*	Aug. 11, 1956	Aug. 14, 1956
26.0	*July 29, 1957*	Aug. 1, 1957	Aug. 1, 1957
24.0	*March 28, 1958*	March 30, 1958	March 30, 1958
24.7	*Aug. 1, 1958*	Aug. 2, 1958	Aug. 2, 1958

Sources: *American Metal Market,* various issues.

advanced by the industry executives corresponds almost precisely
to that in the model; namely, that a price reduction will be so
quickly matched that it will not result in a gain in market share and
price increase unmatched by other sellers would decrease the
market share of the higher-price firm.[4]

However, the latter part of the preceding proposition is inconsistent with an awkward fact. For five and one-half postwar years,
there was excess demand for primary aluminum; that is, at the

[4] The argument corresponds closely with the following testimony of Mr. Rhoades,
a vice president of Kaiser:

Q. [by Mr. Emmerglick, Government Counsel] "To get rid of any of this
accumulation [of inventory] that you had in mid-1949 before you saw the upturn,
did you try to sell anybody by giving him the pig aluminum at a penny below the
market price?

A. No, I don't think so.

Q. If you had sold it would you have been able to make money at a penny below
the market price?

A. Yes, I think our costs could stand it.

Q. [by Judge Knox] Suppose you had reduced the price by a cent, did it occur
to you as a business man that Reynolds and Alcoa would do the same?

A. They would probably meet competition. I do not see how they could afford
to have us selling under them. I mean, then, you would get right down to the
same point again.

See Record, pp. 1456–1457, United States v. Aluminum Company of America, 91
F. Supp. 333 (S.D.N.Y. 1950). Cited hereafter as *Remedy Record.*

current price the buyers were willing to buy more than the current output. Excess demand was indicated by a price for secondary aluminum that was significantly higher than the price for primary aluminum (see Fig. 4). Thus, the demand was such that the price of a somewhat inferior substitute, sold by a large number of sellers, none of whom could administer the price, sold at a higher price. The rationing of aluminum by the primary producers, the backlog of orders, and the existence of a resale market for primary aluminum at higher than the list price are further manifestations of excess demand. In these periods, a primary producer need not sell at the same price as its rivals in order to maintain its current market share.

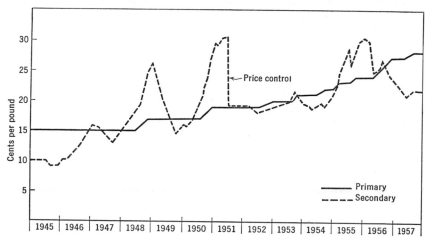

Fig. 4. Primary and secondary aluminum ingot prices, 1945–1957. Secondary aluminum ingot prices are for no. 12 alloy and primary aluminum prices for 99 per cent ingot.

Source: *Metal Statistics, 1958* (New York: American Metal Market, 1958), pp. 619, 625.

Yet, only one instance of nonuniform list prices occurred in these years. Traditionally, aluminum has been sold at a uniform delivered price. On October 28, 1948, Kaiser discontinued its transportation discount and henceforth sold its products f.o.b. plant location. In this way Kaiser increased its net realized price by some 5 percent. On January 1, 1949, Reynolds made the same change in selling terms. Neither Limited nor Alcoa matched this price increase, thus confirming their roles as the lower-price preference firms.[5]

[5] See *Remedy Record*, Defendant Exhibit 238, p. 2875, for a description of these price changes.

As long as the excess demand continued, such price differences could have no immediate effect on sales. Even though the typical buyer paid more by purchasing from Reynolds and Kaiser, their price was still below that prevailing in secondary aluminum markets or in the resale market for primary aluminum. With a decline in demand in the spring of 1949, Reynolds on April 11 and Kaiser on April 20 reinstituted the transportation allowance. Henceforth their prices were uniform with those of Alcoa.[6] This one instance of nonuniform prices was achieved through a change in the transportation discount rather than the more visible change in list prices. Price uniformity despite the excess demand may be explained by the long-run consequences for future sales of a label as the higher-priced firm during a shortage.

Secret price changes are another possible departure from price uniformity. There is no evidence of "secret" price increases during periods of excess demand. Similarly, the executives of the primary producers have disclaimed secret price reductions on aluminum ingot and pig during periods of declining sales.[7] (As discussed subsequently, there may have been some secret price reductions in the foreign market or in various fabricated products.)

The limited occurrence or even nonexistence of secret price-cutting in aluminum pig or ingot can be explained in part by the fewness of sellers. With only three primary producers, even secret price cuts may be sufficiently visible to insure the matching of such reductions. Furthermore, the price-oriented buyers of a standardized industrial product such as aluminum may make price reduction so effective a competitive weapon that it increases the certainty that

[6] On July 19, 1950, Reynolds announced a price increase which was withdrawn 48 hours later. The day after the announcement President Truman issued a general request to industry to avoid price increases in order to prevent an inflation during the Korean War. The next day Reynolds canceled its plans for a price increase. See A. D. H. Kaplan, Joel B. Dirlam, and Robert F. Lanzillotti, *Pricing in Big Business: A Case Approach* (Washington: The Brookings Institution, 1958), p. 33.

[7] Perhaps the best evidence is in House Select Committee on Small Business, Subcommittee No. 3, *Hearings, Aluminum Industry*, 85th Cong., 2nd Sess., 1958. Hereafter cited as *Small Business Hearings, 1958*. Aluminum company executives testified to the absence of price cutting even during the 1957–58 recession. See p. 58 (Q. "Does Alcoa ever sell below the published price [of primary metal]?" A. [by Mr. Wilmot, vice president of Alcoa] "We do not in the United States."); p. 74 (Q. "Has there ever been any variation that you know of between the published price and the price for which primary aluminum was sold?" A. [by Mr. Rhoades, vice president of Kaiser], "I do not know of any.") and p. 21 ([Mr. McConnell of Reynolds] ". . . I know of no instance in which the market price and the published price are not the same.")

competitors will match a price cut. With a high probability of rivals matching a secret price concession, such reductions would decrease the market price without increasing the market shares of the price cutter. At the same time, the short-run inelasticity of demand precludes an increase in aluminum sales sufficient to increase the total revenue of the sellers. Still another factor is that the periods of slack sales in these years have been of short duration.

The Canadian Complications

The preceding section sets forth an extremely simple pattern of price-making: price leadership by Alcoa and price uniformity at all times. Nothing was said about the three primary producers that have entered the industry since 1955, for each has merely followed Alcoa's price leadership for the short time they have been in existence.

But Limited's role in the setting of the market price cannot be dismissed so cavalierly. For the most part the company has followed Alcoa's leadership. It has absorbed the American tariff to maintain a delivered-price uniformity with the domestic producers. Yet the record shows Limited has played an important, though complex role in price-making leadership, and indeed, it accounts for most of the deviations from Alcoa's leadership listed in Table 5.

The price increase in the summer of 1948 formally led by Kaiser is perhaps the clearest example. On June 28, Alcoa announced a one-cent increase. Kaiser then announced a two-cent price increase on July 7, which Reynolds matched on July 15. For the next three months, Alcoa sold aluminum at a price one cent less than Kaiser, Reynolds, and Limited.

Kaiser's leadership, however, was based upon the presumption that Alcoa would soon follow its price, for the published dates fail to identify the actual price leader. At this time Alcoa was buying ingot from Limited under the long-term contract later to be set aside by Judge Knox as part of the remedy decision.[8] This contract allowed Limited to increase its price to Alcoa upon sixty days' notice with the further stipulation that Alcoa could cancel the contract if Limited's selling price exceeded Alcoa's current list price.

Under this provision, on May 19, Limited notified Alcoa of a one-cent price increase per pound of aluminum ingot, effective

[8] This contract is reproduced in *Remedy Record*, Exhibit 96, pp. 1841–1842.

September 2.[9] On June 28, Alcoa raised its own prices by the same amount. On July 2, Limited announced another one-cent price increase, also effective September 2.[10] Thus, in early July, Kaiser and Reynolds knew that, as of September 2, Alcoa would be paying 16 cents per pound while without a change in its current price it would be selling at 15 cents per pound. Aluminum products at that time were generally in short supply, so that Alcoa by reselling Canadian ingot at the same price could maintain its position in the ingot market without depriving its own fabricating facilities. With a price differential, however, these transactions would reduce Alcoa's profits.[11]

Kaiser's assumption of price leadership then could be predicated upon the high probability that Alcoa would soon increase its price to that of Limited's, as in fact it eventually did. Hence, even though Kaiser provided the formal domestic price leadership in the American market, Limited was the actual price leader. Limited may have also been the de facto leader for the increase in January 1955, which again was formally led by Kaiser. Limited increased its selling price in Canada immediately preceding Kaiser's announcement of a price increase. Limited did not change its American price, however, until after Kaiser had announced a price increase.[12]

But the most interesting and complex case of Limited's de facto leadership was the price reduction of March 1958. On March 27,

[9] House Committee on the Judiciary, Subcommittee on Monpoly Power, *Hearings, Study of Monopoly Power, Aluminum*, 82nd Cong., 1st Sess., 1951, p. 439. Cited hereafter as *Monopoly Power Hearings*, 1951.

[10] *Monopoly Power Hearings, 1951*, p. 441.

[11] At this time Alcoa wrote Limited, "While, of course, we dislike the idea of paying $0.16 per pound when the going price for aluminum in the United States is $0.15 per pound, nevertheless, we haven't much option in the matter." *Monopoly Power Hearings, 1951*, p. 441.

[12] Regarding this price increase, Mr. Rhoades, vice president of Kaiser, testified:

"The Canadians raised their price in Canada; as I recall it was something like three-quarters of a cent a pound. We had under review the price of aluminum, pig aluminum, in the United States, for quite some time.

"I believe that Reynolds came out with an announcement of an increase of 1 cent a pound for pig, and appropriate increases for other products. I presume that they were talking about a percentage increase on fabricated products that sell for a higher price, and they would apply a percentage, the same percentage that 1 cent a pound was to the price of pig, apply that percentage to the fabricated products. I do not know, because I do not know definitely what they had in mind.

"Shortly after that, we came out with a price increase of 1 cent a pound across the board — 1 cent a pound on pig, 1 cent a pound on fabricated products. I do not know whether Alcoa came out the same time, or a day later, or a week later. But that is my recollection of the sequence of, let us say February, or at least the latest price increase on aluminum." *Small Business Hearings, 1955*, p. 313.

Limited announced that as of April 1 its Canadian prices would be reduced by about two cents. The company made no statement about its American price, simply stating "specific prices in different markets served by the company will be announced on or before April 1st." [13] The next day Alcoa reduced its prices by two cents, according to a trade paper "promptly taking the hint," [14] and Kaiser and Reynolds followed two days later. On April 1, Limited announced an American price schedule identical to that of the domestic producers. [15]

This is the sole case of a price reduction in the postwar years. The American producers argued before government agencies and in press announcements that this price cut was an initial manifestation of Soviet economic warfare. [16] Certainly the Russians were a precipitating factor, though a review of the history hardly supports such strong language. The Russian entry into the world market began in 1955, when small quantities of Russian aluminum were sold in Western Europe. Since this was a period of great shortage, the Russians were able to realize substantial premiums over the list price. During the first half of 1957, when demand for aluminum began to decrease, Russian export agencies began to offer sizable quantities of aluminum in British, German, and Belgium markets at less than Limited's list price. [17] (Limited was the major seller in all three markets.) Limited met this competition by offering a loyalty discount. In return for buying 80 percent of his requirements from Limited, a customer would receive a 2 percent rebate on all purchases at the end of the year. [18] The Russians then began making at least some sales at 22.5 cents per pound compared to Limited's list price of 23.1 cents after the loyalty discount. Perhaps as a consequence, Limited's share of the English market declined from 82 percent in 1951 to 75 percent in 1958. [19]

But the Russians were not the only new sellers in the British market. All the American producers apparently made at least some offers to sell in Western Europe. Alcoa, for example, made two offers

[13] As quoted from a Limited press release reprinted in F. L. Church, "What the Price Cut Will Mean," *Modern Metals*, Vol. 14, No. 3 (April 1958), p. 80.

[14] *Ibid.*

[15] *Ibid.*

[16] See [The United States Aluminum Producers], *World Trade and the Aluminum Industry* (New York: United States Aluminum Producers, 1958), p. 30.

[17] Church, "What the Price Cut Will Mean," p. 80.

[18] *Small Business Hearings, 1958*, p. 148–149.

[19] Church, "What the Price Cut Will Mean," p. 80.

at 24.25 cents a pound, slightly below Limited's list price and 1.75 cents below its American price.[20] Reynolds bought an interest in a British fabricator and thus displaced Limited as the ingot supplier.[21] Still, the sales of American producers were extremely small compared to the 12,000 tons sold by the Russians in the United Kingdom during the first half of 1958.[22]

Belgium, Holland, and Germany also had an influx of Russian aluminum at prices less than Limited's current list price. (These countries, as well as England, have either no or nominal tariffs on primary aluminum.)[23] At the same time, Limited reported that American producers were making offers in Spain, Brazil, and India, which were at least in some cases at a price less than Limited's list price.[24] Similarly, Norwegian and Nationalist Chinese producers were seeking to make sales in some of these markets.[25] Hence the Russians were only one among others seeking to invade Limited's traditional markets through price reductions.

This new interest of American producers in export sales is explained by a lower domestic rate of sales accompanying the recession, further accentuated by the reduction in the output of manned aircraft. Between 20 and 30 percent of American reduction capacity was closed down at the end of 1957, while Limited had between 15 and 20 percent of its capacity idle.[26] Unused capacity elsewhere in the free world was considerably less, perhaps 5 to 10 percent.[27]

Such excess capacity, of course, explains why the American firms were willing to accept a lower price abroad. At the same time, these price reductions were relatively modest compared to the marginal costs of the aluminum production. The prices cited at Congressional hearings were all above 20 cents per pound,[28] well above the 12 to 14 cents marginal cost of aluminum pig.[29] Thus, there was no full-scale price war. Rather, the oligopolistic rationale prevailed

[20] *Small Business Hearings, 1958,* p. 151.
[21] *Ibid.,* p. 150.
[22] Church, "What the Price Cut Will Mean," p. 80.
[23] *Small Business Hearings, 1958,* pp. 150–153.
[24] *Ibid.,* p. 158.
[25] *Ibid.*
[26] Church, "What the Price Cut Will Mean," p. 82, and *Small Business Hearings, 1958,* p. 156–157.
[27] At least free-world consumption was off only 3 percent in 1957. Church, "What the Price Cut Will Mean," p. 80. At the same time world capacity was increasing. It is clear the decline in output was concentrated in Canada and the United States.
[28] *Small Business Hearings, 1958,* p. 159.
[29] See Chapter VI.

sufficiently to keep prices substantially above marginal costs, despite the excess capacity.

The effect of the Russian exports upon the American market was limited to the indirect effect of changes in world prices upon the domestic price. Russian aluminum itself did not enter the United States. American producers, however, argued that Western European fabricators, utilizing Russian pig, had been able to cut their prices and so increase their sales in the United States.[30] The figures on the imports of fabricated aluminum bear this out to a limited extent. American imports of mill products for the first four months of 1958 were 7470 tons compared to 5880 for a comparable period in 1957. Yet, this increase represented only 2 percent of the domestic output.[31] It was further argued that import statistics failed to show the extent of the competitive injury, for even a small volume of imports can demoralize the price structure.[32] This is a difficult contention to evaluate, but as discussed in the subsequent chapter, the prices of many fabricated products had already become chaotic because of domestic competition, and the addition of only 2000 tons, less than 1 percent of current domestic production, probably intensified the price competition by very little. The imports, however, were concentrated in the New York City area, so that they may have had a significant impact upon prices in this local market.

Limited's officials offered quite a different interpretation of the factors that created the price reductions. Excess domestic capacity caused increased and intensified competition resulting in "a weakening of the price structure" and, further, "a price reduction will make aluminum more competitive with other materials."[33]

These are the generalities. More specifically, the sequence of events suggests that Limited's list-price reduction was an effort to meet various special offers made in its markets by the Russian, the Norwegian, and the American producers. By the volume of sales and the extent of the price reductions, the Russians were perhaps more aggressive in such offers than their capitalist competitors.

Once it became necessary for Limited to cut its Western Euro-

[30] Letter to the Secretary of Commerce from the American primary producers, dated July 28, 1958.

[31] U. S. Department of Commerce figures cited in F. L. Church, "Aluminum Imports: How Great the Threat," *Modern Metals*, Vol. 14, No. 7 (August, 1958), p. 68.

[32] See letter to Secretary of Commerce.

[33] Nathaniel Davis, "The Free World's Stake in Aluminum" (address delivered by the president of Aluminium Limited, before the Executives' Club of Chicago, September 26, 1958).

pean price, the price concession was necessarily extended to the American market. Otherwise a world price of 22.6 cents plus a 1.5 cent tariff would total 24.1 cents, yielding a margin of 1.9 cents under the then prevailing American price. With such a margin, it would probably pay to import aluminum from Western Europe for resale in the United States.

A further factor was that the price reduction in the American market provided some relief to the independent fabricators. As discussed in the next chapter, the prices of products such as extrusions declined in the early part of 1957, while ingot prices remained unchanged. This narrowed the margins of the extruders. Since Limited's American sales were largely to the independents, the company had a stake in the economic difficulties of its customers. Furthermore, these independents are apparently Limited's political allies on the American scene. In any case, the Aluminum Extruders Council, a trade association of the independents, "heartily endorsed" the price reduction.[34]

It is implicit in the foregoing discussion that the author discounts the arguments of the American producers that the price reduction is the result of "the use of aluminum exports as a tool of war." [35] Instead the evidence appears more consistent with Limited's view that "to anyone who subscribes to traditional economic theory [the price reduction] has come as no surprise." [36] Granting that the Russians played some role in precipitating the price reduction, a price reduction of 7.6 percent still does not seem abnormal for a high fixed-cost industry during a period of substantial excess capacity. Neither the American nor Canadian producers operated at a loss. If the Russians were intent on bankrupting the three American producers or Limited they surely could do better than such modest price reductions and shipments amounting to less than 1 percent of the free-world output.

Yet the issue of Russian economic warfare has considerable political importance. The three American producers petitioned the Secretary of State for protection for the aluminum industry from the alleged economic warfare.[37] Among their proposals were a quota on imports, a study of antidumping legislation, and a study of ways

---

[34] Quoted in Church, "What the Price Cut Will Mean," p. 82.
[35] *World Trade and the Aluminum Industry*, p. 30.
[36] Davis, "The Free World's Stake in Aluminum," p. 4.
[37] Letter to the Secretary of State, July 14, 1958.

in which the world aluminum surplus might be used to aid economic development. Shortly thereafter the president of Limited said (in a speech), "If the appearance of Russian exports is used as a pretext for protectionism applied against friendly nations, the Soviet Union will have achieved a notable victory in the cold war." [38] As of the fall of 1958, no government action had been taken.

The Politics of Price Leadership

A discussion of the merits of the proposals of the American producers is reserved for the concluding chapter. Of concern here are the modifications required in the price-preference model by the existence of Limited's special role in price-making. If Limited were an American firm, or if free trade were completely and irrevocably established, then it may well be that Limited would now be the price leader. It has the characteristics of the low-price preference firm; it is the lowest-cost and largest producer, it has a secure financial position, it has the highest rate of expansion so that it might well be the most concerned about the effect of prices on the growth of demand. (In 1948, of course, Limited instigated a price increase. But at that time the company's size and financial position were more nearly comparable to that of Reynolds and Kaiser.)

In fact, Limited is a foreign company and so a price reduction initiated by Limited would be subject to tariff retaliation. This possibility has been repeatedly voiced by the president of Limited, and, as events cited above indicate, this is no idle fear.[39] Nor was 1958 unique. In 1949, when domestic demand slackened, Reynolds

[38] Davis, "The Free World's Stake in Aluminum," p. 7. It should be noted that Limited has asked the United Kingdom to impose a tariff against Russian aluminum.

[39] Mr. Nathaniel Davis, president of Limited, testified as follows: "Generally speaking, it has been our policy to sell our products at the price at which others are selling their products, and by 'others' I refer to the three producers, Alcoa, Reynolds, and Kaiser. . . . We feel that if we did not sell our products at the American price, the duty would be increased." (*Monopoly Power Hearings*, 1951, p. 440.)

Somewhat later he testified: "We have gone on record to the effect that if the American price were to skyrocket, we don't think we would follow them along. We are in a very different situation, because if we were to quote in this country below the United States' prices, there would be an immediate application for an increase in the tariff — it doesn't seem large viewed as 1¼ cents per pound, but I believe it is pertinent to note that we have paid nearly $27 million in tariff in the last 5 years, importing our ingots into this country. . . . But if we could be assured, that the tariff wouldn't immediately be put up against us, if we were to enter price competition with others, I think we would be somewhat encouraged to do so. . . ." (*Small Business Hearings*, 1955, pp. 157–158.)

and Kaiser petitioned the Tariff Commission to eliminate certain tariff reductions granted as part of the reciprocal trade program and to impose quotas on imports.[40] Upward price leadership by Limited may be similarly ruled out because it would put the onus of a price increase upon a peculiarly politically vulnerable company.

Nor are the consequences of isolating Limited by a tariff barrier limited to price leadership. Other aspects of Limited's behavior can be explained in terms of efforts to obtain domestic political allies. The long-term sales contract between Limited and Alcoa from 1947 to 1950 created a community of interest between the two firms, at least to the extent that Alcoa did not join the other two producers in the 1950 petition to the Tariff Commission. In recent years Limited has apparently formed political alliances with the independent fabricators through concentrating its sales to these customers. The independents have been the important supporters of a low tariff on ingot. (The pattern of Limited's American sales is further discussed in Chapter VIII.)

Yet such inferences may exaggerate the political nature of market behavior in the aluminum industry. There is no evidence to show that these so-called alliances existed consciously in the minds of the participants or that the actions described were not the result of mutual economic interests based upon more limited business consideration. Still, the dividing wall between politics and economics in the behavior of the aluminum industry is apparently a low and broken one. We have attempted to include this kind of behavior in our model through what is termed the leverage effect, the ability of high-price preference firms to utilize nonmarket pressures upon a price leader. In the case of Limited, the tariff may be the device for such leverage.

The Level of Prices and the Short-Run Market Equilibrium

Up to this point the discussion has dealt only with the mechanism by which prices are set rather than the level of those prices. Implicitly, however, this discussion indicated that the prices do not equate short-run supply and demand. With such an equilibrium price there would not be a substantial number of excluded buyers willing to purchase at the prevailing price as in the periods of excess

[40] See *Application of the Reynolds Metals Company before the United States Tariff Commission* (Washington, 1950).

demand, nor, conversely, would there be sellers who are willing to supply additional quantities at the current price, as in 1957.

As indicated earlier, secondary aluminum is a close but inferior substitute for primary aluminum and is sold in a highly competitive market of numerous sellers, no one of whom is large enough to influence the market price by his own actions.[41] Hence, the relation between the prices of secondary and primary aluminum indicates the short-run disequilibriums in the primary-aluminum market. The normal price relation, when both products are freely available, is for primary metal to sell at a slight premium over secondary aluminum. Hence, when secondary metal sells at a premium over the primary ingot price, it indicates there is an excess demand for primary aluminum. When secondary sells at a substantial discount from the primary price it indicates there is an excess supply of primary aluminum. The extent of the price differential, however, indicates only roughly the magnitude of these disequilibriums.

From Fig. 4 it is apparent that excess demand occurred frequently in the postwar decade, for the price of secondary aluminum exceeded the price of primary for five years between 1947 and 1957. At the fabricated stage of production, the backlog of orders for fabricated products and the rationing instituted by the producers indicated that excess demand also occurred here.[42]

Some of these market disequilibriums were due to government intervention. Price control existed for 1951, 1952, and part of 1953. At other times, the pending antitrust action and the government stockpiling of aluminum may have had some indirect effect upon pricing decisions by increasing the caution with which any large firm viewed the political impact of a price increase. But the degree of underpricing seems to have been of such a magnitude that it cannot be explained by these events.

Rather, the occurrence of excess demand would seem to have followed from the basic dichotomy between the inelasticity of the short-run demand function and the high elasticity of the long-

---

[41] As one secondary-metals executive summarized the situation: ". . . the price of primary is apparently a managed price and becomes a fictitious price in periods of heavy demands. Secondary aluminum prices are based on a free market influenced only by supply and demand." (*Monopoly Power Hearings, 1951,* p. 591).

Office of Defense Mobilization, National Production Order *M-22,* January 23, 1951, lists 32 firms, but this includes the smaller firms.

[42] *Remedy Record,* Government Exhibit No. 47 and 17 (p. 43) shows order backlogs for fabricated products.

run demand function set forth in Chapter III. This is illustrated in Fig. 5. The vertical axis represents price while the horizontal axis represents both current sales and the long-run rate of growth of future sales. By plotting these two variables on the same axis we can portray both the short-run and the long-run demand functions in the same figure. D_1D_1 and D_2D_2 are short-run demand curves, indicating by their steep slope the inelasticity of this function. RR represents the long-run demand curve, stated in terms of the relation between the price and the long-run rate of growth in

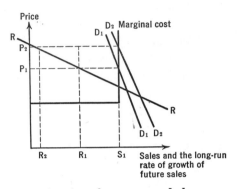

Fig. 5. The short-run and long-run
equilibrium of the firm.

sales. The gradual negative slope of this function depicts the fact that a lower price will induce a significantly higher rate of growth in sales or, in other terms, the long-run demand function is highly elastic. The marginal cost curve is L-shaped, indicating constant marginal costs up to the designed capacity (S_1) and the inability to produce beyond this capacity, a point empirically verified for aluminum reduction in Chapter VI.

Assume an initial equilibrium of the firm at P_1 where sales are S_1 and the rate of growth R_1. Subsequently, an unexpected upward shift in the short-run demand curve to D_2D_2 occurs. If the objective of the firm is only short-run profits, then the price will be increased to P_2. This price change has the corollary that the rate of growth will decrease to R_2.

Yet this outcome would not represent an equilibrium if there were a combination of: first, a rate of growth of sales highly sensitive to price increases; second, a firm with an interest in future profits and sales; and third, an inelastic demand so that substantial price increases with their adverse effect on future sales are required to clear the market. Rather the equilibrium will be at some price less than P_2 for which the value of the growth of future sales offsets the higher short-run profits that the inelastic demand function indicates could be earned. Such a price will not clear the market but instead will create excess demand. Primary aluminum would appear to fulfill all three of these conditions. Furthermore, as shown in Chapter III, price variations, apart from their amount, discourage the growth in sales. This factor, in conjunction with a capacity limitation upon increases in output, further contributes to the existence of excess demand.

In the aluminum industry then, excess demand appears as an inevitable consequence of the demand functions, the time lag in the construction of new capacity, and the existence of firms oriented toward long-run profits. The duration of the excess demand depends upon the behavior of investment, a topic discussed in Chapter X.

None of these characteristics are unique to the postwar period, so that it is not surprising that excess demand also occurred in the aluminum industry during the 1920's, another period of increasing sales. Excess demand was indicated by the decline in the difference between the prices of primary and secondary aluminum from five cents to one cent per pound.[43] As further evidence, imports of primary aluminum increased, and imported aluminum generally commanded a premium over Alcoa's list price,[44] the "spot" price in New York for aluminum exceeded Alcoa's list price, and there was a substantial order backlog.[45]

The opposite condition, excess supply, is explained by the short-run inelasticity of demand, for by definition a price reduction here reduces the revenue of the industry. At the same time, a price reduction is so promptly met as to yield no differential advantage to the price cutter. A dramatic illustration of the price stability in

[43] Donald Wallace, *Market Control in the American Aluminum Industry* (Cambridge: Harvard University Press, 1937), p. 253. The secondary-aluminum output increased from 32,800,000 pounds in 1922 to 92,600,000 in 1928. (The First Boston Corporation, *Aluminum—The Industry, and the Four North American Producers* (New York: First Boston Corporation, 1951) p. 78.

[44] Wallace, *Aluminum Industry*, p. 240.

[45] Mr. A. V. Davis, then president of Alcoa, testified there was a shortage of 55,000,000 pounds of primary aluminum in 1925 and 42,000,000 in 1927. From the context it is apparent that this was a shortage at the going price. (Brief of the United States, p. 204, United States v. Aluminum Company of America, 148 F 2nd, 416 (2d cir. 1945).

the aluminum industry is provided by the early 1930's when the list price of aluminum remained unchanged despite the sharp decline in sales. The 1957 period of excess supply is discussed above.

The Level of Prices and the Price Policy of Alcoa

Thus, the market price bears little relation to the current demand and supply situation. But this negative conclusion does not indicate the factors that determine the market price. According to the oligopoly model set forth at the outset of this chapter, the market price will be the price preferred by the lowest-price preference firm. Alcoa is apparently the low-price preference firm in the aluminum industry, so the market price is a reflection of Alcoa's price policy.

Price policy implies a long-run view in price decisions. The nature of demand for aluminum as described in Chapter III makes any other approach to pricing irrational. Demand is multiperiod, that is, this year's price affects next year's sales. (Otherwise, there would be no long-run demand function.) Given the short-run inelasticity of demand, it is possible to increase current profits by increasing the current price. Yet, given the long-run high elasticity of demand, such price increases jeopardize further sales and future profits.

As a result, pricing decisions involve a choice between present

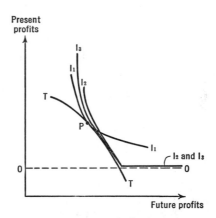

Fig. 6. Conditions of choice between
present and future profits.

and future profits. Such a decision can be represented by Fig. 6. A transformation curve, *TT*, depicts the conditions of choice; that is, successive increments of present profits are achieved at the cost of successively larger reduction in future profits. TT does not intercept the axes because, at some point, further price increases will decrease current profit. Similarly, at another point, further price decreases will have no effect upon future sales. Since a firm will select neither a reduction in both present and future profits, nor less present profits and no greater future profits, the transformation curve has not been extended beyond these points. Notably, however, if the firm were only a short-run profit maximizer, there would still be positive future profits, or if the firm were oriented only to future profits there might well be positive present profits. The important point here is that price policy operates in the range in which there are trade-offs between future and present profits.

A formal solution is indicated by drawing a profit-indifference map. The point at which the transformation curve is tangent to the highest indifference curve indicates the choice with maximum utility. The firm that is here has by definition the most preferred combination of present and future profits obtainable. Such a point would be P on I_1I_1. Such a solution is, however, devoid of content, for there is no disputing tastes and so all solutions seem equally likely.

A less general formulation may produce a more operational conclusion. A firm cannot allow its present profits to fall below a certain level if for no other reason than to avoid bankruptcy. In addition, a certain rate of current profits is required to meet current dividend needs and provide retained earnings for expansion. Future profits are not substitutable for these immediate financial requirements, particularly given the uncertainty of the realization and the unknown amount of future profits. This lower present profit limit is indicated by OO in Fig. 6. But, once these needs are met, the utility of additional present profits declines rapidly, and the future profits become extremely attractive. This rapid change in the marginal rate of substitution of future for present profits is indicated by the kink in the indifference curves I_2 and I_3. These kinked indifference curves will be tangent to a wide range of possible transformation curves at the same level of present profits OO.

Given the proposition that most demand curves are multiperiod (a proposition implicit in the long-run elasticity of demand) and that high present profits may entail fears of entry, government action, and union pressure, the choice between present and future profits frequently occurs. Hence, what Professor Simon calls "satisficing" profits (i.e., attempting to reach some preconceived level of acceptable present profits) rather than maximizing profits may be an administrative simplification to reflect the time preferences of a firm in a very complex and uncertain situation.[46] The empirical form of "satisficing" may be to set prices to yield a desired current rate of profits. All further gains are then taken in the form of future profits. This leaves unresolved the question of what determines the desired current rate of profits. In general, the businesswide standards of good profits, the specific expectations of the stockholders, and the management knowledge of the effect of present prices upon the growth in demand and upon the development of new competition shape the standard for present profits.

It remains to be shown that this model corresponds to the behavior of Alcoa. Statements of Alcoa executives support the three key propositions: the long-run character of pricing, the importance of low prices in expanding the market,[47] and the use of a "planned" rate of return on investment to set prices.[48]

But these generalized statements are not as meaningful as an examination of the administrative procedures by which these general policies are translated into business behavior. (For this purpose the discussion borrows largely from a Brookings Institute Study,

[46] This kind of model of rational choice is discussed at great length in Herbert A. Simon's "A Behavioral Model of Rational Choice," *Quarterly Journal of Economics*, 69:99–118 (February 1955).

[47] According to Mr. Wilson, president of Alcoa:

". . . the whole objective of Alcoa over the whole period of years has been to keep the price trend down, so as to broaden the market and why we are quite content today with the market broadened to the extent that it is with a much less spread between mill cost, as an example, or complete costs and selling prices.

"As far as Alcoa is concerned, it sets its price as low as it consistently can and make a fair profit . . . because we believe that that will insure a maximum development of the aluminum industry. . . . That policy will make the aluminum industry, and that is what is making the aluminum industry today." *Monopoly Power Hearings, 1951,* pp. 678, 632, 634. The following interchange is equally illuminating:

Q. Now at that time when you did not raise the price, is it your opinion that your primary metal was competing with secondary metal, then bringing 24 cents a pound?

A. [by Mr. Wilson, president of Alcoa] Very definitely.

Q. Price-wise?

A. Yes, I would say yes, certainly.

Q. Is it your understanding, Mr. Wilson, then in a competitive market, sellers try to obtain as much money as they can for their products and the buyers try to pay as little as possible.

A. . . . I think there is a distinction between an immediate short-term consideration and a long-run consideration.

Remedy Record, pp. 1266–1267.

[48] See the subsequent discussion in this chapter.

Pricing in Big Buiness.[49]) Alcoa's price making begins with a target price based upon the cost plus a desired profit margin. As Table 6 indicates, most of these costs are relatively easily determined by

TABLE 6. Target price and performance on a fabricated aluminum product, Aluminum Company of America, 1956[a]

Elements	Target price (cost estimate)		Actual cost and price	
	Dollars per Pound	Percent	Dollars per Pound	Percent
Metal value (including commercial metals)	0.261	29.0	0.243	27.0
Prime Cost of Fabrication				
Direct labor	.038	4.2	.040	4.4
Direct material	.145	16.1	.167	18.6
Factory burden at standard rates	.125	13.9	.131	14.6
Total prime cost of fabrication	.308	34.2	.338	37.6
Transportation allowance	.015	1.7	.016	1.8
Allowance for idle facility cost[b]	.029	3.2	.032	3.6
Allowance for plant administrative expense	.032	3.6	.035	3.8
Total works cost	.645	71.6	.664	73.8
Allowance for general administrative and selling expense	.039	4.3	.040	4.4
Total cost	.684	76.0	.704	78.2
Allowance for profit margin	.216	24.0	.196	21.8
Price	.900	100.0	.900	100.0

[a] Figures rounded.
[b] For determining target costs and price, the norm is 70 percent of full capacity. Since the itemized costs are figured on the basis of full capacity, a general allowance is made to spread the full burden of the facilities over output averaging 70 percent of full-capacity use.

Source: A. D. H. Kaplan, Joel B. Dirlam, and Robert F. Lanzillotti, *Pricing in Big Business: A Case Approach* (Washington: The Brookings Institution, 1958), p. 29.

a conventional accounting system. The costs computations are determined upon the assumption of a full capacity rate of production. The idle facility cost, however, is an allowance for the difference

[49] A. D. Kaplan, Joel Dirlam, and Robert F. Lanzillotti, *Pricing in Big Business: A Case Approach* (Washington: The Brooking Institute, 1958), pp. 21–39.

in allocating overhead upon a full-capacity rate of production and a rate of production of 70 percent of capacity which is considered the long-run normal volume.

The profit margin is determined by a "desired" rate of return on the capital invested in the production of each product. The applicable rate of return, in turn, is determined, according to Mr. Wilson, president of Alcoa, as follows:

> In setting our prices we set them so that if and when we have a normal expected load [volume] in our plants, we will make approximately 15 to 20 per cent return on the capital used in connection with operations for producing that particular aluminum commodity.
> Now that results after taxes — over a long period of time — in a profit to the company of about 10 per cent on the equity capital in the business. That is the history that has been shown and litigated over in the antitrust case and I think is not disputed at all, but that is the basis upon which we set prices." [50]

This describes only the determination of a planning norm. As Table 6 shows, the actual performance will depart from the goal. The important point then is the response of the firm to departures from the norm. If the norm is markedly bettered, the history of the 1920's suggests that prices will be reduced in the expectation that this will expand the market for aluminum. But, in the postwar period, the economy-wide inflation has meant that costs have been continually increasing and so actual profit performance has probably fallen short of the norm. As Table 5 indicates, prices have been adjusted upward at about six-month intervals.

Unfortunately, data are not available to compare actual performance with these norms. Mill costs per pound of aluminum pig are the only time series of costs available for the postwar years. Mill costs include labor, depreciation, materials and their transportation, and electric power, and exclude general overhead, research, selling expenses, and transportation of the product.

The gross margin as a percent of the pig price is computed in Table 7. (Gross margin is the difference between the mill cost and the price.) The general trends outlined here are fairly simple to explain. The margin declined until 1952, reflecting a lag in the adjustment of prices to the inflationary trend of costs and aggravated by government price control in 1951, 1952, and 1953. Despite the slight downturn of business in 1954, the margin began to increase

[50] *Monopoly Power Hearings, 1951*, p. 634.

so that by 1955 the gross margin was greater than in 1947. (This does not necessarily mean greater net profits because indirect costs may now be a greater fraction of the total price.) Perhaps all this table demonstrates is that there is a sufficient variation in the relation of direct costs and prices so that the "target" price and the planned rate of return are administrative devices for pricing decisions that have a large number of exceptions and lags.

TABLE 7. The relation of the mill cost of aluminum pig
to its list price

Year	Price (cents per pound)	Mill cost (cents per pound)	Gross profits as a percent of the price
1947	14.0	9.04	35.4
1948	14.5	10.21	29.7
1949	16.0	10.94	32.0
1950	16.6	11.38	31.9
1951	18.0	12.29	31.7
1952	18.4	13.72	25.5
1953	19.7	14.07	28.5
1954	20.2	13.63	32.6
1955	21.9	13.43	38.7

Sources: prices, ingot-price series shown in *Metal Statistics*, 1958 (New York: American Metal Market, 1958), p. 619, as corrected for mill prices shown in *United States v. Aluminum Company of America*, 153 F. Supp. 132, 151; costs, *United States v. Aluminum Company of America*, 153 F. Supp. 132, 185.

The evidence examined here, as well as that in subsequent chapters, suggests three additional observations about price policy. First, this target-price system corresponds to the preceding model of the firm in two respects. There is an emphasis upon a desired current rate of profits. The statements of the primary producers stress the adverse effect of higher prices upon the volume of sales, although admittedly these same practices are equally consistent with the fear that higher profit will create entry or government intervention. Second, the actual prices seldom exceed the target prices, thus creating the periods of excess demand noted earlier. Actual prices, however, have been less than the target price. This may be because of specific competitive situations in the various fabricated products, and certainly the ingot price decrease of 1958 was hardly part of the target-price system. Likewise, actual prices have lagged behind the rising costs until 1954, but the narrowing of the unit profit margin was offset by the high utilization of capacity. Third, the price relation between the various aluminum products is more rigid than the strict application of the target-price system to each product would suggest.

Some of these points will be discussed further in subsequent chapters. At this point, it suffices to say that the translation of over-all price policy into administrative practice is complex, and that any price policy is only the baseline for the numerous exceptions. Nevertheless, the crucial item, the desired rate of return as translated into a target price, may well be the device by which the top management communicates its long-run preference between present and future profits to marketing executives. Exactly why a particular percentage becomes the planned rate of return for pricing decision remains unclear, although it appears that the desired rate of profit may represent a rough equilibrium between the necessity of retained earnings for financing expansion and a low price for market expansion.

This explanation corresponds to the preceding model of price leadership. The higher-price preference firms by definition have a greater preference for present profits than do the price leaders. This, in turn, reflects in part a need for greater retained earnings even at the possible expense of future growth. The factors placing Kaiser and Reynolds in this position have already been touched on in the preceding section and will be discussed again in the subsequent chapters. At present, we wish only to underline the connection, presented in this chapter, between the analysis of price leadership and the behavior of the firm.

V

THE PRICING OF

FABRICATIONS

WITH all the sizes, shapes, and variations of each type of fabricated product, there are several thousand prices at the fabricated level. Fortunately, prices generally move together within each product category. The problem is further simplified by the existence of two distinct patterns to which the prices of most fabricated products can be assigned. The prices of some fabricated products move in timing and in amount with the changes in the price of aluminum pig. These will be termed rigid prices. The prices of other products follow a more independent pattern with neither the timing nor the amplitude of the price changes corresponding to the changes in the price of pig. These will be termed flexible prices.

Rigid and Flexible Prices: The Empirical Evidence

The distinction between rigid and flexible prices is solely an empirical one. The nature of each pattern is discernible from the behavior of Alcoa's prices for 17 principal fabricated products shown in Table 8. With 13 of these products, every change in the fabricated price coincides in time with a change in the price of pig (that is, within 15 days). As Table 9 indicates, 9 of these same products have had percentage changes in the six years from 1949 to 1955 that differ by less than two points from the percentage change in the price of pig. The prices of these products will be classified as rigid.

Two products, extrusions and aluminum powder, have distinctly different price histories. Each had two or more price changes that did not coincide in time with changes in the price of pig. Further, the prices of these products increased by only 10 and 11 percent

TABLE 8. Number of price increases in fabricated aluminum products occurring within 15 days of increases in pig aluminum, January 1, 1949, to June 30, 1955, The Aluminum Company of America[a]

Date of pig price increase	No change	Price increase equal to pig price increase	Price increase less than pig price increase	Price increase more than pig price increase
May 22, 1950	4	11	1[b]	1
Sept. 25, 1950	1	1	0	15
Aug. 4, 1952	0	4	0	13
Jan. 23, 1953	2	1	0	14
July 15, 1953	1	0	0	16
Aug. 5, 1954	1	0	0	16
Jan. 13, 1955	1	15	1	0

[a] Some product price changes did not coincide with increases in the pig price, as follows: one product price changed independently once; one product price changed independently twice; two product prices changed independently three times; the other thirteen product prices changes coincided with the pig price change.

[b] Reduction in price.

Source: Computed from data in House Select Committee on Small Business, Subcommittee No. 3 on Minerals and Raw Materials, *Report, Small Business and the Aluminum Industry,* 84th Cong., 2nd session, H.R. No. 2954, 1956.

from 1949 to 1955 as compared to the 34-percent increase in the price of pig. Therefore, these prices are classified as flexible.

As in any two-fold classification system, there are intermediate cases. The prices of six products have had increases from 1949 to 1955 that were 2 or more percentage points less than the change in the price of aluminum pig, and some of these six have had price changes that did not coincide in timing with a change in price of pig. Yet the difference between the behavior of the prices of these products from that of the rigid-price group is not so marked as in the case of the prices of extrusions and powder cited above. Notably, the percentage advances in the prices of these intermediate products, while well above extrusion and powder, are significantly lower than those for the rigid-price group.

The prices set by Reynolds and Kaiser were generally identical to those of Alcoa. Unfortunately, there are sufficient differences in the specific products for which prices were reported to the House Small Business Committee that direct comparisons cannot be made. The prices of the fabricated products listed by Reynolds and Kaiser exhibit the same division among rigid, flexible, and intermediate patterns. Within generic product categories, these patterns were the same for all three firms.

TABLE 9. Alcoa's base prices in cents per pound, aluminum products,[a]
January 1, 1949, and March 1, 1955

	Prices		Increase	
	1949	1955	Amount	Percent
Pig, 99-percent minimum average purity	16.0¢	21.5¢	5.5¢	34%
Rigid-price group				
Ingot, 99 percent plus, 30-pound	17.0	23.2	6.2	36
Extrusion billet, 6063 solid, various diameters	18.8	25.5	6.7	36
Reroll slab, 5052, 3¾ by 16 by 30 inches	22.5	30.7	8.2	36
Reroll coils, 3003 F, 0.125 by 17 to 48 inches	20.8	28.2	7.4	36
Foil stock, 1145-H 18, 0.026 inch coiled by 12 to 48 inches	22.6	30.7	8.1	36
Foil, 0.0035-inch plain coiled, various widths	40.0	54.0	14.0	35
Sheet 3003 machine finish, 0.020 by 12-inch coiled	27.7	37.1	9.4	34
Intermediate group				
Forging stock 2014, clas. 1, 2-inch diameter	29.5	39.3	9.8	33
Electrical conductor cable, No. 4, 7/1 A.C.S.R.	22.69	30.0	7.31	32
Tube blooms 3003, 2-inch schedule 40 pipe	27.5	36.0	8.5	31
Rod 2017 screw machine stock 1-inch diameter	35.5	46.3	10.8	30
Bar, 2017-T4, 1.438 to 0.689 inch by 1.001 to 1.500 inches	39.5	51.5	12.0	30
Wire, 2117, rivet wire 0.130, 0.203-inch diameter	37.0	47.9	10.9	29
Tubing 3003, 1-inch outside diameter by 0.65-inch wall	46.0	57.8	11.8	26
Redraw rod E. C., H14, ⅜ inch diameter	22.5	28.0	5.5	25
Highly flexible group				
Extrusions 6063, solid shapes, factors 27–28, 0.1 to 0.2 pounds per foot	40.4	44.5	4.1	10
Powder, standard paste 205	39.5	44.0	4.5	11

[a] Grade of purity, alloy, dimension, gage or shape of each product was that most typically used or demanded of Alcoa.

Source: House Select Committee on Small Business, Subcommittee No. 3 on Minerals and Raw Materials, *Report, Small Business and the Aluminum Industry,* 84th Cong. 2nd Session, 1956, H.R. No. 2954, p. 71.

Data on prices of fabricated products are unavailable for the years after 1955 in the same form. *Steel, the Metal Working Journal* publishes the market price (that is, the list prices of the primary producers) for various aluminum fabrications products in the rigid-price group. These data indicate that changes in the prices of these products continued to correspond in timing and amount to the changes in the primary price even during the recession year of 1957.[1]

The trade press does not publish the prices of products in the flexible group, which is perhaps one index of their flexibility. However, prices here do decrease with a decline in demand as, for example, extrusions for which the list price was reduced by 6 percent in 1957.[2] Yet the most significant price reductions have occurred through deviations from the list price.

The division of total fabricated aluminum output between those products with rigid prices and those with flexible prices is not easily determined. If all extrusion, wire and cable (which show some flexibility), and cast products are included in the flexible-price group, then this group accounts for 53.87 percent of the fabricated output (see Table 10). This is an overstatement of the relative size of the flexible-price group. Within the general class of extrusions, subclasses like hard-alloy extrusions have a rigid-price pattern even though these products generally have a flexible-price pattern. On the other hand, within the major commodity groups in the rigid-price group, no examples of flexible-price behavior were discovered. Perhaps all that can be concluded is that both categories include a sizable fraction of the total output and that products in the rigid-price group probably account for the largest share of the output.

An Explanation of Rigid Price Behavior[3]

Products with a pattern of rigid-price behavior are distinguished by the preponderance of their production by the primary producers. In contrast, products with the flexible-price histories are characterized by a relatively large number of independent fabricators that account for at least one-third of the total production. For example, 16 independents account for but 6 percent of the sheet and plate output and here a rigid-price pattern prevails. In contrast, 80 independents produce over one-half the output of extrusions, a product with a flexible-price pattern. There are two exceptions. Cable, an

---

[1] Commenting on the prices for these aluminum products during the recession, *Modern Metals* added, "Mills can take on more flat stock (sheet) business, but price cutting is not the accepted way of doing business — yet." "Looking Ahead," *Modern Metals*, Vol. 13, No. 2 (March 1957), p. 127.

[2] *Ibid.*

[3] This material is based upon interviews in the trade, as are other parts of this chapter.

TABLE 10. Shipments in the United States by integrated and nonintegrated producers of various semifabricated aluminum products, 1954

Product	Integrated producers[a]		Nonintegrated producers[a]		Total shipments	
	Number of producers	Percent of total shipments	Number of producers	Percent of total shipments	Pounds	Percent
Rigid-price group					1,209,083,000	46.13
Sheet and plate	3	94	16	6	1,057,485,000	
Foil	3	69	9	31	151,598,000	
Flexible-price group					1,414,574,000	53.87
Wire and covered cable	3	57	44	43	72,251,000	
ACSR and bare cable	3	75	12	25	147,166,000	
Extruded shapes and drawn tubing	3	47	80	53	523,248,000	
Powder, flake, and paste	2	58	7	42	46,909,000	
Castings[d]	1	9[b]	3800[c]	91		
Total[d]					2,623,657,000	

[a] Integrated producers of aluminum primary metal. Nonintegrated producers of aluminum products exclude captive companies, using most or all of their aluminum for end products. In 1954 these included 6 producing sheet; 1, wire; 1, foil; and 23, extrusions or tubing.

[b] Based on production by Alcoa reported to Subcommittee No. 3. Kaiser and Reynolds do not produce castings.

[c] Over 3800. Based on U. S. Census report for 1950.

[d] Includes some double counting in the weight of reroll sheet stock shipped to nonintegrated producers of foil, reflected in foil shipments and in sheet shipments.

Source: House Select Committee on Small Business, Subcommittee No. 3 on Minerals and Raw Materials, *Report, Small Business and the Aluminum Industry*, 84th Cong., 2nd Session, H.R. No. 2954, 1956, p. 72.

intermediate case, is subject to competition from copper cable. Powder and paste, a product with a flexible-price history, is produced by only 7 independents, who, however, jointly supply 40 percent of the market.

These differences in the relative share of the output by the independents are correlated with the character of the independent fabricator's pricing behavior. For such products as sheet, the independents follow the prices of the primary producers and generally adhere to their list prices.[4] Even if they did not, the small share of the independents means that any off-list pricing by these firms need not be matched by the primary producers. Therefore, the independent fabricators have had little effect upon the amount or timing of price changes.

Rather, the primary producers have set the prices. Since rigid prices change as a unit with changes in the price of ingot, the general model developed in the last chapter to explain the pricing of aluminum ingot is applicable here. Thus the differences between high- and low-price preference firms, the interaction of these differences to set a pattern of price leadership and followership, and the importance of the price policy of the leader, Alcoa, determine the prices of these fabricated products.

An Explanation of Flexible Price Behavior

It is primarily the pricing actions of the independent fabricators that create the flexible prices. The pricing of extrusions is the most obvious illustration of this proposition. Here, however, establishing the role of the independents in pricing is complicated by the decline in the cost of extruding due to various technological changes. This factor alone might lead to some price reductions. But the chronological sequence of events underlines the crucial role of the independent extruders in determining the price of this product.

Initially, the primary producers' list prices of extrusions were adopted by the independent extruders. It was only with declines in demand, as in 1954, and 1957, that the role of the independents became apparent. During the initial decline in demand, the independent fabricators granted concessions from their list prices to retain customers and gain new business. Once these concessions

---

[4] See the testimony of independent sheet rollers, Record, pp. 2000ff., United States v. Aluminum Company of America, 91 F. Supp. 333 (S.D.N.Y., 1950), before Judge Knox (hereafter cited as *Remedy Record*) and interview information.

became widespread, the primary producers reduced their list prices to meet this competition from off-list prices.[5] (As *Modern Metals* observed after one list-price reduction, industry executives hoped the "market" price would now increase sufficiently to equal the new lower list price.)[6]

The logic of such behavior is that each of the 80 independent extruders is individually so small that a single firm can expect that its off-list price will not be matched by changes in the list price by the primary producers. This expectation is likely to be fulfilled initially, since the loss in market share of a primary producer because of the price reduction of a single independent fabricator will be extremely small, given the size and the localized character of the sales of the typical extruder. As a result, primary producers find it unprofitable to meet such price cuts with an across-the-board reduction in list price. At the same time, large firms find it difficult to cut prices only to the potential customers of a particular fabricator, because of the internal administrative complications, the adverse reaction of other customers, and the legal dangers of selective price cutting.[7] The secrecy of off-list pricing itself does not seem to be a major factor, for the existence of such price reductions is generally known. The exact price reductions offered individual customers is, however, confidential.

After several independent fabricators have made off-list price reductions, the primary producers attempt to protect their market shares by reducing their list prices. This is necessary because in extrusions the independents have one-half the market, so that their off-list prices can be quite widespread. In contrast, in a rigid-price product such as sheet, the independents have but 6 percent of the market so that off-list pricing could be ignored by the primary producers.

The short-run elasticity of demand for aluminum products means that the firms have less revenue after the price reduction. Conse-

[5] See F. L. Church, "In Questionnaire Replies Fifty-One Extruders Say," Modern Metals, Vol. 13, No. 7 (August 1957), pp. 8off. Perhaps the best summary view was the following statement of one extruder: "A few of the independents and one of the integrated aluminum companies depend more on the proselytizing of good extrusion customers by means of price cutting than they do on the development of new applications for their own sales volume. Actually it has been price cutting that precipitated the published price reductions by the 'Big Three.' " *Ibid.*, p. 92.

[6] "Looking Ahead," *Modern Metals*, Vol. 13, No. 2 (March 1957), p. 127.

[7] One primary producer stated "price cutting does not allow large volume sales in competition with 'independent extruders' who cut prices to stay in business." F. L. Church, "In Questionnaire Replies Fifty-One Extruders Say," p. 84.

quently there are frequent injunctions by leading independent fabricators for others to sell at book prices. But, if everyone else follows this advice, one firm can profit from off-list prices. If numerous independents act upon this assumption, as they have, the speeches are of little avail.

Once sales begin to increase, the price concessions tend to disappear and the list price becomes the market price. The pattern of subsequent price advances, however, is sufficiently modest that, as noted earlier, from 1949 to 1955 the price of extrusions increased by only 11 percent whereas the price of ingot increased by 34 percent. Furthermore, as Table 11 indicates, the share of primary producers

TABLE 11. Shipments of aluminum mill shapes by integrated producers, 1950–1955 (percent of totals)[a]

Mill shapes	1950	1952	1953	1954	1955	1956	1957
Sheet and plate	96	95	94	94	93	91	90
Foil	73	68	69	69	71	73	75
Wire and covered cable	—	61	60	57	59	51	52
ACSR and bare cable	76	73	72	75	74	60	61
Extruded shapes and drawn tubing	65	60	57	47	48	39	39
Powder, flake, and paste	74	62	55	58	—	—	—

[a]The difference between 100 percent and the percent given is that made by nonintegrated producers.

Sources: House Select Committee on Small Business, Subcommittee No. 3 on Minerals and Raw Materials, *Report, Small Business and the Aluminum Industry*, 84th Cong., 2d Sess., H.R. 2954, 1956, p. 17. House Select Committee on Small Business, Subcommittee No. 3, *Hearings, Aluminum Industry*, 85th Cong., 1st and 2d Sess., 1958, p. 451.

in extrusions has fallen from 65 percent in 1950 to 39 percent in 1957. This is due in part to the role of the primary producers as reluctant price cutters, for in the interim between the list reduction and the initial off-list pricing, the independents apparently increased their share of the market. This gain in market share was retained when demand increased.

Castings, another product with a flexible-price history, represent a different pattern of price-making. Alcoa, the sole primary producer making castings, has no price list, but rather each salesman quotes an individual price for each order, based partly upon a formula reflecting the costs of each order and partly upon a judgment of the state of the market. Each order tends to be an individual bargain, much like the net price after the trade-in allowance in the retail sale of automobiles. When demand is high, the market price tends to follow the cost formula, just as automobile dealers obtain their "Blue Book" prices in the same situation. When demand is slack, prices are shaded almost immediately. Likewise, just as with automobiles, castings can be selling well in Los Angeles and poorly in Boston, with corresponding regional differences in prices.

Such a method of price-making is partially due to the market structure. There are some 3000 foundries with 93 percent of the market, a condition almost approaching pure competition. Therefore it is to be expected that prices will be highly flexible, as these methods of price-making exemplify. The nature of the product is a further factor in creating the individualized character of pricing. Castings are custom designed and so resemble more a job-shop operation than a standard manufacturing process. Finally, the independent foundries utilize largely secondary aluminum that fluctuates greatly in price, and these cost changes, in turn, create adjustments in the prices of castings.

There is, however, one important qualification of the above description. The total output of castings is divided between die, sand, and permanent-mold casting. Die-casting requires a larger over-all capital investment, and larger individual orders are required to make the high investment in the dies economical.[8] In this segment there is more price stability, partly because both the number of buyers and sellers are fewer, and partly because the most important customers, the automobile companies, buy on yearly contracts.

A third example is aluminum wire, a product with a price history intermediate between the rigid and the flexible pattern. With this product, the smaller role of the independents is partially offset by the greater importance of interproduct competition with copper wire. Events in 1949 illustrate the operation of such competition. In May, the published price of copper wire decreased by one cent, and it continued to decrease by that amount at about fifteen-day intervals until mid-July.[9] Aluminum-wire prices remained unchanged until May, when they decreased by one-half cent.[10] Copper-wire prices

---

[8] There were 125 die-casters who are members of the Die Casting Institute, of whom 10 produce 43.7 percent of the total output. House Select Committee on Small Business, Subcommittee No. 3, *Hearings, Aluminum Industry*, 85th Cong., 1st and 2nd Sess., 1958, p. 194. Henceforth called *Small Business Hearings*, 1958.

[9] See American Metal Market, *Metal Statistics, 1952* (New York: American Metal Market, 1952), for these prices.

[10] *American Metal Market* (June 3, 1950), p. 5.

then began to increase with the upturn in sales, passing their May 1949 level in June 1950. Aluminum-wire prices remained unchanged until May 1950, when with the increase in aluminum ingot price, the original differential between wire and ingot prices was restored.

As these two products are close substitutes, the differing price behavior under the same demand conditions underlines the relative rigidity of the prices of these aluminum products. Furthermore, though off-list pricing in aluminum wire does occur, it appears limited compared to that in extrusions and copper wire. Notably, copper wire has two or three times the forty-odd sellers of aluminum cable and wire, and both the share and the numbers of the independents in extrusions are greater than in wire. Even so, the interproduct competition creates more flexible prices here than with other products with rigid price histories, such as aluminum sheet.

This example demonstrates that interproduct competition and the nature of the products have a bearing on the existence of flexible prices. Even so, the castings market without the independents would be a quite different market while a larger number of independent wire-makers might well mean that the fluctuations in wire prices might be initiated in the aluminum industry alone. Instead changes in aluminum-wire price represent only a limited defensive response to the variations in copper-wire prices.

The difference between the behavior of the rigid and flexible prices indicates the decisive importance of the competitive fringe of firms, individually small enough to be unaffected by an oligopolistic recognition of mutual interdependence, yet collectively large enough to influence market price. This suggests that the solicitude extended to small firms by politicians is not justified merely by a nostalgic belief in the small man, but rather provides the emotional support for an important restraint on the pricing of large firms.

The "Price Squeeze" upon the Independent Fabricators

At the same time, complaints by independent fabricators indicate that the existence of small firms has created a new set of public policy problems. It is clear that since 1949 the smaller percentage advance of prices for products with flexible-price history compared to the percentage increase in the price of pig has narrowed the margin between the two prices. As a result, the independent fabricators, and particularly the extruders, have complained of a price squeeze.

Such charges have a venerable history in the aluminum industry. A price squeeze is usually defined as a condition in which the margin between the prices at which firms both buy and sell narrows as the result of the actions of one firm with substantial market power in both the buying and selling markets. The prewar aluminum industry was found by the Court to be such a case. The margin between Alcoa's list price for aluminum sheet and pig declined markedly from 1927 to 1931. Although this jeopardized the economic viability of the independent fabricators of sheet who sold in competition with Alcoa while at the same time buying ingot from Alcoa, it is more doubtful whether the intent was to exert a price squeeze.[11]

The present difficulties of the aluminum extruders are only superficially analogous to the conventional price squeeze. Extruders buy extrusion ingot from the primary producers and sell their products in competition with these same firms. It is also clear that the margin between the buying and selling price has declined markedly since 1947.[12] Beginning in 1953, the extruders have regarded the margin between buying and selling price as unsatisfactory, and a considerable number have voiced forceful complaints of a price squeeze.[13]

Of course, it is almost universal for businessmen to regard their profit margins as unsatisfactory. Yet some standard of comparison is indicated by the fact that, in a survey in 1955 by the House Small Business Committee, only 3 of 18 independents producing sheet, foil, and cable reported an unsatisfactory margin between the pig and the fabricated price compared to 12 of 24 extruders.[14] Sheet

[11] This price squeeze may well have originated in Alcoa's attempt to protect its sheet market from competition from new steel alloys rather than any intent to eliminate competitors. Still, as Wallace observers, "the effect on the independent fabricators can be just as disastrous as one with an intent to eliminate competitors." Donald Wallace, *Market Control in Aluminum Industry* (Cambridge: Harvard University Press, 1937), p. 398. Judge Caffey in the 1937 trial found Alcoa had not intended to monopolize the sheet market by the price squeeze. Judge Hand, however, found that the price squeeze was an unlawful exercise of Alcoa's monopoly power. United States v. Aluminum Company of America, 198 F. 2d, 916.

[12] This is of course implicit in the 11-percent rise in extrusion prices compared to the 34-percent rise in ingot prices. For 1958, *Modern Metals* cites 15.7 cents per pound as the ingot price compared to 38 cents per pound for a typical extrusion, or an absolute margin of 22 cents. For 1957, the ingot price was 27 cents and the extrusion price 48 cents, a margin of 21 cents. *Modern Metals*, cover, Vol. 13, No. 7 (August 1957). In constant dollars, of course, this is an even greater decline.

[13] House Select Committee on Small Business, Subcommittee No. 3 on Minerals and Raw Materials, *Report, Small Business and the Aluminum Industry*, 84th Cong., 2nd Sess., 1956, H.R. 2954, pp. 93-97. Henceforth this report is cited as *Small Business Report, 1956*.

[14] *Small Business Report, 1956*, pp. 93, 103, 105.

and foil have rigid-price patterns. This perhaps underlines the absence of a classic price squeeze, for it is those products with rigid prices in which selling price is most influenced by the primary producers. Here there are fewer complaints of a price squeeze.

Rather the difficulties of the extruders stem largely from the competition between themselves through off-list pricing rather than a price squeeze exerted by the primary producers. To be sure, to some independents the primary producers appear as the price cutters. Price-cutting was sufficiently localized that some independents were forced to reduce their prices only when primary producers reduced their list prices. Furthermore, for 1957 and 1958, there were allegations that the primary producers participated in the off-list price cuts.[15]

Still, the absence of a bona fide price squeeze is indicated by considering how the extrusion market would operate in the absence of the primary producers. The one-half of the capacity now held by the primary producers would be distributed among the existing independents and new entrants. This would mean an even more atomistic market structure and so the price-cutting would be more extensive, thus aggravating the so-called price squeeze. The fact that one-half the capacity is held by three large firms makes this market less price competitive than it would otherwise be.

Furthermore, extrusion production was until 1954 highly profitable, judging from the gross margin then prevailing. At the same time output was increasing at about eight times the rate of all aluminum fabrications.[16] High profit margins and an expanding market combined with relatively low barriers to entry served to attract new firms.[17] The number of independent extruders increased

[15] See the testimony of representatives of the Aluminum Extruders Council, *Small Business Hearings, 1958,* pp. 227ff. Aaron J. Naisuler, chairman, Market Study Committee, stated: "From the cumulative experience of many of its members, the council recently concluded that there was prima facie evidence of price discrimination among customers, and sales below cost or at unreasonably low prices, with the purpose and effect of eliminating the competition of independent custom extruders, on the part of each of the Big Three." No details are given for he requested that "the Committee not call upon us at this time to discuss the basis of our complaint filed with the Department of Justice, lest the ability of the Department to effectively investigate, and, if appropriate, prosecute, be impaired by public disclosure of matters in the course of investigation." *Small Business Hearings, 1958,* p. 228.

[16] The *Small Business Report, 1956,* p. 92, states that one-sixth of the extruders had assets of less than $250,000.

[17] *Small Business Report, 1956,* p. 41.

from 4 in 1940, to 43 in 1952, and to 88 in 1955.[18] The rapid rate of expansion of extruding created conditions for price-cutting, once demand ceased to expand, for in 1954 and 1957 at least some of the newcomers cut prices in order to have the revenue to meet their loan payments on newly bought presses.[19] (Furthermore, despite the price cuts, existing extruders continued to have ambitious plans for expansion.)[20] Accustomed to the profit rates of an expanding industry, extruders may well grumble at the austerity of periods of slack demand.

This explanation does not mean that the extruders are without a legitimate grievance. They do buy in a highly oligopolistic market and sell in a highly competitive market. The decline in their margin reflects that fact rather than a price squeeze by the primary producers. It is indicative of the market power of the primary producers in primary aluminum, however, that price reductions in extrusions have not spread back to aluminum pig.[21]

The smelters of secondary aluminum and the producers of aluminum castings have also made allegations of a price squeeze. The smelters, of course, buy aluminum scrap and melt it to produce secondary aluminum. The foundries in turn buy well over one-half of the secondary-aluminum output. In this sector the primary producers are conspicuously absent, neither selling secondary ingot nor making more than 10 percent of the castings. Even though this would preclude the classical price squeeze, there is still a narrowing of profit margins which can be attributed in part to the indirect effects of actions by the primary producers.

The primary producers influence the secondary aluminum prices through the setting of the primary prices. Secondary aluminum is a close but inferior substitute for primary aluminum. Whenever both types of metal are freely available, secondary aluminum sells for

---

[18] *Small Business Report,* 1956, p. 10.

[19] As one extruder noted, "Too many late-comers to extrusion business are cutting prices to maintain operations." F. L. Church, "In Questionnaire Replies Fifty-One Extruders Say," p. 92.

[20] For example, in 1955, 30 of 39 extruders interviewed would expand capacity if assured ingot, despite a recent period of price-cutting. Eight had installed new presses in the last two years. (*Small Business Report,* 1956, p. 93ff.) Similarly, 21 of 51 extruders planned to expand in 1957, a period with even more price cutting. F. L. Church, "In Questionnaire Replies Fifty-One Extruders Say," p. 88.

[21] Even the hard-alloy extrusions made only by the primary producers were not subject to the same price reductions as the soft alloys. See *Small Business Report,* 1956, p. 93.

a few cents below the price of primary aluminum. During the post-war periods of excess demand for primary aluminum, secondary-metal prices have been substantially above that of primary aluminum. As a result, the foundries with established records of purchasing primary aluminum have had a cost advantage through their use of primary aluminum that enabled them to undersell their rivals sufficiently to generate complaints from the smaller foundries.[22] The smelters have expressed concern over their long-run market position because their customers wholly dependent on secondary have been at a competitive disadvantage.

But the complaints from this sector of the industry have focused largely upon the fact that the primary producers have increased their purchases of secondary aluminum for their own fabricating operations during periods of shortages. Such purchase would further increase the price of secondary aluminum. As Chapter VI indicates, the primary producers buy about one-quarter of the total secondary output and tend to concentrate their purchases in times of shortages. By using the scrap market to meet the peak demand for fabrications rather than building additional primary capacity, the primary producer can increase his average rate of utilization of the high-fixed-cost reduction plants. Yet the purchases of the primary producer have aggravated the instability of the price of secondary aluminum, and such price fluctuations have increased the business uncertainties for the smelters and their customers. This places these firms at a competitive disadvantage vis-à-vis the primary producers and their customers.

A further complication is the practice of tolls and conversions. When the price of secondary aluminum reached its peak, the primary producers apparently reduced their purchases of secondary metal. However, it is alleged that the primary producers encouraged their fabricator-customers to buy secondary ingot or scrap for conversion by the primary producers into the first-stage fabricated products, thus freeing their primary output for their own use.[23] In this way, the primary producers could continue to participate indirectly in the secondary-aluminum market without paying the high price of secondary aluminum. The extent of such practices cannot be estab-

[22] House Select Committee on Small Business, Subcommittee No. 3. *Hearings, Aluminum Industry,* 84th Cong., 1st Sess., 1955, p. 109. Henceforth called *Small Business Hearings, 1955.*

[23] *Small Business Report, 1956,* p. 100–101.

lished without more detailed quantitative evidence than is publicly available.

These are the more general and long-standing complaints. In 1954 and 1955, there was a sequence of events that intensified the complaints from a sector of the industry. As shown in Table 12,

TABLE 12. United States exports and imports of aluminum scrap, 1939–1954 (in short tons)

Year	Exports	Imports	Net balance (export balance underlined)
1939	476	5,046	4,570
1940	955	648	307
1941	57	55	2
1942	32	24	8
1943	14	241	227
1944	413	1,784	1,371
1945	802	5,168	4,366
1946	640	14,541	13,901
1947	788	15,719	14,931
1948	438	71,742	71,304
1949	396	40,221	39,825
1950	799	68,247	67,448
1951	6,280	16,479	10,199
1952	1,027	6,997	5,970
1953	4,582	26,724	22,142
1954	39,338	14,725	24,613

Source: House Select Committee on Small Business, Subcommittee No. 3 on Minerals and Raw Materials, *Report, Small Business and the Aluminum Industry*, 84th Cong., 2nd Sess., H.R. 2954, 1956, p. 69.

from 1945 to 1950 the United States was a substantial net importer of aluminum scrap because the domestic scrap prices were higher than the world price. In 1954, however, the economic expansion in Western Europe increased the European scrap price sufficiently that the United States became for the first time a substantial exporter of scrap. Superimposed on the existing shortage of primary aluminum, the shift in the international trade situation further increased scrap prices.

The burden of the adjustment to the world shortage of aluminum fell almost entirely on the American secondary-aluminum industry for two reasons: the primary industry with a private rationing system based upon historical allocation did not accommodate the new exporters, and the tariffs on primary aluminum in the importing countries discouraged the purchase of primary metal.[24] The Aluminum Smelters Research Institute, a trade association, proposed a limitation on scrap exports, combined with the requirement that additional exports be distributed between primary and secondary aluminum in proportion to the production of each in order to distribute the burden of adjustment to changing international trade between primary and secondary aluminum.[25] By 1957, however, world demand eased sufficiently to reduce the volume of American exports of scrap.

Although this crisis has passed, this event as well as the others described above are indicative of the position of the secondary market in the total structure of the aluminum industry. It is essentially an overflow market for all types of firms — primary producers, fabricators, and exporters — in which aluminum is always available at the market price.[26] Such an overflow character creates marked instability in the price of secondary aluminum with resulting difficulties for the long-run occupants of the secondary-aluminum market — the smelters and their foundry customers. No measure is available of the extent of these difficulties, but given the preference of most business firms for stability in the prices at which they purchase, these firms are at a competitive disadvantage vis-à-vis the sellers and the users of primary aluminum.

The problem of this sector and that of the extruders are essentially the same. Both are flexible parts of an otherwise rigid-price industry, thus creating for them special burdens in the adjustment to changing demand. No real solution for either problem exists short of a structural reorganization of the aluminum industry, but as discussed in the concluding chapter, this is a complex action that may not be worth its costs or in any case that ought not to be undertaken lightly.

Profits in Aluminum Fabricating

A further feature of the price structure of the aluminum industry is that the return from investment in fabricating capacity has been

---

[24] *Small Business Hearings, 1955*, p. 113.

[25] See the testimony of Carl H. Burton, secretary of the Institute, *Small Business Hearings*, 1955, pp. 106–126.

[26] As Mr. Burton testified, "I do not know of nor have I been able to find, one single case where any foundry man or diecaster has been unable to get ingot from smelters if he is willing to pay the quoted market price. . . . Market prices for smelters' ingot are not arbitrary figures picked out of the air. . . . Scrap prices are determined by the law of supply and demand." *Small Business Hearings, 1955*, p. 108.

generally higher than the return from investment in primary capacity. Officials of all three primary producers have so testified, and *Fortune,* that insider of the business press, states, "It is out of the fabrication of their own aluminum, and not out of the sale of pig and ingot that the big three make their important money." [27]

A rough estimate of the difference in profit rates at the two stages of production can be made in the following way. In 1948, Kaiser derived but 6 percent of its revenue from activities outside the aluminum industry, while aluminum sheet was the only fabricated product produced in substantial volume. The capacities at the reduction and fabricated stages were approximately the same, and facilities at both stages were operated at full capacity, with practically none of the primary aluminum sold in the open market.

TABLE 13. Profit margin on aluminum ingot and fabricated products

Price per pound of pig	$0.1500[a]
—Mill cost per pound	$0.1117
=Gross profit per pound of pig	$0.0383
×Pounds of pig produced	256,200,000
=Gross profit on pig	$9,781,460
Annual gross profits	$25,470,000
—Gross profit on pig	$9,781,460
=Gross profit on sheet	$16,689,510
÷Pounds of sheet produced	263,000,000
=Profit per pound of sheet	$0.0635

[a] The price of aluminum pig was 14 cents the first six months of 1948, 15 cents the next four months, and 16 cents the last two months. Fifteen cents per pound has been taken as a rough average price.

Source: Data from Carl M. Loeb, Rhoades and Company, *Aluminum. An Analysis of the Industry in the United States* (New York, 1950), pp. 38–40.

Under these conditions, the difference between the mill cost and market price of pig constitutes the unit gross profit of the primary production stage. The unit profit times the annual output yields the total gross profit at this stage of production. The over-all company profits minus the pig profits, in turn, yields the profits

[27] Robert Sheehan, "Look at the Reynolds Boys Now," *Fortune,* Vol. 48, No. 2 (August 1953), p. 100. Rep. Sidney R. Yates (Illinois), member of Subcommittee No. 3, said to Mr. Reynolds, president of Reynolds Metals Co., who agreed: "There is no question but that the fabricating part of your business is the part that makes the money." (*Small Business Hearings, 1955,* p. 244.) A Kaiser product manager says, "Pig, ingot and billet are the lower profit products." W. B. Griffin, "Man of the Year: Kaiser Aluminum's Dusty Rhoades." (*Modern Metals,* Vol. 11, No. 12 [January 1956], p. 110.) And finally, Mr. Wilmot, vice president of Alcoa, states, "The (profit) margin for the production of intermediate products is low in relation to the margin of the finished sheet." (*Small Business Hearings, 1955,* p. 266.)

assignable to sheet production. Dividing this figure by the annual output indicates the profit per pound on aluminum sheet. These computations are shown in Table 13. Such a method involves two relatively minor errors; the profits on nonaluminum business is credited to sheet production while the administrative and selling costs are assigned to sheet production.[28]

These profits can be related to an investment base through the use of the capital coefficients as computed by the Inter-Industry Analysis Branch of the Bureau of Mines.[29] Such figures contain a large margin of error, but they may still be superior to the balance-sheet figures. Aluminum rolled products required a capital input of $495 per ton of output while aluminum ingot required $463 per ton (both in 1947 prices). Using this data on profits and these figures as an investment base, the rate of return on capital is 16.3 percent at the ingot stage of production and 27.6 percent at the fabricated stage of production.

It is not possible to make similar computations for other fabricated products. The statements cited previously indicate that the rate of return on investment was generally higher at the fabricated stage of production. From the behavior of the prices of products in the flexible group, however, the rate of profit must have fallen on these specific products since 1948. Furthermore, the general pattern of prices and cost changes since 1948 may have resulted in profit rates of the ingot stage nearer those in fabricating.

The figures above are, of course, crude approximations, only substantiating that profits are significantly higher at the fabricated stage of production. If the preceding model of pricing is at all correct, then this profit differential reflects the price policy of Alcoa. Three factors could explain a price policy creating these profit differentials; the historical legacy of the antitrust case, the nature of vertical integration in the aluminum industry, and the possible higher risks in investing in fabricating capacity.

[28] Nonaluminum sales were only about 6 percent of total sales and general administrative costs about 5 percent of total costs. The low magnitude of both these items means the error cannot be too great. The bias is, of course, toward understating sheet profits since the profits of nonaluminum sales were considerably less than the general administrative costs. Any allocation of such common costs between various divisions would be highly arbitrary.

[29] Pierre Citosson, Gregory Zec, and Francis Kelley, "Capital Coefficients for the Integrated Aluminum Industry," U. S. Department of the Interior, Bureau of Mines, Office of Chief Economist, Inter-Industry Analysis Branch Item Number 43 (mimeographed material), 1953.

Alcoa reduced the aluminum price of ingot from 18 to 15 cents per pound in 1942.[30] This price reduction was at the insistence of the Reconstruction Finance Corporation which, as the principal buyer of aluminum ingot through the Defense Metals Corporation and as the owner of the newly built aluminum plants through the Defense Plant Corporation, occupied an especially strategic bargaining position vis-à-vis Alcoa.[31] There was no corresponding reduction in the prices of fabricated products.

No direct evidence exists of why the prices of fabricated products were not changed at the same time. The record of the antitrust suit against Alcoa contained evidence that the price spread between ingot prices and fabricated prices during 1927–1931 had narrowed sufficiently to jeopardize the survival of the independent fabricator.[32] This record may have restrained the RFC from urging a simultaneous price reduction for fabricated products and may have made Alcoa equally reluctant to reduce these prices (over and above its obvious interest as a fabricator). Furthermore, in all the court proceedings and public discussions, the allegation was always against Alcoa as a monopolizer of aluminum ingot and not of the various fabricated products. Therefore, the quasi-political pressures on the ingot price may not have existed on fabricated prices.

These historical factors may still be present, for Mr. Wilmot, vice president of Alcoa, explained the differing profit margins as follows: "The margin for the production of intermediate products is low in relation to the margin of the finished sheet. And that is for no other reason than to allow room for that nonintegrated fabricator to exist." [33] It should be added that Alcoa operates under Judge Hand's mandate not to repeat the price "squeeze" of 1927–1931 (that is, narrowing the price spread between the ingot price and fabricated price). To overprotect against such a charge, a generous profit margin may be maintained on fabricated products, although all the court apparently requires is no lower profit margin on fabricated products than on ingot. There may also be an element of administrative lethargy in that the idle capacity allowance on fabricating facilities may have been greater than on primary capacity, largely because prewar fluctuations in sales were greater at this stage. But, for much of the postwar period, utilization has been

[30] *Materials Survey: Aluminum*, p. IV–6.
[31] *Remedy Record*, p. 989–999.
[32] See Chapter II.
[33] *Small Business Hearing*, 1955, p. 266.

limited only by the availability of ingot, so these idle capacity allowances have in fact been additional profits.

Yet, this price policy may also endure because it is profitable for the primary producers. To the extent that the vertically integrated firms consume their own primary aluminum production, it is a matter of indifference at what stage of production the profits occur. However, to the extent they are buyers of ingot, the primary producers' interest lies in low ingot prices. The primary producers have never quite been net buyers of primary aluminum ingot and pig. Their heavy purchases of ingot from Limited, as described in the subsequent chapters, did, however, reduce the profitability of ingot price increases. Limited could be expected to increase its selling price whenever the primary producers changed their prices as in fact it did. Finally, low primary price discourages entry of new producers, although this may not be its intent.

A final factor that may explain the higher profit rates at the fabricating stage is the possibility that greater risks are involved in investment in fabricating capacity. Fabricating capacity is subject not only to the general fluctuations in the over-all demand for aluminum but also to the shifts in the demand for specific products. But the higher fixed costs in aluminum reduction add to the riskiness of investment in reduction capacity and partially offset the possible difference in the risks created by differences in demand conditions.

This differential in the rates of profit at the two stages of production, whatever its causes, is of considerable importance. Its implications for market behavior are discussed in subsequent chapters.

THE OUTPUT AND INVENTORY PRACTICES OF THE PRIMARY PRODUCERS[1]

THE preceding two chapters espouse a variant of the full-cost theory of pricing. Such theories offer an alternative to the marginalist view of pricing, but unlike the marginal theories they do not provide a simultaneous explanation for the determination of price and output. For some industries it may suffice to dismiss the question of the volume of output with the statement that, at a price determined by full costs, firms will supply the current demand. For the aluminum industry, however, the cost and the time required to alter the rate of production, the sharp fluctuations in demand, and the peculiarities of the short-run cost function create a more complex pattern of output behavior.

Aluminum Ingot: The Pattern of Output and Inventory Behavior

The fluctuations in demand for aluminum are in part merely a reflection of the character of the end uses for aluminum; that is, most aluminum is used for producers' capital goods and for consum-

---

[1] Some of this material is in Merton J. Peck, "Marginal Analysis and the Explanation of Business Behavior Under Uncertainty: As Case Study of Inventory-Output Behavior in the Aluminum Industry," in Social Science Research Council, Committee on Business Enterprise Research, *Expectations, Uncertainty and Business Behavior*, ed. Mary Jean Bowman (New York: Social Science Research Council, 1958), pp. 119–133.

ers' durables. But underlying the sharpness of these fluctuations are the sudden shifts in the level of inventories held by purchasers of aluminum. Although no time series of buyers' inventories of aluminum is available, the inventory origins of demand fluctuations is recognized in the statements of executives of primary producers.[2] Some part of the changes in the level of inventories can be explained by the acceleration principle; that is, if the buyers maintain a constant ratio of inventories to sales, changes in the rate of their sales will produce magnified variations in their purchases of aluminum as the buyers alter their inventories to correspond to the new level of sales. But a greater part of this demand has been for inventories to serve as a hedge against the recurring shortages of aluminum products. Although the stability of list prices precludes conventional price speculation, this demand for inventories has a price dimension. During a shortage, a resale market develops in which aluminum consumers sell from their inventories to other users, often at considerable profit.[3] This "gray" market obviously represents a further incentive for inventory investment on an upswing of demand. Once demand begins to decline, the speculative rationale for hold-

[2] On the downswing of a sales cycle, according to Mr. Wilson, president of Alcoa, "We always do have these periods when business starts dropping off, and it is like a snowball, they always gather momentum. When everybody thinks that their inventories are possibly a little out of adjustment, why nobody wants to buy for a period of time until they adjust their inventories. Then when they have a little pickup in business, their inventories are a little inadequate, and they want to crowd in as much as they can in a short period." (*Record* p. 1141, United States v. Aluminum Company of America, 91 F. Supp. 333 [S.D.N.Y., 1950], Henceforth cited as *Remedy Record.*) On the upswing of demand, Mr. Reynolds, president of Reynolds Metals, reports, ". . . as the volume steps up, the inventories of necessity step up—but I also think that people are trying to build up their pipelines, we will call it." (House Select Committee on Small Business, Subcommittee No. 3, *Hearings, Aluminum Industry,* 84th Cong., 1st Sess., 1955, p. 237. Henceforth cited as *Small Business Hearings,* 1955). Some idea of the magnitude of the inventory accumulation is given by the following testimony of Mr. Wilmot, vice president of Alcoa: "By the latter part of 1954 all fears of any sort of recession had vanished, confidence was restored, business became buoyant, and there was a rush on the part of all to replenish these inventories. Some rather ridiculous situations occurred. For example, a number of customers insisted on placing orders with us for pig and ingot, in amounts from 5 to 10 times greater than they had given us in 1954, for shipment in the same length of time. In short, there was a concentrated attempt to recoup in a few weeks' time an inventory position which they had spent something over a year in reducing." *Small Business Hearings,* 1955, p. 257.
[3] "Here and There," *Modern Metals,* Vol. 4, No. 2 (March 1948), p. 10. In 1948, sellers of aluminum in this market were known as the "forty-cent sheet boys." Since the list price of aluminum was then about thirty cents per pound, the title suggests a substantial premium over the list price. It was estimated that 3 percent of the current aluminum sheet went through this market in 1948.

ing high inventories no longer applies, so that inventory levels are reduced markedly.

Such a speculative demand depends upon business expectations. Relatively little is known about such business expectations except that they are both variable and relatively unpredictable. It follows, then, that the current sales of aluminum products have these same characteristics, so that the primary producers must adopt policies to adjust to frequent, relatively unpredictable, and substantial variation in their rate of sales.

In this situation, the technology precludes a primary producer from simply varying production with the current rate of sales. Primary-aluminum reduction requires a lead time of a month or two to restart production, and in addition, there are also significant start-up costs in reopening a pot line.[4] But the most important factor is the preponderance of fixed costs at the ingot stage of production.

The Short-Run Costs of Aluminum Reduction

The significance of fixed costs is apparent from an examination of the short-run cost function for aluminum.[5] Data are not available to estimate statistically the cost function. It is possible, however, to determine the percentage composition of the various components of the mill costs of aluminum at full capacity and to classify each cost as fixed or variable, as in Table 14. Obviously, at production at less than full capacity, the fixed costs will become proportionally more important. Figure 7 depicts the cost function corresponding to the cost data shown in Table 14, with the vertical intercept corresponding to the 46 percent of the mill costs at full capacity. This is a notably high proportion of fixed costs.

This method of costing has two apparent limitations. First, a cost has either been classified as fixed or variable, permitting no intermediate cases. Each cost that is classified as fixed, however, is sub-

---

[4] These start-up costs are in the order of $100,000 per pot line.

[5] A short-run cost function states the variation of costs with changes in output for a given capacity, in contrast to the long-run cost function that indicates the variation in costs with a change in capacity. This conceptual distinction corresponds to the empirical conditions in the aluminum industry, for existing reduction capacity cannot be modified without clearly observable investment, while the technology does not permit a volume of production much greater than the designed capacity. For a further discussion see George Stigler, "Production and Distribution in the Short Run," reprinted in *Readings in the Theory of Income Distribution,* ed. William Fellner and Bernard F. Haley (Philadelphia: Blakiston, 1946), pp. 120–121.

TABLE 14. The percentage division of various components of aluminum costs at designed capacity into fixed and variable categories[a]

Cost Component	Fixed	Variable	Total
Aluminum Reduction			35
Direct production labor		7	
Administrative and maintenance salaries	3		
Depreciation, insurance, state & local taxes	25		
Alumina			20
Purchase of coal, limestone, and soda		4	
Bauxite, labor & other mining costs		3	
Depreciation and local taxes	3		
Processing:			
Labor, supplies, elec. power		5	
Depreciation & maintenance	5		
Electric power			15
Demand charges	10		
Current charges		5	
Carbon rods		12	12
Transportation		18	18
Totals	46	54	100

[a] Explanation of the classification and sources of data:

Aluminum Reduction: Direct production labor — each pot line has a specified crew. Since the variation in production is made by changing the pot line in operation, this is a directly and linearly variable cost. Administrative and maintenance salaries — with short-run fluctuations in output this labor force is not changed so that it is a short-run fixed cost. Depreciation, insurance, state & local taxes — this is largely a fixed cost in the short run. This explanation of aluminum reduction costs is based upon Nathaniel H. Engle, Homer E. Gregory, and Robert Mossé, *Aluminum: An Industrial Marketing Survey* (Chicago: Richard D. Irwin, 1945), pp. 436–439.

Alumina: Purchase of coal, limestone, and soda — these materials are used in fixed proportions and so they are a linear variable cost. Bauxite, labor & other mining costs — bauxite is mined largely by open strip methods. These costs are largely directly proportional to output. Depreciation and local taxes — a fixed cost. Alumina Processing: Labor, miscellaneous supplies, electric power — (alumina plants often consist of two or three complete and self-contained production units. Output variation is usually accomplished by closing down units. Hence these are linear variable costs.) Depreciation and maintenence — a fixed cost item. This explanation of alumina costs is generally based upon Engle, *Aluminum: An Industrial Marketing Survey,* p. 217. Alumina-processing costs are dealt with in the testimony of Mr. Wilson, president of Alcoa, *Record,* p. 1086, U. S. v. Aluminum Company of America, 91 F. Supp. 333 (S.D.N.Y., 1950), henceforth cited as *Remedy Record.* Mr. Wilson testified as follows: "The plant [the Hurricane Creek alumina plant] is so laid out that all of the process costs and all of the process efficiencies would be just as good at that low rate of operation as they are at full operation." This is, of course, an example of built-in flexibility.

Electric Power: This is bought under long-term contracts which at full-capacity operation typically require two-thirds of the payment as a demand charge. This is a fixed payment during the life of the contract regardless of actual consumption. This fixed payment reflects the high fixed costs of electric power generation. Hence, roughly the same proportion would apply when the power facilities are owned by the primary producers. Current charges — electric power charges which vary directly and linearly with current consumption. These proportions are based upon the figures in Reynolds power contract for the Jones Mill Plant (*Remedy Record,* Defendant

ject to various conditions that prevent its reduction within the few months' time relevant to an output decision. These conditions are set forth in Table 14. It is immaterial for the output behavior examined here whether some of these costs are variable within a two-year, or five-year, or twenty-year period. Conversely, the variable costs can be reduced almost immediately with a reduction in output, as the explanation in Table 14 indicates.

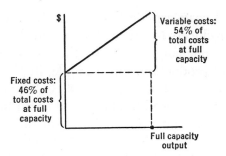

Fig. 7. The short-run cost curve for aluminum reduction.

Second, as shown in Fig. 7, it is assumed that the variable costs can be reduced in direct and constant proportion to the reduction in output. This seems a realistic assumption because of the character of the technology: an electrochemical process that specifies fixed proportions of the inputs of capital and materials for alumina and aluminum production. This precludes any adaptability through changing the proportions of inputs with different rates of production.

Rather, the rate of production is varied simply by changes in the number of pot lines in operation. Each pot line is a discrete production unit, which must be either operated 24 hours a day at its designed capacity or closed down. The primary producer has several pot lines, so that aluminum reduction comes close to the textbook definition of a situation of complete divisibility of the produc-

---

Exhibit 275, p. 3378). A check of other power contracts shows these proportions are typical.

    Carbon Rods: These are used in fixed proportions to current output and so are linear variable costs. Based upon *Remedy Record,* Defendant Exhibit 182, p. 2705.

    Transportation: Transportation of bauxite and alumina. These shipments are in direct proportion to output and bought at constant transportation rates. Hence these charges are linear variable costs. These figures are based upon House Committee on the Judiciary, Subcommittee on Monopoly Power, *Hearings, Study of Monopoly Power. Serial No. 1, Part I, Aluminum,* 82nd Cong., 1st Sess., 1951, p. 885.

tion process, defined as a large number of machines in a large plant. Not only does the combination of zero adaptability and complete divisibility create a linear cost function in the reduction process itself, but the technology has somewhat the same character in alumina reduction and bauxite mining.

The Significance of High Fixed Costs for Output and Inventory Behavior

The high fixed costs explain the output and inventory responses of the primary producers to the fluctuations in demand. Fixed costs by definition are unchanged and so their existence reduces the costs of continued production. For example, in 1948, the additional cost of continued production was only 6 cents per pound, and for this 6 cents, the primary producers received an addition to inventory worth 15 cents at existing prices. With both the long-term growth in demand and the oligopolistic market structure that prevents a collapse in prices,[6] it is almost certain that any inventory could eventually be sold at the existing price. The substantial margin between price and marginal cost makes it profitable to incur a substantial interest and storage cost in accumulating inventory.

As a result, the decision when and how much inventory to accumulate is not based upon the specific expectations of future sales. Instead, the producers tend to continue production whenever sales decline and so build up substantial inventories. Then, and only then, is the cessation of inventory accumulation considered. For the usual fluctuation in demand, this practice of continued production will be the most profitable policy. For the declines of demand of long duration and great magnitude, a more optimal policy would be to close down several pot lines at the outset of the decline in demand and then to reopen these facilities shortly before the initial increase in demand in order to reduce the interest and storage costs of inventory accumulation. This more optimal policy, however, requires a precise forecast of future sales in order to make a differentiation from the outset between major and minor declines in demand. Given the primitiveness of the art of demand-forecasting,

---

[6] For various public relations reasons, companies are unlikely to stress this element. One statement that does is from the 1932 *Annual Report* of the Canadian firm, Aluminium Limited, which was outside the direct reach of the Sherman Act. "World stocks of aluminum are not excessively large. They are in firm hands and do not weigh unduly upon the world market." (Quoted by Donald Wallace, *Market Control in the Aluminum Industry* [Cambridge: Harvard University Press, 1937], p. 321.)

the less ambitious policy of initially continuing production during each decline in demand is probably the most profitable in the long run. This is a highly institutionalized, long-run adjustment to uncertainty, rather than an action determined by the expectations of each situation.

It remains to be shown that this explanation corresponds to the actual business behavior. The affirmative evidence seems clear. The statements of the primary producers correspond to the rationale set forth here,[7] but perhaps more significantly the variations in the rates of primary output are minimal compared to the fluctuations in consumption. The substantial changes in the levels of inventory held by the primary producers further indicate the operation of such a policy.[8]

In fact, an investigation of the history of the aluminum industry since 1924 shows but three instances of a deliberate closing down of production. For these three situations, the precipitating factors may be described as an external event. This point is best clarified by further considering the nature of the cost-profit relation of production for inventory. With a given set of expectations of future sales, the marginal-cost function of production for inventory is continuously increasing from the outset — for the larger the inventory, the longer the time period it must be held, and so the greater the interest and storage charges. Unprofitable inventory accumulation occurs when this marginal-cost function intersects the constant marginal-revenue function. (Prices are, of course, unchanged during short declines in demand.) At what levels of inventory this point occurs is ordinarily extremely uncertain, since it depends on the length and duration of the demand downturn.

However, outside events may create sharp upward shifts in the marginal-cost function. Even though a firm's expectations of future

---

[7] Perhaps the two most explicit statements are the Reynolds Metal Company, "If a primary producer continues production during a buyer's market, he builds up inventory which does have value, but if he closes down he must pay fixed costs, in exchange for which he has nothing" (*Application of the Reynolds Metals Company before the United States Tariff Commission,* 1950, p. 50) and the *Annual Report* of Alcoa in 1932, "Due partly to a desire to assist in the employment situation, and partly to the fact that the heavy fixed charges for hydropower must be paid whether the plants are in use or not, the plants producing aluminum have been operated somewhat in excess of sales."

[8] No complete monthly figures on producers' inventories are available. A comparison of annual apparent consumption and output indicates substantial inventory accumulation. See House Committee on the Judiciary, Subcommittee on the Study of Monopoly Power, *Hearings, Study of Monopoly Power,* 82d Cong., 1st Sess., 1951, p. 911. Henceforth called *Monopoly Power Hearings, 1951.*

sales may be unchanged and uncertain, the sharp shift in the marginal costs of further inventory accumulation indicates that the relation between marginal cost and revenue has significantly worsened and that the profitability of further inventory accumulation must be carefully considered. If inventory is already several times its normal level, the outcome of such a reconsideration is likely to be the cessation of further inventory accumulation. This explanation of business behavior again emphasizes a minimum of actions based on future expectations, for these breaks in the marginal-cost function are present and pressing events rather than future expectations.

A concrete example perhaps clarifies the nature of these outside events and how they create discontinuities in the marginal-cost functions. With the sharp fall in the level of sales in the first half of 1947, the inventory of ingot held by The Reynolds Metals Company increased from 15,000,000 pounds in January to 52,000,000 pounds in July.[9] This inventory accumulation was financed by a successively depleting cash balance, a bank loan of $12,000,000 and finally a sale of a subsidiary.[10] Only at this point did Reynolds close down one of its reduction plants. According to the testimony of Mr. Reynolds, this was not a revision of expectations but rather "we just didn't have any more cash to put in there." [11]

Of course, additional capital could have been obtained at a higher rate of interest. Since Reynolds ceased inventory accumulation at the point at which capital was unavailable at existing terms, it suggests the company was confident enough of an expected marginal revenue and cost relation to continue inventory accumulation at the existing cost of capital, but not sufficiently confident to incur the sharp rise in marginal costs due to capital rationing.

A second example is provided by the even sharper decline in demand in 1931. Alcoa accumulated a total of six months of output, financing this through a bank loan of $27,000,000.[12] Only then did

[9] *Remedy Record,* Government Exhibit No. 18.
[10] *Remedy Record,* p. 157.
[11] More fully, Mr. Reynolds' testimony was as follows:

Q. . . . when you closed down your Longview plant, you thought that the business depression, if you call it that, was going to exist longer than it did?

A. [by Mr. Reynolds] "We didn't think that. We just didn't have any more cash to put in there. If we had had the money, we would have continued to pile up the metal."

Remedy Record, p. 222.
[12] Wallace, *Market Control,* p. 327.

Alcoa close some of its plants, which suggests, again, that capital rationing may have also been decisive in the decision.

The third and final instance of deliberate closing down of capacity occurred in the 1957 recession. Here the weather provides the outside event forcing the decision and creating the cost discontinuity. Substantial inventory had already been accumulated when low water in the Northwest created a power shortage and the consequent closing of aluminum-reduction plants. When power did become available, inventories were even more substantial, so these plants were not reopened.[13] Here, the start-up costs provided the upward shift in the marginal-cost function. However, as sales continued to decline, there was the shutdown of an additional volume of capacity, so that by June 1958, 30 percent of the capacity of the industry was not operating.[14]

For aluminum ingot, then, the marginal cost–price relation makes profitable the accumulation of the substantial inventory for most of the future sales patterns that have occurred. Even for those times for which inventory accumulation would better have been postponed, the normal behavior (to accumulate inventory initially and avoid production shutdowns) still occurs. Once the inventory levels are clearly abnormal, shutdowns of pot lines do occur, and here the timing of the shutdowns is determined by outside events.

Output and Inventory Behavior at the Fabricated Stage

The output and inventory policy of the primary producers at the fabricated stage is much more conventional. Output is varied with the current level of sales, and inventory accumulation is limited to the amounts necessary to meet the inevitable administrative and technical delays.[15] Such a hand-to-mouth policy is in sharp contrast to the inventory policy at the ingot stage.

It is easy to see why this should be so. The conversion of aluminum ingot into fabricated products is a more conventional manu-

---

[13] U. S. Bureau of Mines, *Minerals Yearbook* (Washington, 1958), Vol. I. p. 167. Similarly, a work-stoppage at a Kaiser plant in September 1957 resulted in a lengthy shutdown. On December 31, 1956, producers' ingot inventories were 102,496 tons and on December 31, 1957, 71,142 tons compared to 15,020 tons on the same date in 1955. *Ibid.*, p. 176.

[14] [United States Aluminum Producers], *World Trade and The Aluminum Industry* (New York: [United States Aluminum Producers], 1958), p. 43.

[15] For data on inventories of aluminum sheet, see *Remedy Record* Government Exhibits 17 and 47. These inventories are modest compared to those of ingot, and their variations are small. Sheet accounts for 40 percent of the total output and other fabricated products have about the same pattern of inventory fluctuations.

facturing process than the electrochemical reduction process. Labor costs are about 75 percent of the total manufacturing cost at the fabricating level.[16] Since most of the wage payments are for direct operating labor, this is largely a variable cost.

The narrow margins between variable cost and selling price, of course, do not justify incurring the interest cost of inventory accumulation. Furthermore, holding inventory in fabricated form involves gambling on the future sales pattern of a specific aluminum product rather than the future sales pattern of aluminum products generally. In contrast, inventories of ingot can be converted into the proportions of fabrication required by current demand. Finally, ingot can be stored much more cheaply than most fabricated products.

Output Behavior and Vertical Integration

The coexistence of these two different types of inventory policies at each stage of production has obvious consequences for the pattern of vertical integration. If a substantial inventory is accumulated at the ingot stage, there must be some additional capacity to fabricate this inventory over and above that required for current production. Otherwise the ingot inventories could not reach the market. The greater this excess capacity, the shorter the time lag in converting the accumulated ingot inventory into sales, once demand has returned to a more normal level. This means the greater the excess of fabricating capacity, the lower the risks of ingot inventory accumulation, for the shorter time lag permits disposing of inventory before the demand cycle might reverse itself.

Furthermore, excess fabricating capacity permits the production of the particular types of fabrications in current demand.[17] Indeed,

---

[16] *Monopoly Power Hearings, 1951*, p. 891.

[17] This explanation generally corresponds to the statements of the executives of the primary producers. Mr. Wilson, president of Alcoa stated: "The principal and certainly the major reason [for excess fabricating capacity] is that you practically never experience the coincident demand for all the fabricated products at a maximum at the same time . . . and furthermore . . . we desire fabricating capacity in excess of our smelting or reduction capacity because we buy metal in the market in addition to our own production; we have built up our inventory of aluminum during the period of easing demands upon us for aluminum, and we certainly expect and hope to turn that inventory into fabricated products which we can sell when the business demand is such that it can be sold." *Remedy Record*, pp. 983–984. The explanation here attaches less importance to the coincident demand, because in fact during much of the postwar period all aluminum products have been in great demand. Furthermore, one product, sheet, accounts for 40 per cent of the fabricated output. In either case, of course, as Mr. Rhoades of Kaiser replied in response to

some part of the excess fabricating capacity is not excess capacity in the economic sense. Rather it permits the adjustment of the product mix to cyclical changes in the composition of demand. This kind of excess capacity occurs in other processing industries such as steel and chemicals.

Yet fabricating capacity in the aluminum industry is so markedly greater than ingot capacity that it exceeds the requirements for a hedge against product mix changes. The primary producers have stated that each pound of ingot capacity should be matched by two pounds of fabricating capacity.[18] In 1950 they had in fact nearly this one-to-two ratio.[19] By 1956, they held only slightly more fabricating than ingot capacity, but in these years there was a government-required sale of ingot.[20]

A one-to-two capacity ratio means that on the average a considerable proportion of the primary producers' fabricating capacity would not be utilized. Such idle capacity reduces profits by considerable amounts. For example, in 1948, Alcoa, with nearly a one-to-two ratio, realized only a 6 percent return on investment compared with Kaiser, which, as noted earlier, had one-to-one ratio of capacity and a return on invested capital of about 15 percent.[21]

---

query on excess fabricating capacity, "The problem in this industry, as I see it, is to be in a position to sell your metal." (*Remedy Record*, p. 1480.)

[18] Mr. Rhoades, vice president of Kaiser Metals, testified, "I think in general if we can hit about two-to-one, in that neightborhood is the right ratio, two fabricating to one reduction. . . . It is kind of an endless chain. . . . You will get more fabricating capacity, and when your ratio possibly gets above two to one, then you get over onto the metal capacity, and you bring that up. . . . (*Remedy Record*, p. 1384, p. 1480.)

[19] As of 1950, Alcoa's finishing capacity as a percent of primary capacity was 183; Reynolds, 170; and Kaiser, 195. Carl M. Loeb, Rhoades & Co., *Aluminum: An Analysis of the Industry in the United States* (New York: Loeb, Rhoades, 1950), p. 36. The measurement of capacity is a traditionally elusive concept. In aluminum fabricating, capacity depends on product mix, but the peacetime variations in this mix are not sufficient to change markedly these figures. There is also some double counting, for items like foil are processed through both sheet and foil mills.

[20] In 1955, Alcoa had 1,604,000,000 pounds of fabricating capacity and 1,520,-000,000 pounds of ingot capacity; Reynolds 973,000,000 pounds of fabricating capacity and 839,000,000 pounds of ingot capacity; and Kaiser 838,000,000 pounds of fabricating capacity and 816,000,000 pounds of ingot capacity. House Select Committee on Small Business, Subcommittee No. 3 on Minerals and Raw Materials, *Report, Small Business and the Aluminum Industry*, 84th Cong., 2d Sess., H.R. 2954, 1956, p. 35. Henceforth cited as *Small Business Report, 1956*). For a discussion of these government programs, see Chapter VII.

[21] These rates of returns are based on book value adjusted upward for accelerated depreciation and the purchase of government plants, but less than construction cost. Even though these adjustments may be questionable, they affect all companies relatively equally. These figures, including the adjustments, are from Loeb, Rhoades & Co., *The Aluminum Industry*, p. 45.

(The Kaiser capacity ratio does not indicate a departure from the industry norm, for in the next two years it acquired additional fabricating capacity.) Even though fabricating is not as capital intensive as ingot reduction, still substantial sums are involved.

If this kind of vertical integration is costly in terms of foregone profits, then the offsetting gains must be substantial. The primary producers, of course, are willing to accumulate substantial ingot inventories, so that considerable investment in reducing the risks of such inventory accumulation may well be profitable.

Furthermore, the use of purchased aluminum permits a higher rate of utilization for this excess fabricating capacity. Secondary aluminum is typically purchased by primary producers for fabricating once the accumulated ingot inventory has been consumed.[22] Since such purchases come at the peaks of demand, these actions by the primary producers further accentuate the price swings in the secondary market.[23] Given the construction of excess fabricating capacity for use in disposing of ingot inventories, the primary producers still find such purchases profitable as long as the sum of the marginal cost of fabricating plus the price of secondary aluminum is less than the selling price of fabrications.

The purchase of primary aluminum also serves to increase the utilization of the excess capacity. If a primary producer foresees several years of high demand, then this excess fabricating capacity can be utilized by negotiating a long-term purchase contract with Limited. As noted elsewhere, Alcoa has signed three such contracts and Kaiser two. Of course, a long-term contract reduces the insurance character of the excess capacity, in that considerable fabricating capacity must be diverted to the fabrication of the purchased

---

[22] The concentration of secondary purchases in periods of high demand is apparent from Reynolds' secondary purchases of 5,152,000 pounds in 1947 (a poor year) and 25,883,000 pounds in 1948 (a peak year). See United States v. Aluminum Company of America, 91 F. Supp. 333 at 360. Alcoa's purchases actually declined from 1947 to 1948, but this is explainable by large purchases of primary ingot from Limited. For a general statement of the industry practice in the timing and extent of secondary purchases consistent with these assumptions, see the testimony in the *Remedy Record,* p. 1092, as well as Leonard Doyle's "Industrial Economic Problems in the Post-War Aluminum Market in the United States," *The Journal of Industrial Economics,* Vol. 1, No. 3 (July 1953), pp. 212–230.

[23] These purchases are sufficiently large that even one producer can affect the price. For example, Alcoa bought 38,000,000 pounds of secondary in 1948 when the total production was 191,000,000 pounds. (*Monopoly Power Hearings, 1951,* p. 911.) Lately the primary producers have purchased scrap, rather than the secondary aluminum itself, but this does not alter the argument.

aluminum. For this reason, these contracts are based upon the expectations of relatively long periods of high demand.

These purchasing activities, even though reducing the insurance cost of excess capacity, are profitable in their own right. This is so because of a price structure that yields higher returns on fabricating capacity. Such differential returns, however, insure that other primary producers and particularly new entrants will tend to follow the existing pattern of vertical integration.

The Welfare Economics of Excess Capacity

In evaluating these output practices, accumulation of ingot inventories clearly minimizes the real costs of aluminum production. Fixed-cost industries such as ingot reduction should be operated much more continuously than high variable-cost industries. Marginal-cost pricing would create something analogous to the existing pattern of ingot production. Such price variations would encourage counter-cyclical price speculation and the accumulation of ingot inventories. Once such inventory accumulations occurred, the construction of excess fabricating capacity would be necessary in order to utilize this inventory at a time when it is desired. And the lower capital costs at this stage of production mean that it is here that the capacity to meet peak demand should exist. Furthermore, the peak demand is better met with the increased use of secondary aluminum rather than the construction of additional capital-intensive reduction facilities.

The tendency of the primary producers to construct two pounds of fabricating capacity for one pound of reduction capacity, however, appears to be excess insurance in terms of its social cost. The cost of this idle capacity is built into the prices, and this may well be a case in which the monopoly profits are realized in risk reduction rather than in direct profits. Furthermore, part of the costs of these output policies is exported to the permanent buyers and sellers in the secondary market who must adjust to the resulting price fluctuations.

Finally, the present level of excess fabricating capacity creates a precarious situation for the independent fabricators. Whenever there is a high demand for aluminum products, the primary producers are reluctant to sell ingot, particularly once their accumulated ingot inventories have been consumed, for then every pound of ingot can be used more profitably through internal fabrication. To further intensify the shortage of ingot for independents, the primary producers tend to be net purchasers rather than sellers during periods with a high volume of sales. As a result, the supply of ingot for the independents becomes precarious at the very time that sales opportunities are at their maximum.

VII

THE SUPPLY OF INGOT FOR THE INDEPENDENT FABRICATORS

D<small>URING</small> the years 1946 to 1958, the primary producers have often been reluctant sellers of ingot. The combination of an excess demand for aluminum products and an excess fabricating capacity has meant that the primary producers profited more by fabricating their ingot production.[1] As was to be expected, the independent fabricators have complained repeatedly and at length of the inadequacy of their supply of ingot.[2] As of 1957, the dispute over the

[1] See the preceding chapter.

[2] The full citations of the principal Congressional hearings and reports are as follows:

House Committee on the Judiciary, Subcommittee on Study of Monopoly Power, *Hearings, Study of Monopoly Power, Serial No. 1. Part 1, Aluminum,* 82d Cong., 1st Sess., 1951. Henceforth cited as *Monopoly Power Hearings, 1951.*

Joint Committee on Defense Production, *Defense Production Act Progress Report No. 20. Aluminum Program,* 82d Cong. 2d Sess., 1952. Henceforth cited as *Defense Production Report No. 20.*

Joint Committee on Defense Production, *Defense Production Act Progress Report No. 24. Aluminum Expansion Program and Competition,* 82d Cong., 2d Sess., 1953. Henceforth cited as *Defense Production Report No. 24.*

House Select Committee on Small Business, Subcommittee No. 3, *Hearings, Aluminum Industry,* 84th Cong., 1st Sess., 1955. Henceforth cited as *Small Business Hearings, 1955.*

House Select Committee on Small Business, Subcommittee No. 3, on Minerals and Raw Materials, *Report, Small Business and the Aluminum Industry,* 84th Cong., 2d Sess., H.R. 2954, 1956. Henceforth cited as *Small Business Report, 1956.*

House Select Committee on Small Business, Subcommittee No. 3, *Hearings, Aluminum Industry,* 85th Cong., 1st and 2nd Sess., 1958. Henceforth cited as *Small Business Hearings, 1958.*

House Select Committee on Small Business, Subcommittee No. 3. on Minerals and Raw Materials, *Report, Small Business Problems in the Aluminum Industry,* 85th Cong., 2d Sess., H.R. 2716, 1959. Henceforth cited as *Small Business Report, 1959.*

availability of primary ingot subsided, for the recession made the primary producers eager to sell aluminum in any form.

Yet the problem of the adequacy of the supply of ingot for the independent fabricators has more than historical interest. The primary producers continue to have the excess fabricating capacity that makes fabrication rather than the sale of ingot more profitable whenever the demand permits. And, as the report of the House Small Business Committee observed, "The growth and continuation of small business in the aluminum industry depends very heavily on the ability of the small non-integrated fabricators and processors to acquire a continuous supply of the basic metal in all economic cycles in the aluminum industry." [3]

The Distribution of Ingot: 1946–1954

The independents' share of the total of both secondary and primary aluminum output decreased from 33 to 27 percent from 1946 to 1954. (See Table 15) Although often cited, these statistics are

TABLE 15. The ingot supply of the nonintegrated users.

Year	Noninte- grated ingot supply (millions of pounds)	Share of total U. S. supply of primary and secondary aluminum (percent)	Domestic primary aluminum (millions of pounds)	(Percent)	Secondary aluminum (millions of pounds)	(Percent)	Canadian imports (millions of pounds)	(Percent)
1946	572	33	173	30	396	69	3	01
1947	720	36	186	26	533	74	1	00
1948	639	30	210	33	389	61	40	06
1949	426	24	168	39	239	56	19	04
1950	688	29	263	38	360	52	65	09
1951	796	31	239	30	441	55	116	15
1952	948	34	327	34	470	50	151	16
1953	1157	30	381	33	527	46	249	22
1954	1074	27	380	35	460	43	234	22

Source: House Select Committee on Small Business, Subcommittee No. 3 on Minerals and Raw Materials, *Report, Small Business and the Aluminum Industry*, 84th Congress, 2d sess., H.R. 2954, 1956, p. 14.

meaningless since substantial quantities of primary aluminum were stockpiled by the government from 1950 on and so never reached any type of fabricator. [4] In terms of ingot available for fabrication, the independents fared well. The independents' share of the total fabricating output increased from 10 percent in 1946 to 15 percent in 1950 and to 24 percent in 1957. [5] This relative expansion involved

[3] *Small Business Report, 1959,* p. 11.
[4] *Small Business Hearings, 1955,* p. 364.
[5] Computed from data in *Small Business Hearings, 1958,* p. 450.

a six-fold increase of the independents' output from 1946 to 1957.

In the period from 1946 to 1954, there were marked shifts among the independents' sources of ingot, as shown in Table 15. The decline of secondary aluminum from 69 to 43 percent of independents' total supply was an inevitable consequence of the depletion of the stock of World War II scrap aircraft.[6] (In this respect, the Korean war was not as productive.)

TABLE 16. Sales of primary aluminum and acquisition of primary aluminum by domestic primary producers (millions of pounds)

	Alcoa		Kaiser		Reynolds	
	1946–50	1951–54	1946–50	1951–54	1946–50	1951–54
A. Primary metal only						
Sales of Primary Metal to Domestic Noninte- grated Users	802	456	64	401	134	476
Acquisition of Primary Metal by Purchase, Tolls, and Conver- sions	819	511	75	168	185	138
Percentage — Acquisi- tions to Sales	102	112	117	42	138	29
B. Sales of primary aluminum and acquisitions of primary and secondary aluminum						
Sales of Primary Metal to Domestic Noninte- grated Users	802	456	64	401	134	476
Acquisitions of Primary and Secondary Metal by Purchase, Tolls, and Conversions	1390	901	147	341	448	289
Percentage, Acquisitions to Sales	174	198	230	85	335	61

Source: House, Select Committee on Small Business, Subcommittee No. 3 on Minerals and Raw Materials, *Report, Small Business and the Aluminum Industry,* 84th Cong., 2d sess., H. R. 2954, 1956, p. 15.

The primary producers have increased their contribution to the total supply of ingot for the independents by 5 percentage

[6] The aggregate figures on secondary aluminum obscure the changing nature of the scrap sources. Old scrap, junked aircraft, discarded cooking utensils, and so forth decreased from a 1947 peak of 328,000,000 pounds to an annual rate of between 130,000,000 and 160,000,000 pounds since 1950. Conversely, new scrap created in fabrication has increased with the expansion of the aluminum industry, but not sufficiently to offset the decline in old scrap. See data in *Small Business Report, 1956,* p. 55.

points. Alone, this statistic is misleading, for the primary producers simultaneously purchased secondary and primary aluminum to such an extent as to be net buyers until 1950. As a result the primary producers made no contribution to the independent's supply of ingot. (See Table 16.) After that date, Kaiser and Reynolds were net sellers, but this change reflects in part the government policies described later in this chapter.

During most of these years the sale of ingot meant a loss in profits for the primary producers, for demand was such that a primary producer could usually utilize all the available ingot in fabricating. This point is borne out by the testimony of Mr. Wilson, president of Alcoa. "Had we refused to ship that material [ingot] and put it into fabrication for ourselves, our accountants estimate that our income after taxes would have been five million dollars greater in 1948." [7]

In the long run, however, the sale of ingot may reduce the fluctuations in a primary producer's sales, in that the demand for ingot may vary countercyclically from the demand for aluminum fabrications. The buyers of ingot produce largely castings and extrusions, and furthermore, the independents are likely to have established connections with certain end-product manufacturers. Consequently, as the President of Alcoa testified, ". . . there will come a time when sooner or later the business conditions may well be such that we could not sell all of our production or all the metal available to us in fabricated form, and the market then for the pig and ingot is a very valuable market." [8]

In order to sell ingot at a later date, it is necessary for a primary producer to continue to sell ingot to established customers in times of excess demand. Hence, such sales can be viewed as profitable in the long run. The simultaneous purchase of ingot at least serves to reduce the loss in profits from such sales at a time when ingot output could more profitably be fabricated.

For the independents as a group, the simultaneous purchase and sale of ingot by the primary producers obviously makes no contribution to the supply of ingot. The algebraic addition of sales and purchases, however, overlooks two mitigating factors. For some purposes, primary ingot is preferable to secondary and a substantial

[7] *Record* p. 785. United States v. Aluminum Company of America, 91 F. Supp. 333 (S.D.N.Y., 1950), henceforth cited as *Remedy Record*.
[8] *Remedy Record,* p. 787.

fraction of the primary producers' purchases were bought under long-term contracts with Limited. This ingot might not have been otherwise available to the independent fabricators.

It was the increase in Limited's sale of ingot to the independents from a token 3,000,000 pounds in 1946 to 234,000,000 pounds in 1954 that made possible the expansion of the share of independents in total fabricating output. In some respects Limited is a "natural" source of supply.[9] The high tariff on fabrications means Limited must export to the United States in ingot form. Hence, Limited is not in direct competition with the independent fabricators, and from Limited's point of view these customers are valuable because they cannot substitute their own ingot production for purchases at times of slack demand.

But Canadian aluminum has its drawbacks. The independents are dependent upon not only a single seller, but one with interests in other markets to which its aluminum output might be diverted. Limited has sold a substantial volume to the American primary producers, often under long-term contracts.[10] Even as late as 1954, Limited's sales to the integrated producers were 45 percent of its total American sales. Such transactions permitted an American primary producer to utilize his excess fabricating capacity and assured Limited a long-term market that facilitated the financing of its expansion. Whatever their other merits, these long-term contracts, of course, reduced the immediate availability of ingot for independent fabricators. New contracts of this type could mean Limited would no longer be an important source of supply of ingot for the independent fabricator. Finally, Limited, as discussed earlier, is vulnerable to tariff retaliation.

The Independent Fabricators and Their Discontents

In view of the precarious nature of their supply of ingot, it seems paradoxical that the independents not only exist but have expanded both absolutely and relatively. Apparently, for some types

[9] The "natural" fit of Limited and the independents was stressed by Mr. Davis, president of Limited, as follows: "In the United States we have energetically solicited the business of the rapidly growing independent (non-integrated) fabricators. We have done so in the belief that the independent fabricators would look upon us as a natural supplier, not competing with them in the United States fabricating business—and that we on our part could look to them as steady buyers in both good and bad times—in comparison with those who produce their own ingot requirements." (*Small Business Hearings, 1955*, p. 144.)

[10] These contracts are described in Chapters II and IX.

of fabrication, the small firm operates at no discernible cost disadvantage, and entry on a small scale is relatively easy. During periods of high demand, the small firms are attracted into the industry and those already in operation expand to the extent that ingot is available, despite the possible difficulties in the long-term outlook for the supply of purchasable ingot.

The attributes of small business in the aluminum industry are perhaps best exemplified by castings.[11] The process itself is utilized for a wide range of metals, so that the existing foundries provide a ready-made supply of entrants. The capital outlay for a minimum-sized economical foundry operation is estimated at $200,000, and further economies of scale appear to be relatively insignificant. The product itself is often individually designed for each customer and so requires flexibility of decision-making and continuing close contact with the customers, skills presumed to flourish best in the smaller firm. Finally, castings are traditionally made from secondary aluminum, the most secure of the independents' source of supply. The comparative advantage of the small firm is perhaps best demonstrated by the fact that neither Reynolds nor Kaiser has entered this field, while Alcoa's share has been continually declining to its present 9 percent.

Aluminum sheet is a contrasting example in which the large firms are at an advantage. The capital outlay for a single plant is substantial. For example, Alcoa's new rolling mill at Davenport, Iowa, is reported to cost approximately $36,000,000.[12] The product is fairly standardized and the economies of scale significant. Hence this sector is dominated by the primary producers. Even the 6-percent market share assigned to independent fabricators in most tabulations is misleading, for only two of the fifteen independent fabricators have a complete sheet operation, and the remainder buy reroll sheet and execute only the final stages of cold rerolling.[13] Similarly, the independent fabricators of foil and wire and cable usually buy semifabrications rather than the ingot. This division of products between large vertically integrated firms and independent fabricators also occurs in other metals, with, as in aluminum, the vertically integrated firms dominating the output of rolled prod-

[11] The subsequent discussion is limited to castings and extrusions, the two largest small-business sectors. Apparently, powder and cable are less natural in small-business sectors as defined by the above characteristics than either of the other two.
[12] *Small Business Report,* 1956, p. 42.
[13] *Ibid.*

ucts (97 percent of the output in steel and 68 percent in copper) and the independents dominating other products (76 percent of the total steel casting output and 57 percent of the copper wire output.)[14]

In contrast to castings and sheet, extrusions are a sector in dispute between the independents and the primary producers. Indeed, the complaints and difficulties of the independent fabricators are, on closer inspection, largely those of the extruders. It is not surprising that this should be so.

Like castings, the investment requirements for extruding are nominal, with a single extrusion press costing approximately $25,000. Again, as in castings, sales have a job character and there appear to be no significant economies of scale.[15] The high profit margins in extruding up to 1953 encouraged the entry of new independents and the expansion of established extruders. The primary producers, however, have shown little inclination to abandon extruding to the independents, as they have done in casting, but instead they have expanded their capacity and output by 40 percent from 1950 to 1957.[16] This may be because the demand for extrusions has been increasing markedly. Extrusion output increased five-fold from 1950 to 1955 compared to the 60 percent increase in the output of all fabrication.[17] Such a growing market is not lightly abandoned.

It is this high rate of growth of demand that underlies the complaints of the extruders. Of the 39 extruders answering a 1955 House Small Business Committee questionnaire, 33 considered their ingot supply situation unsatisfactory, yet only 3 reported receiving less ingot than in the preceding year.[18] The meaning of unsatisfactory is disclosed by the reply that 30 of the 39 would expand if an assured and increased supply of ingot were available, even though all but 8 had expanded their capacity in the last two years. Granted that such complaints may seem trivial compared to a reduction of the existing level of ingot supply, still businessmen can be expected to resent a restriction of their growth. Indeed, the accumulated

[14] *Ibid.,* p. 20.

[15] As Mr. Pickens, president of the Texas Aluminum Company points out, "You can buy a small one [extrusion press] that will fit maybe on this table top of three or four hundred tons, or you can buy 1 self-contained up to the large size of 3,000 to 3,500 tons which then puts you in competition with the three large producers . . . you are able to compete nicely. You can give service at somebody's back door when the others, the big ones have to ship from great distances, et cetera." *Small Business Hearings,* 1955, p. 102–103.

[16] *Small Business Hearings,* 1958, p. 450.

[17] Based on data in *Small Business Report,* 1956.

[18] *Small Business Report,* 1956, pp. 88–97.

resentment of the extruders is substantial. For example, one impassioned extruder wrote, "The primary producers have broken faith with the American people . . . a permanent change should be made so that the independent producers don't have to appeal to the Office of Defense Mobilization 3 or 4 times a year for metal necessary for survival." [19]

All this is in contrast to the responses of the independent fabricators in the slow growth sectors. Of 23 companies in sheet, cable, and foil production, only 6 characterized the supply of metal as unsatisfactory, and only 7 reported postponing expansion because of a shortage of metal. Perhaps a better index of relative satisfaction is offered by the percentage of responses to the Committee's questionnaire. Only one-third of these fabricators replied, whereas two-thirds of the extruders did so.[20]

The Private Rationing of Aluminum

The fact that the extruders rated the ingot supply unsatisfactory whereas the other fabricators did not is largely a reflection of the system of private rationing. Allocations were based upon past purchases, so those sectors with a lower rate of the growth in demand lost fewer opportunities for expansion.[21] With the total output of ingot increasing, firms with a relatively stable demand might even obtain all the ingot they desired.

Historical allocation is perhaps the most administrable standard for rationing and its use is understandable for this reason alone. There was a collateral advantage for primary producers. They were the largest fabricators of the products with a low rate of growth. Therefore, when they applied the rationing formula to themselves, as they did, historical allocation insured more ingot for internal fabrication than would a standard based upon current demand.

A further factor in the extruders' discontent was that the administrative friction inherent in any rationing system was concentrated among these customers. This was not intentional; rather there seems to be no discernible pattern of discrimination in operation of the private system. The extruders, however, as befits a growth industry, account for a disproportionate number of the new

[19] *Ibid.*, p. 96.
[20] *Ibid.*, pp. 102–104.
[21] *Ibid.*, pp. 30–31. Each primary producer made exceptions for hardship cases.

firms without established contacts within the sales organizations of the primary producers. Furthermore, the extruders are generally smaller firms and are easier to lose in the administrative process.

Private rationing does contain an important protection against administrative error, for an independent fabricator may be the customer of several primary producers. Of the sample of 36 extruders, only one relied upon a single supplier, so that errors of one firm might be offset by the generosity of another. For example, statements such as, "Alcoa has been very cooperative as source. Kaiser cancelled total 190,000 pounds for second and third quarter," are in juxtaposition to, "With the exception of Kaiser who are correctly following the allocation pattern, our efforts to get relief from the other three have been unsuccessful." [22]

These instances perhaps illustrate the inherent unpopularity of the operator of a rationing system be he a fellow businessman or an OPA bureaucrat. Rationing administered by a competitor, however, involves a unique conflict of interests, particularly when, as one independent stated, "All of the prime producers are frank to admit that it is more profitable for them to fabricate and sell than it is to sell raw materials." [23]

To the primary producers, these complaints undoubtedly seem ungracious. Even though some errors may have been made, and a historical allocation was more favorable to the primary producers than some other standard would have been, the most profitable policy, at least in the short run, would have been for the primary producers to have fabricated most of their ingot production. Yet, a policy of fair shares though private rationing seems taken for granted by all concerned — Congressmen, government officials, independents, and primary producers. Perhaps this demonstrates concretely the changing standards of business morality, for in the 1920's Alcoa could meet the shortages of ingot without formal rationing or any necessity of justifying its actions. Some of this change is in the businessmen's personal code of conduct, for the testimony of company officials gives the impression of a sincere and personal concern over fairness. At the same time, of course, the prospect that policies will be questioned before Congressional committees, that the extruders have advocates among their local Congressmen, and that the primary producers are involved in

[22] *Ibid.*, p. 90.
[23] *Ibid.*, p. 30.

various government contracts may have made some type of rationing system inevitable.

Long-Term Contracts for the Sale of Ingot

Long-term contracts for the sale of ingot became increasingly common after 1950. Such contracts served not only to formalize the historical pattern of allocation, but they also offered obvious advantages for both parties. The independent fabricator obtained an assured source of ingot and the primary producer was guaranteed a market.

These contracts do not appear to have aided the independents as a group. The nonsigners, of course, were simply farther back in the queue as a result of the priority granted the signers. It might be argued that such contracts served to increase the total supply made available to independents. The data on the sales of ingot hardly bear this out, nor are the origins of these contracts consistent with that result. Long-term contracts became common only when government action required the sale of ingot to independent fabricators. Furthermore, the long-term contracts represented an indirect increase in price, for the independents committed themselves to either a fixed amount or a share of their purchases and so assumed some of the risks of market fluctuations.[24] However, they still paid the current list price.

The general objection to long-term contracts is the reduction in the mobility of buyers to transfer their patronage from one seller to another. For this reason, the courts have viewed such contracts with suspicion although long-term contracts have never been illegal per se.[25]

In examining the effect of competition, the long-term contracts in the aluminum industry should be clearly distinguished from such cases as *Standard Stations* or *American Can,* for the independent fabricators can and do simultaneously sign several contracts with various primary producers. As to the relative importance of long-

---

[24] There is considerable variation in the forms of contracts. Reynolds apparently has emphasized fixed volume contracts (*Small Business Hearings, 1955,* p. 473), whereas the others have stressed minimum-maximum contracts. Little information is available concerning the volume terms of the contracts, although the minimum amounts were sufficiently sizable to deter firms from signing.

[25] The leading cases here are U. S. v. American Can Co., 87 F. Supp. 18 (D.C. Cal. 1949), and Standard Oil Company of California v. U. S., 69 Sup. Ct. 1051 (1949). Both of these cases involved exclusive contracts and "substantial" amounts of commerce.

term contracts, it is apparent that a substantial fraction of the sales of ingot was covered by these contracts. (It is difficult to state the amounts covered by the contracts because of the requirements character of many contracts. According to a House report, maximum contract commitments were 540,000,000 pounds in 1955, nearly one and one-half the 1954 level of ingot sales.)[26]

The important question is whether long-term contracts, despite their inauspicious origins, will eventually encourage the primary producers to sell more ingot and thus increase competition. These contracts may facilitate competition in the fabricating market, through insuring a greater ingot supply to the independents, and therefore be worth the loss in the short-run mobility of the buyers in the ingot market.[27] Within the context of the present market structure of the industry, at best these long-term contracts may foster a greater degree of competition; at worst, they are merely a manifestation of the market power already held by the primary producers. Thus, these contracts do not appear to be worth striking down by government action.

Government Protection for the Independent Fabricator

Congressional hearings were not only a forum in which the independents could vent their complaints. The hearings also created a Congressional interest in the fate of the independents that insured the inclusion of several provisions in contracts between the General Services Administration and the primary producers.

The major objective of the contracts was the expansion of aluminum reduction capacity to meet post-Korean defense requirements. As an inducement for the expansion, the government contracted to purchase any unsold output from new facilities for the first five years of their life. The primary producers also received five-year certificates of accelerated amortization so that their new investment was assured a market until fully depreciated. The interest of the independents was to be protected by a provision that two-thirds of the production from the new facilities should be

[26] *Small Business Report, 1956,* p. 34.

[27] It might appear that long-term contracts, by assuring buyers of their supply, would reduce the fluctuations in demand. These fluctuations are mostly caused by the inventory accumulation as a hedge against shortages. However, ingot buyers account for a small part of the demand, and there has been little use of long-term contracts for purchases of fabrications, which is in volume the major factor in inventory cycles.

reserved jointly for the nonintegrated user and the government for the first five years of the life of the contract. For the next fifteen years one-quarter of this production would be reserved exclusively for the nonintegrated users.

This provision appeared to insure a substantial increase in the supply of ingot for the independent fabricator. All concerned seemed satisfied, and a 1952 report of the Joint Committee on Defense Porduction concluded, ". . . there is no basis at this time for any claim that the future of independent aluminum fabricators is being jeopardized." [28] Yet, in fact, this provision was largely a legal fiction that could have little influence upon the allocation of ingot.

This was most obvious in the treatment of the long-term contracts for the sale of ingot. The primary producers were to offer ingot on a first-come first-serve basis, except that the existence of private rationing was recognized by permitting a primary producer to reduce a disproportionately large order. Hence, as the 1952 Congressional Report correctly stated, the ingot is available without "the necessity of any additional commitments or contracts by either the Government or the independent fabricator." [29] But two clauses later, the contract between the GSA and the primary producers stated, "It is recognized that the Contractor has made and intends in the future to make contracts with such of its customers who are nonintegrated users" . . . and "such commitments for any applicable period may be deducted from the quantity which the contractor is obligated to make available to other nonintegrated users . . ." [30] Significantly, there was no over-all limit on the amount of contract sales that might be credited to the required sales of ingot. As a result, the primary producers signed a sufficient number of long-term contracts that in 1959 the volume of obligated sales to the independents could be met by simply fulfilling long-term contracts for the purchase of ingot. In the last section, it was concluded that long-term contracts on net balance may contribute to competition by increasing the supply of ingot for sale. But here the provisions of a government contract required the sale of ingot. Per-

[28] Defense Production Report No. 20, p. 10.
[29] Ibid.
[30] Small Business Hearings, 1955, p. 841. The contract did limit the volume of sales to any one customer that might be credited towards the obligated share to 500,000 pounds without GSA prior approval. But this limit was no serious handicap on contract sales. The provision requiring 25 percent of output to be sold for the next fifteen years after the five-year period is silent on the inclusion of contract sales.

mitting long-term contracts in these circumstances served only to shift the risks of demand fluctuations forward to the fabricators and to freeze out the nonsigner customers.

The argument over the inclusion of long-term contracts in the share of ingot earmarked for the independent fabricators became academic because the share itself had little meaning. During the first five years, the required share of two-thirds of the total output from the new facilities was assigned jointly to government purchase and to the nonintegrated users. With a high volume of government purchases, the residual share for the independents could be zero. This was not a hypothetical danger. The residual required to be sold to the independents was minus 7,000,000 pounds and minus 10,000,000 pounds in the last two quarters of 1954 when the government was vigorously accumulating a stockpile of aluminum.[31]

Furthermore, the provisions of the GSA contract did not insure the net increase in the independents' share that the Congressional report suggested. Rather, these provisions applied only to the output of the new facilities, and the primary producers could distribute the output from the capacity existing prior to 1950 as they pleased. Therefore, the primary producers, by consuming all their output from the older facilities, could still sell less ingot to the independents than they had before the contracts were signed.[32] Such a drastic conclusion undoubtedly understates the indirect influence of these contracts, for from 1950 to 1954 the primary producers sold a volume of ingot consistently greater than the combined amount of their legal obligation and their 1950 level of sales from the old capacity.[33]

Yet the voluntary character of the sale of ingot left the government without authority over the sale of ingot. The stockpile relief program of 1955 illustrates this point. Early in 1954, business activity declined sufficiently that the demand for aluminum was less than capacity for the first time since 1950. Consequently, the government began purchasing a substantial volume of aluminum for stockpiling. (These purchases had been postponed until then because of the high demand for aluminum.)

Later in the year, the general level of business activity recovered sufficiently that aluminum products were again in great demand.

[31] *Small Business Report, 1956*, p. 73.
[32] Based on data in *Small Business Report, 1956*.
[33] Based on data in *Small Business Hearings, 1955*, p. 184.

Government purchases were credited against the required ingot sales. Although the primary producers sold considerably more than their obligations required, the total sales of ingot to the independents declined by some 30 percent in 1954. The independents protested vigorously at the reduction of their supplies and as a result the General Services Administration issued an order for "stockpile relief" by canceling the government purchases.

Yet, since the contracts between the GSA and the primary producers covered only new facilities, these cancellations did not create an obligation for the primary producers to increase their sales of ingot. Kaiser's distribution of ingot illustrates why this is so. The company's 1950 sales of ingot were 73,000,000 pounds, and this volume of sales over and above the contract obligations was maintained throughout this period. The cancellation of government orders freed another 60,000,000 pounds. By simply maintaining the sales to the independents from its old facilities at the existing level of 73,000,000 pounds, Kaiser met its legal obligation for the sale of 60,000,000 pounds of ingot. Hence, the additional metal made available by the cancellation of government orders could be distributed as Kaiser might decide.[34]

Thus the government was placed in a peculiarly powerless position. It could either continue its stockpile puchases and ignore the complaints of the independents, or it could carry through the stockpile relief and trust that the primary producers would voluntarily increase their sale of ingot. Another alternative, that of taking possession of ingot and then distributing it to the independents was only formally available, for the government lacked a distributive organization as well as the political support for such government intervention. At best, the government could and did attempt to negotiate a voluntary settlement whereby the primary producers would increase the sale of ingot. Alcoa accepted such an agreement while Reynolds and Kaiser did not. The stockpile relief was finally applied to all three producers, while the government, according to the GSA General Counsel, "tried on a voluntary basis to see if we could negotiate with the companies. . . ."[35]

But, lest Reynolds and Kaiser be accused of utilizing a legal technicality, their arguments should be noted. Both companies claimed they anticipated the stockpile relief through increased

---

[34] *Small Business Hearings, 1955,* p. 184.
[35] *Ibid.,* p. 186.

shipments to the nonintegrated firms.[36] Therefore, they argued that further sales of ingot would divert ingot from their own fabricating operations and prevent them from serving their customers for fabrications. The fragmentary data available substantiate Reynolds' and Kaiser's claim to have anticipated the relief, in that their sale of ingot increased in 1954.[37] In contrast, Alcoa had in that year the lowest volume of ingot sales in nine years.[38] The fact remains that the primary producers had the power to make the decisions on the distribution of aluminum.

The final and perhaps greatest oversight in the wording of these contracts was in the definition of nonintegrated user. The issue arose initially in 1952, when Alcoa requested the General Services Administration to amend the contract to include the purchases of semifabrications such as reroll sheet and redraw rod as part of the share reserved for nonintegrated users.[39] Such a request had a superficial equity in that the contract did not include an explicit provision for such buyers. Their market position is the same as a buyer of ingot, for they sell the completed fabrications in competition with the primary producers who are their suppliers. Thus arguments justifying protection to the independent fabricators applied equally to this group.

Upon this rationale, the Defense Production Administration concurred in Alcoa's request, stating that the basic objective (in contract administration) should be ". . . the insuring of a source of supply of aluminum to users at the earliest stage of fabrication at which the operations of any given nonintegrated user begin." [40] Upon a more pragmatic basis, the Department of Justice and the Federal Trade Commission opposed any enlargement of the products

[36] See Kaiser's letter of May 18, 1955, to the Subcommittee No. 3 (*ibid.*, pp. 182–183) and Reynolds' letter of April 13, 1955 (*ibid.*, pp. 180–181).

[37] Calculations based on data in *Small Business Report, 1956*, p. 76.

[38] Apparently Alcoa scored a public relations triumph among the fabricators in agreeing to distribute all the stockpile relics to the independents. In addition, Alcoa sales ". . . have carried a notation on our invoices that the metal is from this particular stockpile source." (*Small Business Hearings, 1955*, p. 258.) As a result, according to the Committee report, ". . . an impression was created that Reynolds and Kaiser were not fulfilling their obligations to the nonintegrated users to the same degree that Alcoa was." (*Small Business Report, 1956*, p. 27.) Mr. Reynolds states, "The next time you can rest assured we will release it after we get some relief. We will not make that mistake again." (*Small Business Hearings, 1955*, p. 236.)

[39] Alcoa's letter of November 19, 1952, to the Administrator, General Services Administration, *Small Business Report, 1956*, pp. 114–115.

[40] Letter of Samuel Anderson, deputy administrator for aluminum, Office of Defense Mobilization, December 15, 1952, *Small Business Report, 1956*, p. 115.

included in the required sales.[41] The needs of the buyers of semi-fabrications were already served from the ingot allocated for the primary producers. From the evidence cited earlier it appears that these fabricators fared relatively well under the private rationing system. Consequently, to include semifabrications now as part of the reserved share would only increase the amount of the ingot available to the primary producers for their internal consumption and thus would reduce the aggregate amount of metal available to the independents. The views of the Federal Trade Commission and the Department of Justice prevailed and semifabrications were not included with ingot in the share earmarked for sales.

As it turned out, there was no need to enlarge the list of products that might be counted as sales to nonintegrated users. A customer for semifabrications might instead buy ingot from a primary producer, take title, but leave the metal with the primary producer to be converted into its semifabricated form. Such arrangements (called tolls or conversion) were a long-standing industry practice, but in the typical prewar transaction, customers would import ingot, usually one of the alloys not available domestically, and then turn the metal over to Alcoa for fabrication, paying a toll or conversion fee for this service. With the postwar shortage of aluminum, these tolls and conversion became more common. In a typical transaction the customer located aluminum abroad, in the domestic grey market, or in the secondary market, and then turned it over to a primary producer for fabrication. The novel feature of toll arrangements here was that the buyer bought ingot from the primary producer and left it for further fabrication. The primary producer could then credit such ingot sales towards its obligated share of ingot sales. Not only could the buyers of semifabricated forms qualify for inclusion in the obligated share, but so could all other customers of the primary producers except the 15 percent or so who bought completely finished consumer products such as foil or building materials.[42]

---

[41] Letter of Edward Hodges, acting assistant attorney general, February 9, 1953, and letter of James Mead, chairman of the Federal Trade Commission, March 19, 1953, *Small Business Report, 1956*, p. 117.

[42] As Mr. Elliot, general counsel of the GSA, explained, ". . . strictly as a matter of contract interpretation, I would think that someone who, let us say, uses sheet normally could be a nonintegrated user who would purchase pig or ingot and have that then made into sheet . . . [the primary producer's] obligation is to offer pig, ingot, and billet. . . . If Mr. X., a purchaser, needs this amount of aluminum for his own operations, and after buying the pig he needs another step done to it, which actually is not done in his own plant, he can have somebody else subcontract it; he could go back to Alcoa if he bought it from Alcoa, he could go to Mr. Singer's

Thus through toll arrangements every customer of the primary producers, fabricators, semifabricators, end-product manufacturers, in fact any firm which used aluminum for further manufacture and did not produce primary aluminum, could qualify for the ingot the primary producers are obligated to offer for sale. Since customers accounting for 85 percent of the primary producers' output were eligible for a reserved share which at the maximum was one-third of the primary output, such an interpretation is equivalent to granting everyone a priority. A priority for all is obviously a priority for none.

Again in practice, the primary producers did not utilize this legal opening to any great extent. The volume of tolls and conversions by the primary producers increased from 11,000,000 pounds in 1952 to 36,000,000 pounds in 1953, 34,000,000 pounds in 1954 and 12,000,000 pounds in the first half of 1955.[43] Nevertheless, the ability of other customers to be included in the reserved share meant that the provisions were essentially voluntary. It may be that this flexibility made some difference in the distribution of ingot, but if so the effect was relatively minor.

The total effect of the contract provisions then was to provide the independent fabricators with no legally mandatory increase in ingot. In fact, it apparently provided nothing at all. But the primary producers consistently exceeded their contractual duties. Even though the primary producers were not legally required to increase their sales to the independents, actual ingot sales were greater than the sum of the 1950 level and the new obligations entailed by the contract. Hence, the volume of ingot available to the independents increased, although it should be added that primary producers stepped up their ingot purchases so that their net contribution to the independents' supply is less impressive. The primary producers through tolls and conversions could have made the required ingot sales to all comers, whereas, in fact, relatively few such transactions occurred. Despite the long-term contracts for sale of ingot, the primary producers retained a share of the ingot for sale on a spot basis.

The behavior of the primary producers then might be characterized as follows. Their attorneys insured that the contracts placed them under little legal obligation. At the same time, the sales depart-

---

company if they are equipped to do it. He could go to Kaiser or whomever." (*Small Business Hearings, 1955*, p. 334, p. 336.
[43] *Small Business Report, 1956*, p. 56.

ments used the more generous interpretations as a standard for voluntary behavior. Voluntary behavior is clearly preferable for them because at certain crucial times, such as in the stockpile relief, the primary producers retained the option of making their own decisions concerning the allocation of metal. Further, most everyone prefers to do his good deeds under the illusion of free will.

The behavior of the government agencies, principally the General Services Administration and the Office of Defense Mobilization, is more difficult to understand. Their role was to protect the independents and it is an understatement to conclude that this was not accomplished. If one starts from the law-school maxim that a contract should anticipate every possibility, avoid ambiguity, and accomplish what each party intended — then surely these contracts stand as classic examples of what not to do. In justifying the government's legal representation, the General Counsel of the General Services Administration pointed out that these contracts were unique in his phrase, "the guinea pigs" [for a new type of government policy.] Furthermore, the distribution of aluminum ingot was at that time directly controlled by the government through the material allocation orders.[44] As a result, he states, ". . . we just did not dwell on the point whether or not the tender to the nonintegrated would be in addition to what would normally be the companies' practices with respect to their old production."[45]

Similarly, the aggregation of the government share and that of the independents was apparently decided somewhat casually. The original plan was to assign one-third of the output to the government, one-third to the independent, and one-third to the primary producer. But, according to the General Counsel, "When we came to executing the contracts, we lumped the two-thirds for the Government and the nonintegrated producers together. The reasons for it were, we felt it would give the government more flexibility in the first place, and in the second place, it was felt it would give the nonintegrated a greater opportunity because the Government, by cutting back its call, could let the nonintegrated have more than one-third."[46] The independents benefited little from these presumed

[44] *Small Business Hearings, 1955,* p. 199. Mr. Elliot adds, "While I cannot point to anything specific in the contract I would certainly feel that the companies have a moral obligation not to substitute wholly their obligation under the new contract for that which they would otherwise be tendering to the nonintegrated, if they had no contract."

[45] *Ibid.,* p. 203.

[46] *Ibid.,* p. 202.

advantages, for they assumed the burden of fluctuations in the rate of stockpiling and a high rate of stockpiling could, as it did in 1954, eliminate the reserved share of the independents.

It is easy to criticize in retrospect, and the environment of post-Korea Washington was hardly favorable to careful legal draftsmanship. Yet the errors consistently favored the primary producers. This is not merely a situation in which the legal talent of the primary producers outmaneuvered that of the government. Rather, as the General Counsel pointed out, these were negotiated contracts so that the outcome was a result of the bargaining strength of the two parties. And, although it is customary to attribute to a government agency great power in dealing with businessmen, this may not have been the case here.

The government required sizable expansion of aluminum capacity and in return was willing to offer a guaranteed market and accelerated amortization. Let us suppose the government lawyers held out for more stringent protection for the independents than the primary producers would accept. This would place the government attorneys in the politically vulnerable position of delaying a defense program, since the initiative for these contracts came from the government. The company, on the other hand, would not be as politically exposed in refusing certain provisions. Its lawyers appear as merely protecting the rights of the stockholders when the company offered its services to the defense program. Furthermore, with only three existing producers there was little chance of playing one company against another.

Indicative of the government's weak bargaining position is that the GSA Counsel testified, ". . . at least one of the companies or some of their representatives were opposed to giving us any enforcement provisions whatsoever." [47] His testimony suggests that it was considered a legal victory that the contract contained a method by which the government could enforce the provisions of the contract. The disparity of bargaining strength may also explain the

---

[47] *Ibid.*, p. 206. As one independent fabricator pointed out, "Now, this stockpiling contract was not made for toll arrangements, nor for sheet manufacturers, or for sheet facilities or for toll arrangements of any kind for aircraft companies or for washing machine companies. This contract was made by the Government to cover new pig-reduction facilities of the three producers and therefore my interpretation is clear that this means the user of metal or extruder of metal . . . this would mean a lot of new customers . . . will buy it [ingot] now in order to have it converted into sheet. And that, in my opinion, would bypass or short circuit the original intent of the stockpiling program." (*Ibid.*, pp. 334, 337.)

peculiarities of legal draftsmanship in that the government may have accepted vague provisions and hoped for the best.

In the administration of the contracts the weak bargaining position of the government agencies vis-à-vis the primary producers may have also played some role. Yet it would seem that the concept of fairness to all sectors of the industry, reenforced by the political pressures upon government administrators, had a greater influence. A case in point is the interpretation of the term nonintegrated used in qualifying for the required ingot sales. The fabricators of ingot urged an interpretation that would restrict the definition to themselves. The General Services Administration replied that such an interpretation would discriminate between firms that bought ingot and those that bought aluminum in other forms. According to the General Services Administrator, "Since it [the contract] was intended to assure some supply of pig, ingot, or billet to nonintegrated users as a class, it may properly be said that it was not intended to foster competition between particular classes of such companies." [48] The GSA correspondence stresses equity to the 17,000 users of aluminum, a number that would include even the end-product manufacturers.

Such an argument implies that a buyer of sheet would receive no aluminum without a place in the reserved share of ingot, yet obviously both the independent fabricators and the primary producers eventually sell their aluminum to such customers in a fabricated form.[49] The less restrictive definition may be dubious logic but it recognizes certain political and economic realities. The direct buyer of ingot is concentrated in the production of certain fabricated products. Consequently, the end-products manufacturers using these products would benefit more from stockpile relief than, say, one using sheet. (This would be so even if the buyers of semifabrications were included in stockpile relief for in such products as sheet the nonintegrated fabricators produce but 6 percent of the output.) The primary producers could alter their product mix to offset changes in the relative output of the independents, but these companies could be expected to be loath to abandon their market

[48] Letter to Congressman Yates, *Small Business Report, 1956,* p. 119.

[49] As Mr. Brile, president of Fairmont Aluminum Company, stated, ". . . they [end product users] are the only beneficiaries of that [stockpile relief], because all that our mills make eventually finds its way into the hands of these consumers. What do we do with the metal except to distribute it to those in that 14,000 [firm] group? So they certainly will benefit to the extent that these mills benefit." (*Small Business Hearings, 1955,* p. 368.)

position in various products. Hence a narrow definition of the term nonintegrated user distorts the allocation of aluminum between various fabricated products.

A government official, however, may not be so concerned with such economic effects as with satisfying the claims of various trade associations for their share of stockpile relief. And it may not be a very satisfactory answer to show that eventually a group of buyers will receive their share through the allocation first to fabricators and the eventual resale of the ingot in a fabricated form.

The pressures upon administrative officials are to preserve the status quo in the name of fairness. In contrast, to change the market structure of an industry requires the willingness to favor one group of businessmen over another. The official of a government agency occupies an overly exposed political position for adoption and execution of such policies. Furthermore, it may be a psychological and sociological impossibility to expect an administrator of an operating agency directly concerned with other objectives to be a fervent promoter of competition.

Yet obviously the market structure in the aluminum industry was changed in that the independent fabricators now have a much larger market share. Whenever the contract provisions were interpreted the Department of Justice and the Federal Trade Commission took a position that favored the users of ingot, not only in defining the products to be included in the obligated share, but in other transactions in the aluminum industry in the postwar years. These officials, unlike those of a procurement agency, have no need for the daily cooperation of all sectors of an industry, and so they can give priority to the promotion of competition. The clearance of policies through the Department of Justice, then, may substantially alter the content of government policy.

The major defenders of the independent fabricators, however, were Congressmen. Congressional insistence was significant in the inclusion of the provisions of the contract requiring the sale of ingot. Furthermore, the primary producers consistently exceeded their legal obligation, perhaps in part because of a fear of Congressional disapproval.

The potency of Congressional disapproval is best demonstrated in the subsequent revision of the contracts with the primary producers. The GSA had carried on negotiations for revision for some time without result, until in the fall of 1957 Senator Robertson of

Virginia interested himself in these contracts. He called a surprise session of the Joint Committee on Defense Production. Shortly thereafter the primary producers agreed to increase the proportion of ingot they were obliged to sell to the independents from 25 to 40 percent for the fifteen-year period. With the other issue of importance to the independents, the definition of a nonintegrated user, the GSA had no success.[50]

Other modifications of the contracts, as described subsequently, represented costly concessions by the primary producers. The only apparent change in the bargaining power of the government administrators was an avowed Senatorial disapproval of the contracts. This could be no more than disapproval, for further investigation would reveal nothing new and no legislation seemed feasible or was suggested. Rather these concessions, and indeed, much of the behavior of the primary producers must be attributed to the political vulnerability of the large firm and particularly to their sensitivity to Congressional disapproval, attributes of the informal system of business-government relations about which relatively little is known.

A Concluding Comment

The particular problems cited above are now history. Beginning with the 1957 recession, aluminum has been freely available. There is also evidence of a more permanent change in the position of the independent fabricators. The ingot market appears to be sufficiently sizable to be of economic value to a primary producer, particularly if such sales are made under long-term contracts. As early as 1956, one primary producer announced that further expansion was planned on the basis that two-thirds of the output would be consumed internally and the remainder would be sold to independent fabricators under long-term contracts.[51] Although this may not be the behavior of an eager seller, it still represents a major change from previous practice.

Similarly, the independents are now sufficiently numerous to have even more of the political power upon which their past growth

---

[50] Mr. Floete testified with respect to the redefinition of a nonintegrated user that, "Mr. Medley [GSA staff member] says that was discussed prior and never could get an agreement on it from the companies." Congressman Yates then asked, "Well, you can see that the term nonintegrated user as it has been interpreted doesn't protect small business very much does it?" Mr. Medley replied, "Not with the introduction of this molten metal question." (These contracts are discussed in the next chapter.) *Small Business Hearings, 1958*, p. 389, p. 390.

[51] *Small Business Report, 1956*, p. 45.

has depended. Finally, the independents are the beneficiaries of the high rate of expansion of aluminum capacity which by 1957 made the primary producers eager to sell aluminum in any form possible. Yet it is unclear whether these changes are sufficient to alter permanently the precarious character of the independent fabricator's supply of aluminum ingot.

VIII

THE MARKETING OF
ALUMINUM

THE sale of ingot to independent fabricators is a small part of the marketing activities of the primary producers. This chapter examines the distribution of other aluminum products and more specifically the marketing activities of the primary producers directed at expanding the use of aluminum, the role of the independent distributors of aluminum, and the impact of the "big buyers" upon the terms of sale.

Market Development by the Primary Producers

Chapter III discussed the dynamics of the growth in demand for aluminum as a learning process. Even though, as stated there, customers learn from one another, the primary producers are active teachers through their efforts to expand the use of aluminum.

Two examples illustrate the content of these teaching activities.[1] In 1950, Kaiser developed two types of covered aluminum conductor wire for use as electrical distribution lines. At that time, almost all distribution lines were copper, primarily because existing conductors created a galvanic action between aluminum wire and a building's electrical system of copper wire. Kaiser had developed new conductors to eliminate the purely technical problem, thus making possible the use of aluminum as a conductor wire. In introducing the new wire, Kaiser set the price at 15 percent below that of comparable copper wire.

The marketing effort for this product was concentrated in 30

---

[1] These examples are from E. Raymond Corey, *The Development of Markets for New Materials* (Boston: Graduate School of Business Administration, Harvard University, 1956), pp. 110–116. This book contains an excellent analysis of the problems of marketing a new industrial product.

field salesmen, each assigned to five electric utility accounts. (Electric utilities are the principal buyers of conductor wire.) These salesmen were assisted by various service engineers to help with engineering problems. The direct sales effort was preceded by a technical report distributed through the Transmission and Distribution Committee of the Edison Institute (of which Kaiser was a member). In addition various technical pamphlets were mailed to potential customers.

The individual salesmen made repeated calls on their accounts. In one utility, there were 19 calls on the specification engineer, 13 on the distribution engineer, and 10 on the purchasing agent. In addition, considerable technical assistance was provided to this utility; the training of line crews, an engineering study of conductors, and a cost analysis of the two types of wire. By 1953, 75 out of the 121 Class I utilities were using aluminum conductor wire. For the rest, the resistance to aluminum copper wire was classified by Kaiser under the following categories: failure to understand the connector problem, 34 percent; crew training, 27 percent; failure to see cost savings, 19 percent; fear of corrosion, 5.5 percent; inventory of copper wire, 14.5 percent. It should be noted each of these reasons except the last is in large part a learning problem.

Alcoa's introduction of aluminum sleeve bearings for diesel engines illustrates the same lengthy learning process with a less successful outcome.[2] In 1937, Alcoa developed alloy 750 for use in engine bearings. Experimental bearings were installed by one diesel engine builder in that year, but all further testing and development was postponed by the war. By 1944 the alloying metal was again available and considerable operating experience had been accumulated, so that Alcoa could begin the full-scale marketing of the aluminum bearings.

These bearings had better corrosion resistance, higher heat dissipation, and lower fatigue failure than the conventional steel bearings. In addition, the softer aluminum bearings did not damage an engine shaft during a failure in the oil supply — an important advantage for the larger diesels where new shafts cost as much as $4500. Finally aluminum bearings were less costly to manufacture and could be machined on common machine tools.

Despite the impressive array of technical advantages, the initial

[2] See Corey, *The Development of Markets for New Materials*, pp. 82–97, for a fuller discussion.

customer response was disappointing. Originally Alcoa planned to market the castings to bearing manufacturers but these firms showed little interest. The sales effort was then concentrated upon the engine manufacturers. Three engine manufacturers that manufactured their own bearings shifted to aluminum primarily because of the easier machinability. So did one engine builder who began making his own bearings. In the 1950's some engine users ordered replacement aluminum bearings, and there was a renewed interest in aluminum bearings by engine builders. Still, aluminum bearings had not become standard equipment by 1954.

The moral of these two examples is obvious. A new component that must be integrated into existing products and processes requires a long and protracted learning period. Hence, products are not simply accepted on their merits, but must be merchandised aggressively.

The marketing activities of the primary producers are directed in large part to this kind of merchandising of new applications for aluminum. Such activities are impressive in their careful rationality, their investment of sales effort for a long-run payoff, their service orientation, and their large absolute size.

Kaiser's sales organization illustrates these features, although they are equally evident in the sales organizations of Reynolds and Alcoa.[3] The conscious rationality is best demonstrated by the general staff of the sales organization, the market analysis group. Each year this group prepares a plan setting forth an estimate of the size of various markets and of Kaiser's desired share. These plans are communicated to the product managers of sheet, foil, and so forth, who have the final authority on pricing, allocation, and sales quotas in accordance with an over-all plan. The actual sales force is located in the twenty-odd district offices, but like the infantry in modern war, this is a relatively small part of the total personnel.

But, to insure that no market opportunity is overlooked, a separate industry section maintains a longer-run sales development programmed on an industry basis — building construction, railroads, automobiles, marine applications, machinery and equipment, and

---

[3] This description of sales organization is based on W. B. Griffin, "Kaiser Aluminum: More Metal for More Products for More People," *Modern Metals*, Vol. 11, No. 12 (January 1956), and E. A. Farrell "Selling Aluminum," *Modern Metals*, Vol. 12, No. 6 and No. 7. (July and August 1956). For comparable description of Reynolds' sales organization see F. L. Church "Man of the Year, David P. Reynolds," *Modern Metals*, Vol. 10, No. 12. (January 1955).

so forth. This group sponsors long-run efforts to develop markets, such as seminars for potential users and cooperative research ventures with manufacturers.

The service orientation of these marketing efforts is personified in the sales engineers, whose number almost equals that of salesmen. The sales engineers ordinarily answer customers' queries on product design and fabricating techniques, but in some cases Kaiser's sales engineers design dies and tools and give technical assistance until the product is in production. Frequently new end-products are described in the trade journals as the joint efforts of a manufacturer and a primary producer.

These sales efforts involve a large absolute magnitude of resources — expenditures of probably $30,000,000 or more for a primary producer.[4] These expenditures have facilitated a better allocation in the relative use of the different metals. Aluminum has become relatively cheaper than other metals since the war. As a result, a large-scale shift toward aluminum, facilitated by these marketing efforts, has occurred. Even without the relative price change, the efficient operation of markets presupposes knowledge by the participants, and this knowledge is effectively distributed by the kind of selling described above.

At the same time, there is little danger of overselling to the businessmen buyers. In many products like aluminum windows or trailers, sales efforts were ineffective until the relative price of aluminum declined to make aluminum clearly the most desirable material. Finally, the total sales efforts, including both the market analysts and the TV spectaculars, is approximately 5 percent of the aggregate sales revenue.[5]

Granted then that this sales effort is socially productive, the question then becomes what forms of market structure are conducive to the socially optimum amounts and direction of marketing activity. The evidence is diffuse and qualitative, but it does appear that the marketing of aluminum is more lively under the postwar oligopoly than it was under the prewar monopoly. This is socially desirable, for the marketing effort is largely directed at the dissemination of technical knowledge.

[4] The annual reports of the primary producers give a total for sales and general administration expenditures. From comments in the trade literature, more than $30,000,000 is the order of magnitude of sales expenditures.

[5] This is only an approximation. Total sales and all general administration expenses are about 10 percent of sales, but the annual reports do not show sales expenses separately.

The virtue of oligopoly, here as elsewhere, is that several organizations are more likely to experiment with differing policies, and if one proves successful, it then becomes industry practice. The differing view of the optimum market strategy is illustrated by the entry of primary producers into end-product manufacture. This is a way for a primary producer both to by-pass and to accelerate by example the learning process of their customers. For instance, Alcoa initially entered fabricating primarily because of the lack of interest in aluminum by existing metal fabricators.[6] In end-products, however, Alcoa followed a general policy of persuading existing end-product manufacturers to produce new aluminum products, and only after indifferent or no success did Alcoa produce end-products, and then only temporarily and on a small scale.[7]

Reynolds, upon its entry into the aluminum industry, adopted the quite different marketing strategy of moving aggressively into end-product manufacturing — furniture, foil, deep-freeze units, venetian blinds, window frames, truck trailers, cooking ware, irrigation pipes, natural gas pipeline, grain bins, and so forth.[8] (Such a strategy, of course, was consistent with the company's origins as a manufacturer of cigarette foil.) Alcoa initially held to its older policy of cooperative activity with the manufacturers, but along with Kaiser it gradually began to move into end-product manufacturing.[9] At present all the companies make a wide range of final products, but Reynolds remains the most extensively integrated into these activities.

Nevertheless, only about 15 percent of the primary aluminum output is consumed by vertically integrated end-product manufacturing. These operations have not always been profitable. For ex-

[6] Donald H. Wallace, *Market Control in the Aluminum Industry* (Cambridge: Harvard University Press, 1937), pp. 8–12.

[7] A classic example of this spin-off process is Alcoa's manufacture of furniture in the 1920's, made only after efforts to interest other manufacturers failed. The furniture operation was eventually sold to a furniture manufacturer. Aluminum cooking ware provides an exception. Alcoa began the production through a subsidiary at an early date and continues to market the Wearever line. The subsidiary, however, was independent of the parent company in its management.

[8] Loeb, Carl M., Rhoades and Company, *Aluminum: An Analysis of the Industry* (New York: Loeb, Rhoades and Company, 1950), p. 9.

[9] Mr. Wilson, president of Alcoa, testified in 1948: "Reynolds has developed many more building products than we have. They have gone into that branch of the field and offered down-spouting, guttering, and clapboards in aluminum, clapboard style and a great many more products in the building industry of their own fabrication than we have. We have worked more with other fabricators and distributors." (*Record*, p. 1091. United States v. Aluminum Company of America, 91 F. Supp. 333 [S.D.N.Y., 1950], henceforth cited as *Remedy Record*.)

ample, Reynolds is estimated to have lost $10,000,000 in end-product manufacturing, and an investment analysis concludes "with a removal of the unprofitable manufactured products, a very substantial increase in over-all earnings should be forthcoming." [10] Nevertheless, Reynolds' manufacture of end-products seems to have accelerated the acceptance of some end-products, particularly in the construction sector.[11]

Vertical Integration and Marketing Effort

Some degree of vertical integration into fabrication is required for the present level and type of sales engineering carried on by the primary producers. Without vertical integration the incentives for sales engineering would be indirect and uncertain. Consider, for example, a primary producer persuading a manufacturer to adopt a new aluminum application. Without its own fabrication facilities, a primary producer could still expect to increase its sales of aluminum ingot to the independent fabricators as a result of the new use of aluminum. Yet, leakages in this process are probable. The end-product manufacturer might buy from an independent fabricator served by another primary producer and the fabricator, in turn, might buy from another primary producer than the one expending the marketing effort.

The fabricators in particular are a weak link, for most fabricators buy from several primary producers, so that a primary producer's sales engineering effort might well show up in the increased ingot sales of a rival primary producer. In the long run, these leakages might be offsetting; but the primary aluminum producers are, after all, profit-making institutions, so that a relatively close correlation between marketing effort and the profit payoff is required for the present level of marketing activity. In addition, the kinds of resistance to learning outlined above would be compounded if a primary producer was also required to persuade the fabricator to produce new types of fabrication required for a new application.

Of course, the independent fabricators would provide some of this sales engineering, as in fact they already do. But individual independent fabricators of roughly their present size could not

[10] Loeb, *Aluminum,* p. 41.

[11] "Critics of Reynolds (and it has its share) complain that it competes with its own customers. Reynolds' men do not deny this, but they argue that their competition usually broadens the market." (F. L. Church, "Man of the Year, David P. Reynolds," p. 110)

support the elaborate sales engineering effort of the primary producers, nor could they afford the present level of effort directed at long-run market development.

A lower level of sales engineering would hardly be disastrous for the aluminum industry; end-product manufacturers have the incentive to seek out profitable aluminum applications; and to assume a complete lack of know-how and energy on their part is unfounded. One example illustrates the semiautomatic character of aluminum growth. Over one-half of the soft-alloy extrusions are manufactured by independent extruders, none of whom carries out the large-scale market development, while the primary producers have not made a concentrated effort in this market. Yet this particular fabrication has one of the highest rates of growth of demand.[12] Likewise, in Europe some aluminum applications are farther advanced than the United States, despite a lower level of sales engineering.[13] In these cases other factors such as the relative price of aluminum may offset the lack of sales engineering, but apparently a high level of sales engineering is not an absolute requisite for the use of aluminum.

Even so, sales engineering serves to facilitate the growth of aluminum as well as a more efficient allocation of resources, so that a loss of a socially desirable service must be counted as one of the costs of a public policy limiting vertical integration.

Marketing Effort and the Rivalry Between the Primary Producers

These marketing activities are also the principal factor in the division of the market among the primary producers. As such they play an important role in the functioning of oligopoly over and above their role in expanding the market for aluminum. The prices of most aluminum products are identical among primary producers, so that buyers choose between sellers partly by accident, partly for a wide variety of historical reasons, and partly because of differences in marketing skill. This method of dividing the market gives a relatively high degree of stability in market shares. There is clearly

---

[12] Computed from data in House Select Committee on Small Business, Subcommittee No. 3 on Minerals and Raw Materials, *Report, Small Business and the Aluminum Industry*, 84th Cong., 2d Sess., H.R. No. 2954, 1956, p. 72. Henceforth cited as *Small Business Report, 1956*.

[13] See "Report from Europe," *Modern Metals*, Vol. 12, No. 6 (July 1956), pp. 44, 48.

a matching phenomenon — if one primary producer creates a high level of effective sales engineering, the other firms match such an effort. Specifically, Reynolds' entry into end-products was quickly duplicated by the other primary producers. Yet, unlike price competition, no firm can exactly duplicate the effort of another, so that one firm may easily show small increases in market share. At the same time, no one firm can quickly dominate the market by marketing efforts because of the reluctance of end-product customers to shift suppliers.

In contrast, the buyers of ingot, that is, the independent fabricators, often buy simultaneously from all three producers and are more likely to shift their supplier in the event of a price difference. The fabricators, as fulltime and established processors of aluminum, have less of a need for the engineering services of a primary producer and as a result place less emphasis upon a continuing relation with a sole supplier.[14] Furthermore, aluminum is a greater proportion of their selling price than for the end-product manufacturers, which means any price difference would be of more significance to them. As a result, if the primary producers should sell ingot largely to fabricators, these buyers would be much more responsive to any small price differences between the primary producers than would end-product manufacturers.

Vertical disintegration, then, would create a situation more conducive to price competition (and particularly secret price concessions) and so might weaken the oligopolistic discipline that now sets the level of aluminum prices. The market power held by the primary producers is greater because they sell fabrications, products which permit more product differentiation than ingot. This is still another factor in evaluating the effects of vertical integration upon the functioning of the aluminum industry, a topic examined in the concluding chapter.

The Aluminum Distributors

In addition to the primary producers, the marketing system in the aluminum industry now includes a sizable number of distributors. The distributor of aluminum is an independent warehouseman selling aluminum for the primary producers. Not until 1929 did Alcoa appoint distributors, and by 1939 this group, now 6, sold no more

[14] See the discussion in Chapter VII.

than 2.5 percent of aluminum output.[15] By 1955, the distributors
sold 10–11 percent of a greatly expanded output of aluminum, and
their number had increased from 6 to 114.[16] In addition, 89 jobbers,
operating without a full-line distributor appointment and generally
selling only a few products, added another one or two percentage
points to the aluminum marketed through independent middlemen.[17]

The increased importance of the distributor can be attributed
to the general expansion of aluminum capacity, to the increase in
selling costs,[18] and to the entry of Reynolds and Kaiser.[19] Both
these firms faced the problem of rapidly building up a market for
their capacity. They began appointing numerous distributors. Since
Alcoa did likewise almost simultaneously, it is difficult to identify
leadership and followership in this marketing strategy. Nevertheless,
the timing is such to support the presumption that the increased use
of distributors was caused in part by the greater rivalry for market
shares between the primary producers. The increase in the number
of distributors supports the proposition that the introduction of
oligopoly generated greater marketing effort.

This rivalry did not extend to the creation of competitors to
the primary producers' own distributing organization. Rather, the
distributors were assigned the role of handling small orders.[20] This
division of the marketing function corresponds to that in steel and
copper, where the metal producers serve the large users directly

[15] Wayne Rising, "A Vital Industry," *Modern Metals*, Vol. 12, No. 11 (December
1955), p. 72. Without the formal title some firms date back much further in
distributing aluminum. A distributor in Portland, Oregon, Pacific Metal Co., added
aluminum in 1890, a year after the Hall process was patented. F. L. Church, "Light
Metals Man of the Year . . . Mr. Distributor," *Modern Metals*, Vol. 12, No. 12
(January 1957), p. 90. Strahs Aluminum Co. in New York City performed distributor
functions for Alcoa since 1917. *Ibid.*, p. 88.

[16] W. Rising, "A Vital Industry," p. 72.

[17] F. L. Church, "Light Metals Man of the Year . . . Mr. Distributor," p. 87.

[18] Robert Welsh, until 1953 with Kaiser (in 1957, secretary, American Steel
Warehouse Association), stated: "Any metal producer could afford calls on reasonably
small customers a few years ago for he had salesmen making $125 to $300 per
month. . . . Today the producers' sales tickets from calls on small accounts cannot
support such calls. . . . The distributor is the answer." Quoted in F. L. Church,
"Light Metals Man of the Year . . . Mr. Distributor," p. 88.

[19] [In 1945 distributors started to increase] ". . . the three producers were
fighting for new markets." *Ibid.*

[20] One contract between distributor and Kaiser specifically states: "[The distributor] is to supplement the effort of the Permanente [now Kaiser] selling organization
by providing a service Permanente is not in a position to offer. This service includes
handling requirements of customers unable to buy mill quantities or customers
which require warehouse service such as special shearing or shifting, special credit
terms, or carrying of customers less than carload inventories." *Remedy Record*,
Government Exhibit 70, p. 291.

from their mills with carload shipments. Transshipping the carload shipments through a distributor's warehouse is an unnecessary step in the distributive process. (Carloads are the lowest cost unit of shipment under the present structure of rail rates.) For the small orders, however, distributors are at an advantage with their inventories warehoused near the customer and their ability to consolidate small orders for carload shipment.

There is, however, a dispute about the dividing point between small and large orders. Orders of less than 4000 pounds are conceded to be distributor business, and carload shipments of more than 30,000 pounds are conceded to be mill (primary producer) business.[21] But for orders in the intermediate size range both the primary producers and the distributors claim to be most efficient.

The issue is in large part one of price structure. The primary producers usually quote a base price in terms of individual orders of 30,000 pounds or more (a carload). For smaller quantities, the primary producers add quantity extras ranging on sheet from 60 cents per pound for orders of less than 24 pounds to 0.002 cents per pound for orders of more than 20,000 pounds. The justification for these price differences is the higher rail rates and the greater handling and shipping costs per pound for the smaller orders. Yet the primary producers' quantity extras are also the important factor in determining the distributor's margin. The distributors buy from the primary producer at the base price less 5 percent and resell at the primary producer's base price plus the quantity extras.[22] But for the larger orders the distributors consider that the quantity extras produce an insufficient margin. As a result, the distributors often sell above the primary producers' list price on such orders, and so the distributor receives relatively few of the larger less-than-carload orders.[23]

[21] Given the existing price structure, individual customers have their own breaking point between distributors and mill orders, depending on inventory policy, speed of delivery, and so forth. For example, Hotpoint Appliance in Chicago buys orders of less than 4,000 pounds from distributors and orders of more than 10,000 pounds from the mill, barring emergencies. In the intermediate range between 6,000 and 10,000 pounds, it depends on the relative cost and the quality of the service. Said one user, ". . . it's much better to be a big warehouse buyer than a small mill customer . . ." F. L. Church, "Light Metals Man of the Year . . . Mr. Distributor," p. 102. But these statements, of course, do not answer the question of social efficiency, since the existing price structure is in dispute.

[22] Ibid., p. 94.

[23] As one user pointed out, "If we want to buy 30,000 pounds of one item, we can buy this from the mill at the same price as the distributor pays for it. So only

The distributors allege that the small orders alone are not sufficiently profitable to support the operations of a distributor and so some larger less than carload orders are required to make a profit. Furthermore, they allege that the quantity extras do not fully reflect the primary producers' costs of handling these intermediate size orders, so that there is economic price discrimination (cost differences unreflected in price differences) against which the distributors cannot compete.[24]

The speeches of the distributors frequently refer to the steel industry where the distributors handle about one-fifth of the total output as compared to the aluminum industry where the distributors handle about 10–11 percent.[25] Similarly, with respect to profit margins, the President of the Aluminum Distributors Association states, ". . . the percentage of profit we obtain on aluminum sales is not commensurate with those of virtually every steel item we carry, and has become a matter of concern to many distributors." [26] In a survey by the Distributors Association, the gross margin on most aluminum products was found to be 20 percent compared to 25 percent to 30 percent on steel products. The costs of handling the two products cannot be ascertained, at least from this survey, because all but two or three distributors included handle steel, copper and brass, as well as aluminum, and most expenses are joint costs. The association survey reports that average costs are higher for distributors handling only aluminum than for those handling only steel.[27]

Despite the inconclusiveness of such data, the distributor's net profit margin may well be lower on aluminum than on steel. Historically, the typical distributor started in steel and added aluminum after World War II.[28] As an additional line over which to distribute overhead, aluminum was welcome, even if it carried a lower gross profit margin than steel. With a growth in sales to a

---

in an extreme situation would we buy it at the premium price the distributors must ask." Quoted in *Ibid.*, p. 100.

[24] A recent presidential speech at the National Association of Aluminum Distributors contained the following statement: "The producers should take a long, hard look at their costs of processing what they term a small mill order. . . ." Wayne Rising, "A Vital Industry," p. 72.

[25] *Ibid.*

[26] Wayne Rising, president of the National Association of Aluminum Distributors, *Ibid.*, p. 74.

[27] "Aluminum Distributors Discuss Outlook for 1955 in Association's Annual Meeting." *Modern Metals*, Vol. 10, No. 12 (January 1955), p. 38.

[28] *Modern Metals*, Vol. 3, No. 1 (February 1947), p. 43.

point for many distributors where aluminum has become more than one-third of their total sales, distributors are less eager to accord aluminum the status of a marginal line. Many now expect a profit margin comparable to that for steel products.[29]

To all this, the primary producers reply that the distributor's natural economic role is the small order and "the distributors lose sight of their primary function — to make a profit on small orders." Here "the producers believe that the discount and the quantity markups are sufficient to enable the distributor to make a better [than average] profit." [30] Although it is easy enough to show that direct mill delivery is cheaper for carload orders, the distributors may well be able to handle the larger less-than-carload orders at a lower cost than the primary producers. Without further cost data this issue cannot be resolved.

There are, however, two factors, apart from relative efficiency, to explain the primary producers' retention of the intermediate-sized orders. First, the distributor does not carry out the same level of sales engineering as a primary producer.[31] But the distributors' current level of marketing effort is at least partially of the primary producers' own making, since the low profit margin of the distributors precludes large sales expenses. The most obvious example is that distributors' salesmen handling both aluminum and steel sometimes receive a lower commission on aluminum sales because of the lower margin to the distributor, certainly an awkward situation for the two competitive metals.[32] Nevertheless, even under most favorable circumstances, the distributors can hardly duplicate the elaborate marketing activities of the primary producers, and from the analysis in the preceding section, the primary producers' sales engineering requires considerable direct contact between the primary producers and the manufacturers.

Second, an increase in volume handled by distributors might

---

[29] There are now only two or three exclusive distributors of aluminum. *Modern Metals* quotes a Kaiser marketing man as follows: "With the aluminum industry in its present stage of development I believe an all aluminum distributor could make a go of it only in highly industrialized areas such as New York, Chicago, and Los Angeles. I don't think the general tendency will be toward the all aluminum setup, not in the short-term at any rate. But as aluminum usage continues to increase, it will be much more feasible to have all aluminum outlets," E. A. Farrell, "Selling Aluminum," Part 2, *Modern Metals*, Vol. 12, No. 7 (Aug. 1956), p. 70.

[30] F. L. Church, "Light Metals Man of the Year . . . Mr. Distributor," p. 94.

[31] An official of a primary producer states the distributors "skim off the cream" and wait for demand to appear rather than develop markets. *Ibid.*, p. 98.

[32] *Modern Metals*, Vol. 10, No. 11 (December 1954), p. 100.

well introduce more price competition. At present the market structure of the distributors is unlikely to produce excessive price competition. Each primary producer has several distributors in areas like New York City, so that the number of sellers is about a dozen.[33] The low margin, however, leaves little range for price reduction and the smaller orders involve a sufficient element of service so that product differentiation rather than price competition divides the market. Apparently, even in 1957, when demand was at a low level, there was little off-list pricing among distributors.[34] But, if the distributors were to handle the intermediate orders and the number of distributors were to increase with the expansion of the distributors' market share, price competition among the numerous small firms would become probable, as the experience with aluminum extruders indicates. As long as the primary producers control the major fraction of aluminum distribution, the possibility of this kind of price competition is prevented.

These, then, are the reasons the primary producers might well find it advantageous to control directly the marketing of the bulk of aluminum products and to assign to the distributors only the small-order function, apart from the real costs of the two methods of distribution. And, although no one states so publicly, the distributors do not have the market power to alter the present arrangements.

In steel, which the distributors frequently use as a norm, the power relations are quite different. A distributor of steel is not the appointed distributor of one producer as in aluminum, but rather buys from several producers.[35] Thus the steel producers are in competition for the segment of the market serviced by distributors, and the distributors can change their shares bought from various producers. Furthermore, a distributor of steel can choose among handling the products of some eight to ten suppliers of steel. In aluminum the only alternative open to a distributor is to resign and seek an appointment as a distributor with one of the two other primary producers. Apparently competition among the three primary producers is workable enough to force them to seek out the dis-

[33] Testimony of A. A. Smith, president of Adam Metal Supply Inc., House Select Committee on Small Business, Subcommittee No. 3, *Hearings, Aluminum Industry*, 85th Cong., 1st and 2d Sess., 1958, p. 310. Henceforth cited as *Small Business Hearings, 1958*.

[34] The distributors in the New York area were particularly affected by price competition from imports in 1957.

[35] *Modern Metals*, Vol. 10, No. 12 (January 1955), p. 37.

tributor, but not sufficient to alter the profit margins nor the kind of market assigned the distributor by the policies of the primary producers.

Notably, the distributors' discount and the quantity extras have remained largely unchanged since 1946. The one reported revision in quantity extras may have lowered the distributors' margin.[36] Another significant change was the introduction of consignment selling. Under this system the distributor buys inventory on consignment and pays each month for items actually sold with the option of returning slow-moving stock to the mill. This reduces the working capital requirements of the distributor as well as the risks of excess inventory, although the discount from list price in this case is 4 instead of 5 percent. This particular change was introduced by Alcoa and quickly matched by Reynolds and Kaiser, illustrating that the matching phenomenon operating in price changes likewise applies to distributor terms.[37]

This history suggests that the distributors are unlikely to develop as independent marketing firms that deal with the primary producers on a basis of near equality. In this, the distributors are analagous to the independent fabricators: holding a market position assigned by the primary producers and so a constant source of friction and speechmaking. Yet, like the independent fabricator, the distributors' position cannot be altered short of either elaborate protective legislation or a radical change in the market structure.

The gains of public policy actions to enlarge the role of the distributors may be fairly limited. Price competition between the distributors might well have some effect on the level of list prices, but as long as the carload orders are directly distributed by the primary producers, the largest volume of sales will be handled by

[36] *Modern Metals* reports, "Price hikes averaging 4.5% were passed from the mill to the warehouse to the consumer, but warehousers' over-all price schedules [apparently the quantity extras] have been readjusted on volume orders. The end effect is a price cut of 0.5 c to 1.0 c to the consumer." E. A. Farrell, "An Aluminum Distributor Looks Ahead," *Modern Metals,* Vol. 11, No. 12 (January 1956), p. 40.

[37] Apparently there was some reluctant followership since, according to *Modern Metals,* "The producers and distributors also disagree on whether consigned aluminum stocks are a good thing. One industrialist says it's a crutch for distributors; that the producers have over $60 million tied up with distributors most of the time; that a small mill cannot afford to consign stocks to distributors. Some say consignment is only useful when a new product is being introduced, or where trial and acceptance is a long process. Others claim that with consignment there's no pressure to sell, and that a distributor functions best when he's 'in hock up to his ears.'" F. L. Church, "Light Metals Man of the Year . . . Mr. Distributor," p. 94–95.

the primary producers. For these carload orders, transshipping through distributors seems clearly an uneconomical channel of distribution.

Even though changes in the distributors' role may add relatively little to the over-all workability of competition, their contentions that their market share is unduly restricted by the price structure set by the primary producers may still be valid. The evidence is insufficient to judge the substantive merits of these issues. But it seems clear that the market power of the primary producers is such that competition does not automatically insure an economical division of function between this small business sector and the primary producers.

The Big Buyers and Hot Aluminum

It has been argued that the market power of the big buyers may force price concessions which spread and affect the general level of prices in the industry. In this way, the market power of big buyers offsets that of the sellers. Professor Adelman's study of the A. & P. case introduced this view of big buyer,[38] and in a more elaborate form it is central to Professor Galbraith's theory of countervailing power.[39] Much as it is desirable to be fashionable, examples of this kind of role for the big buyer did not occur in the aluminum industry until recently.

In the one pre-1950 example, the big buyer paid more than the list price. In 1949, Reynolds negotiated a contract with the National Rural Electric Cooperative Association, an organization of cooperatives distributing electricity under federal sponsorship, for the sale of 475,000,000 pounds of electrical cable over a ten-year period. The price was approximately 3 cents above Alcoa's list price with a further provision for readjustments for any future increase in Reynold's direct costs. The most striking feature of the contract was that Reynolds had neither a cable plant nor the funds to build one. Rather, the cooperatives furnished the capital to build a plant through

---

[38] See Morris Adelman, "The A & P case: A Study in Applied Economic Theory," *Quarterly Journal of Economics*, 63:238–257 (May 1949), and "Competition and the Antitrust Laws," *Harvard Law Review*, 61:1289–1350 (September 1948), particularly page 1300, and "The Large Firm and Its Suppliers," *Review of Economics and Statistics*, 31:113–118 (May 1949). For a contrary view see Joel B. Dirlam and Alfred E. Kahn, "Antitrust Law and the Big Buyer: Another Look at the A & P case," *Journal of Political Economy*, 60:118–132. (April 1952).

[39] J. K. Galbraith, *American Capitalism; The Concept of Countervailing Power* (Boston, Houghton Mifflin, 1952).

a $6,000,000 advance payment. Furthermore, aluminum ingot output was then restricted by a power shortage and it was alleged that the Rural Electrification Administration arranged for Reynolds to receive additional power required to produce the aluminum ingot for the cable.[40]

The contract provisions do not appear so one-sided in the context of the times. Aluminum was in extremely short supply early in 1949 and was rationed by the primary producers. The contract guaranteed the REA an assured supply of 25,000 miles of power line and, according to the REA press release, "relief from the long-term shortage of aluminum cable."[41] This contract is a dramatic example of the increase in the bargaining power of the sellers under conditions of excess demand.[42]

Subsequent big-buyer transactions also involved Reynolds, thus confirming their flair for marketing innovation. Contracts here covered the sale of molten aluminum to Ford and General Motors for the manufacture of castings in a nearby plant owned by the automobile companies. According to *Iron Age*, the first General Motors contract originated in 1948. Buick required aluminum for its Dyna-flow transmissions. And at this time the molten-metal contracts were said to have been formulated.[43]

It is a matter of record that General Motors constructed in 1950 a casting plant at Jones Mill, Arkansas, near the Reynolds reduction plant. The molten aluminum from the Reynolds plant is poured into a thermos tank and trucked about a mile to the General Motors casting plant, where, still in molten form, it is cast into various aluminum parts. These sales were made under a three-year contract requiring daily deliveries and purchases of not less than 7,500 pounds nor more than 25,000 pounds, depending upon the current output of the casting plant. In 1952 a new five-year contract was signed providing for the sale of a minimum of 20,000,000 pounds and a maximum of 40,000,000 pounds annually.[44]

The third General Motors–Reynolds contract was signed in 1957. This contract covered the delivery of molten metal to a General

[40]This contract is described in *Modern Metals*, Vol. 5, No. 2 (March 1949), p. 15, and Vol. 5, No. 1 (February 1949), p. 31.
[41] *Modern Metals*, Vol. 5, No. 2 (March 1949), p. 15.
[42] Professor Galbraith observes that the essence of a sellers' market is the shift of countervailing power away from buyers. Galbraith, *American Capitalism*, p. 111.
[43] *The Iron Age*, Vol. 179, No. 10 (March 7, 1957), p. 91.
[44] "House Committee Takes Another Look at Competition in Aluminum," *Modern Metals*, Vol. 13, No. 11 (December 1957), p. 83.

Motors foundry in Massena, New York. The quantity is stated in terms of the total requirements of this foundry, subject to an annual maximum of 75,000,000 pounds. General Motors, however, must place with the foundry at least one-half of all aluminum castings used for Chevrolet transmissions and one-quarter of all castings used for Chevrolet pistons. The contract runs for ten years with a renewal option.[45]

Prior to the signing of this contract, Reynolds had attempted to obtain a long-term power contract for a proposed reduction plant from the New York State Power Authority. The Authority was reluctant to grant such a contract because the employment provided by a reduction plant was low compared to the amount of power required. The Authority took the position that power should be reserved for industries that offered a greater number of jobs. At this point, Reynolds entered into its contract with General Motors (making the contract conditional upon the signing of the power contract), so that Reynolds could now offer the Authority a package that included considerably more jobs. The Authority then granted the power contract, Reynolds conveyed land to General Motors, and both parties began the construction of their respective plants. According to Reynolds' counsel, "There is no doubt that without the General Motors contract, the power contract would not have been approved."[46]

Reynolds signed still another molten-metal contract with the Ford Motor Company in 1955. It provides for the delivery of 64,000,000 pounds annually for ten years with one five-year renewal option.[47] Again, both Ford and Reynolds constructed the facilities after signing the contract. The contract was conditional upon Reynolds' ability to obtain the necessary capital, and according to a Reynolds executive, "The existence of the contract was one of the conditions required of our company by the lending institution from whom we borrowed $75 million of the amount needed for the expansion."[48]

These contracts became public knowledge as the result of a Securities and Exchange Commission registration statement.[49] There

[45] This contract is reproduced in *Small Business Hearings, 1958*, pp. 408–410.
[46] *Small Business Hearings, 1958*, p. 11.
[47] The contract is reproduced in *Small Business Hearings, 1958*, pp. 411–435.
[48] *Small Business Hearings, 1958*, p. 10.
[49] Reynolds apparently would have liked the SEC to have treated these contracts as confidential. *Small Business Hearings, 1958*, p. 20.

were complaints from independent fabricators, and in 1958 the House of Representatives Small Business Committee held hearings on whether these contracts represented price discrimination and a foreclosure of markets.

The issue of price discrimination was complicated by the method in which prices were determined under each of these contracts. The starting point was the current list price for pig. The average cost of the freight paid by Reynolds in its deliveries to pig and ingot customers was first deducted from the list price. Ten percent of the balance was then deducted. The resulting figure was multiplied by the percentage of casting aluminum in the alloy to determine the "aluminum" price. To this was added the current market price of the alloying metals. The mechanics of this pricing formula are illustrated by an example cited in the General Motors contract and shown in Table 17.[50]

TABLE 17. Example of establishing price per pound of molten metal containing 95 percent aluminum and 5 percent silicon

Current list price 99 + pig (prevailing in 1952)	$0.1800
Freight factor	0.0113
Difference	0.1687
Deduction (10 percent)	0.01687
Difference	0.15183
Aluminum content	0.95
Product	0.14424
Cost of silicon (5 percent at $0.200 market price per pound)	0.01000
Delivered price per pound	0.15424

Source: Contract between General Motors Corporation and Reynolds Metals Company, 1952. Reproduced in *Small Business Hearings, 1958,* p. 404.

The price difference between the list price and that in the contract is not evident from the illustrative example shown in the contract. (See Table 17.) The relevant comparison is not with the price of aluminum pig but with that of the comparable casting alloy. Casting alloy of the same composition as much of that sold under the contract carried a list price of 26.50 cents per pound in 1958 compared to a contract price of 22.63. The price difference reflects not only the freight factor and the 10 percent discount, but also the fact that the alloying metals are included at their market price

[50] Testimony of David Laine, Executive Secretary, American Die Casting Institute, *Small Business Hearings, 1958,* p. 200.

whereas the list price reflects some markup on the alloying components. The 17.5 percent price difference appears to be representative of the price differences created by the contract.

The term price discrimination in economic analysis is limited to price differences that do not correspond to differences in the sellers' costs. The transportation factor is a cost saving to the seller, in that Reynolds ordinarily sells pig aluminum at a uniform delivered price and absorbs the freight. In the molten-metal transactions, the buyer takes delivery at the reduction plant in a large truck equipped with a ladle into which the metal is poured.[51] The buyer trucks the metal to the casting plant in its molten form where it is immediately cast.[52]

Reynolds then does not pay freight upon the delivery of the metal. Furthermore, Reynolds' cost savings here are in large part at the expense of the higher transportation expenses for the buyers. In the past, automobile companies had located their transmission plants in the midwest, and the expense of transporting aluminum pig to these plants was paid by the aluminum producers. In relocating plants at the sites of reduction plants, the automobile companies bore the added cost of transporting the finished castings a greater distance. Ford estimated these extra freight charges at about 1.25 cents per pound, compared to the 0.9 cent it receives as a freight allowance.[53] General Motors presumably fared somewhat better since their New York state plant is nearer the Detroit assembly plant. In view of these extra costs incurred by the buyer and the cost savings of the seller, one would expect a departure from the list price. The freight allowance was a reduction from list price that roughly corresponded to the seller's savings in cost and so created a price difference corresponding to a cost difference. Hence, this is not price discrimination as defined in economics.

In all other sales, however, the buyer of aluminum paid the full list price for metal delivered to his plant. An independent foundry in the same town did not receive a "freight factor" even though the delivery costs were well below average.[54] This is, of course, the

[51] These are delivery terms in the Ford contract. *Small Business Hearings, 1958,* p. 415. General Motors has a similar arrangement.

[52] *Small Business Hearings, 1958,* p. 123.

[53] *Small Business Hearings, 1958,* p. 129.

[54] The testimony is as follows:

Representative Yates: Can a small fabricator, an extruder, for example, who operates in Listerhill, Ala., hard by your producing plant, get the same freight

price discrimination inherent in a system of uniform prices in which distant and near buyers pay the same price although the costs of serving them are obviously different. The automobile companies are the exception to this system. Thus, this exception is in itself discriminatory in the broader sense of the term, even though it is not price discrimination narrowly defined.

The 10-percent discount had no such clear relation to an identifiable cost. The molten-metal process eliminated pigging, the pouring of metal into molds by the primary producer. Estimates of pigging costs by three secondary smelters ranged from 0.25 to 0.33 cents per pound, which was substantially under the approximately 2-cent discount.[55] Similarly, Kaiser and Alcoa officials replied that the cost of pigging is less than 10 percent of the published price.[56] No data are available to measure the cost savings from the reduction in inventories and various sales and administrative expenses. However, in view of the fact that such costs are a small percentage of the sales price, it seems unlikely that these cost savings plus the saving in pigging costs would equal the 10 percent reduction from list price. There appears then to be price discrimination here as the economist defines the term, namely, price differences that do not correspond to cost differences. (This does not necessarily mean there is price discrimination in the legal sense. Law and economics define price discrimination differently and, in any case, the complete facts on costs are not available.)

These contracts were still highly advantageous to Reynolds. Reynolds was guaranteed the sale of aluminum produced in its capacity for at least 10 years. The security afforded by these contracts was important in financing the original investment.

The reduction in risks for Reynolds, however, may have been offset by greater cost and greater uncertainty elsewhere. Such

---

advantages that Ford gets at Listerhill — the freight deduction — or will he pay freight in his bill?

Mr. McConnell [a Reynolds executive]: No. He pays freight allowed to destination, wherever he wants to ship them.

Mr. Yates: So that despite the proximity which he enjoys — while he isn't buying molten metal — he does pay a freight factor that is not paid by Ford Motor Co.

Mr. McConnell: That is right. He does.

Small Business Hearings, 1958, p. 36. One comment may clarify Mr. McConnell's first answer. The mechanics of delivered price are that the buyer pays the actual freight upon delivery and then deducts the cost from his bill from the aluminum company.

[55] *Small Business Hearings,* 1958, p. 215.

[56] *Small Business Hearings,* 1958, p. 59 and p. 76.

arrangements did not eliminate the variations in the consumption of aluminum from fluctuations in automotive output, so the industry-wide burden of uncertainty, idle capacity, and inventory holdings remains nearly unchanged.[57] With plants of the automobile companies providing a fixed volume, the independent die casters would necessarily absorb all the fluctuations in total aluminum consumption.[58] This outcome was facilitated by the purchasing practices of the automobile companies in which on the twenty-fifth of each month the independent die caster is usually given a release specifying next month's volume of purchases.[59] Hence when automotive sales decline, the purchases from the independent die casters could be reduced and a greater proportion of requirements met with the metal under contract.[60] Greater fluctuations in the independents' sales, of course, would create higher costs for the independent fabricators, which should be measured against the cost savings from the elimination of certain steps in the physical process and other reductions in costs for Reynolds and the automobile companies.

The second issue raised at the Congressional hearing was that of market foreclosure. Because of the requirements nature of the General Motors contract, the total volume covered by these contracts is difficult to establish. At a maximum, the three contracts cover the sale of 189,000,000 pounds annually, approximately one-half of the 1957 total production of die castings by the noncaptive die casters.[61] Obviously, if Chrysler and a few nonautomotive firms were to conclude similar contracts, even a greater share of die casting would be produced in captive shops. The secondary smelters would lose a substantial fraction of their potential market, for the

[57] Because the uncertainty and inventory costs are shifted from the primary producers to the die casters, two groups of diverse size, market position, and perhaps managerial practice, the "quantum" of uncertainty and inventory costs in such a shift probably changes. If, as is often said, large firms because of their diversity and size find uncertainty less costly than small firms, the result may be to increase the total social costs by shifting more uncertainty to the smaller firms.

[58] This would be most true in the case of the Ford contract, which specifies a fixed amount. In the G.M. contracts, their requirements nature would mean only a constant share is reserved for Reynolds. On the other hand, when requirements decline, General Motors can minimize costs by continuing to buy the same quantities from its lower cost source. Furthermore, this would increase the utilization of its own investment. The result would be similar to that with a fixed-volume contract.

[59] Testimony of David Laine, executive secretary, American Die Casting Institute, *Small Business Hearings, 1958*, p. 196.

[60] This is emphasized by Laine, *Small Business Hearings, 1958*, pp. 196–197.

[61] "House Committee Takes Another Look at Competition in Aluminum," *Modern Metals*, Vol. 13, No. 11 (December 1957), p. 84.

secondary smelters sold about 70 percent of their output to the independent die casters.

Nevertheless, these contracts did not reduce the automotive sales of the independent die casters. General Motors quadrupled its aluminum consumption from 1951 to 1958. As a result, though General Motors fabricated one-half of its aluminum internally in 1958 instead of one-third as in 1951, the purchase of externally fabricated aluminum increased three times in these years.[62] Indeed, the growth in aluminum usage was an important precipitating factor in these contracts, for it would have required a vast expansion of the die-casting industry, and that expansion might well have raised the prices and created shortages. Furthermore, an expansion of this magnitude could not be supplied through the use of secondary aluminum. For example, Ford forecast that its maximum requirements for aluminum alone would require 25 percent of the current secondary aluminum output.[63] Since the supply of secondary is relatively inelastic, a shift to primary aluminum was inevitable.

The Ford-Reynolds contract contains a separate issue of market foreclosure. One provision of the contract states that Reynolds shall have an opportunity to supply 30 percent of the dollar volume of Ford's annual purchases of aluminum products (sheet, bars, rods, coils, and so on) and 30 percent of the dollar volume of parts assemblies made substantially from aluminum.[64] (Both these figures are exclusive of pig and ingot and aluminum casting, the materials involved in the molten-metal process.) "Opportunity to supply" requires Ford to notify Reynolds of the quantity and specifications of its purchases up to the 30-percent figure and Reynolds can quote a price. Ford must then buy if "Reynolds' quotation is competitive." [65] If Reynolds submits no quotation, Ford may require Reynolds to supply up to 30 percent of its aluminum products at the generally prevailing market price and, for assemblies, at a price not less than the cost of manufacture as determined by Reynolds according to generally accepted accounting practices.[66]

The effect of these provisions is quite unclear. A Reynolds

---

[62] This is all aluminum products. No separate figures are available for castings. Data in *Small Business Hearings, 1958,* p. 11.

[63] Testimony of Earl Ward, vice president of purchasing, Ford Motor Company, *Small Business Hearings, 1958,* p. 118.

[64] This is Section 16. See *Small Business Hearings, 1958,* p. 418.

[65] *Small Business Hearings, 1958,* p. 418.

[66] *Small Business Hearings, 1958,* p. 419.

executive responded to a congressional query with the statement, ". . . I don't think I agree with you that the contract requires Ford to buy 30 percent from us. . . . Maybe that is the final legal commitment but we are not in position to require Ford to do much of anything at the time we try to sell it." [67] Similarly, the Ford executive stressed that this clause is "[merely] an opportunity to quote" that . . . "we would give to Alcoa or anyone else." [68]

Yet, the literal wording of the contract would seem to assure Reynolds 30 percent of Ford's purchases. Most aluminum products are sold at the published list price, which is usually the same for all the primary producers. Hence, Reynolds would "be competitive" and so be guaranteed 30 percent of Ford's purchases if it quoted the list price. At the same time Reynolds' obligation to supply Ford, if exercised, assures Ford of obtaining 30 percent of its requirements. Both parties are then assured protection against market risks for 10 years, but at the expense of the other sellers of aluminum products who cannot compete for this market and of other buyers of Reynolds' aluminum who are without a guaranteed share of its aluminum output. In these provisions, there is no issue of technological change, and hence no clearly apparent cost saving which offsets the reduction in competition.

In the molten-metal arrangements themselves, however, the issues of price discrimination and market foreclosure are occasioned by and comingled with the technological innovation in the use of molten aluminum and the rapid expansion of the consumption of aluminum in the automobile industry. Clearly, such long-term contracts reduce the immediate competition; for a substantial volume of business is foreclosed both from the die casters and the other primary producers. The policy issue is whether the cost savings are worth the reduction in competition. (It is an either/or question since a long-term contract is a prerequisite for the substantial investment by the buyer in a die-casting plant.)

It can be argued they are not. The only physical part of the production process eliminated is pigging on the part of the primary producer and the reheating on the part of the buyer. Pigging is a relatively low-cost process so that the savings here are nominal, and apparently reheating of metal is at least not one of the high-cost stages in production of castings. The net transportation cost

[67] *Small Business Hearings, 1958*, p. 33.
[68] *Small Business Hearings, 1958*, p. 131.

saving is likewise nominal, since the reduction on the pig aluminum is offset by the buyer's increased charges on the shipment of the finished castings. Finally, inventory savings and risk-reduction are substantial advantages for the signers, but, as discussed above, these may be offset by the increased uncertainties of the independent die caster who would now absorb all the fluctuations in automotive consumption.

In sum, these long-term contracts appear largely as part of the pattern of contractual security for the large firms at the expense of the smaller firms. In aluminum, then, the big buyer seems more a fellow beneficiary of market power than a force for lower prices generally, as the big-buyer thesis implies. Most examples supporting the big-buyer thesis are from retailing and wholesaling of consumer goods, highly competitive sectors in both structure and behavior. A more concentrated industry such as aluminum may have a different pattern for the role of the big buyer.

IX

THE EXPANSION OF CAPACITY

✦ In a growth industry such as aluminum, the expansion of capacity is one of the most important forms of business behavior. Yet there is little history from which to infer the character of investment behavior, for the expansion that doubled reduction capacity from 1949 to 1954 was largely under government auspices. There was further expansion from 1954 to 1956, but little information is publicly available for this period. Consequently this chapter is in large part speculation on the nature of investment behavior in the aluminum industry and examination of the government program under which most of the postwar expansion took place.[1]

The General Conditions for the Expansion of Reduction Capacity

Aluminum reduction capacity has a twenty- to thirty-year economic life, so that the return on investment depends on prices and demand over several decades. The upward trend in aluminum consumption insures that additional capacity will be required at some future date so that any overexpansion will eventually be self-correcting. Yet the three-year construction period for new capacity requires largely irreversible commitments for additional capacity well in advance of its use.[2] The present price policy and the high

---

[1] The term investment as used in this chapter denotes the expansion of primary capacity. Little information is available on investment in fabricating capacity or on the replacement of existing equipment.

[2] The following construction periods were cited for complete reduction plants and accompanying power facilities by D. L. Marlett, Deputy Defense Power Administrator: 8–16 months, natural gas engine; 24–30 months, steampower and hydropower. See House Committee on the Judiciary, Subcommittee on Study of Monopoly Power, *Hearings, Aluminum*, 1951, p. 95. Henceforth cited as *Monopoly Power Hearings, 1951*.

fixed costs mean the consequences of excess capacity cannot be off-set by changes in prices or output. Therefore, investment commitments involve a substantial risk.

As a result, investment behavior is likely to be characterized by considerable prudence. Consider first the single firm, setting aside for the moment the problem of rivalry between oligopolists. Investment behavior can be divided into what might be called "normal" and "extraordinary" situations. A normal investment policy is implicit in a long-run price policy that represents a compromise between a sufficiently low price to expand demand and a sufficiently high price to finance the resulting expansion as well as meet current dividend objectives.

This principle may be the most general factor in price, profit, and investment policies, but it is also clear that there may be a large element of custom and inertia in these as in most business policies. Furthermore, the investment funds generated by profit rate depend on the prevailing dividend policy and this, in turn, is likely to be determined by stockholder expectations and the norms of the investment community, as well as the views of the management of the firm. Nevertheless, a "workable" rate of profit that yields a growing demand and the funds to finance expansion is the one likely to survive and be enshrined in the policies of a firm.

Such a price and investment policy meets the routine situation, the steady increase in demand of a growth industry supplied by internally financed investment. In essence, this is a simple acceleration model of investment; that is, increases in demand call forth additional capacity. The capital market has no marked effect on the rate of investment except in a generalized way through its influence on the planned rate of profits. Furthermore, the marginal profits of expansion so important in the conventional economic theory of the firm count for little. Rather the rate of profit is already determined by the long-term price policy so it is the demand at a fixed rate of profit that is relevant to investment decisions instead of changes in the rate of profit. This normal investment behavior may not necessarily be the most profitable one for the stockholders because it does not capitalize on the "leverage" possibilities of using lower-cost debt financing to exploit more fully the growth in demand. Yet it may be sufficiently satisfactory to the management group that controls the firm, for it reduces the risks of investment.

For much of the prewar period the expansion in capacity has in fact been internally financed. Yet an examination of the rate of growth in aluminum consumption indicates three large surges in demand, one in the late 1920's, a second during World War II, and a third since that war. Such a rapid increase in demand cannot be supplied by the expansion of capacity through the traditional policy of internal financing, but instead the use of outside capital is necessary to bring demand and capacity into some sort of balance.

The use of outside capital, mainly in the form of debt, exposes the firm to more risk, since bonds require fixed payment irrespective of current income. In return, debt financing provides higher overall profits since the interest cost is less than the expected rate of return. The firm, then, has a different combination of risk and income from that reflected in its conventional price and investment policy.[3] The higher income alone, given the policy of stable prices and hence a stable profit rate, may not suffice to offset the higher risk. Consequently, the firm may seek additional protection from the risks of market fluctuations. This additional protection has taken different forms. In World War II, the government constructed most of the new capacity and assumed the risks, and in the post-Korean years, government tax benefits and purchase contracts provided risk protection. In the 1920's a substantial volume of excess demand for aluminum at the going price provided a safety margin against a decline in demand.[4]

The existence of oligopoly modifies this statement of investment behavior in the following way. Assume, as in Chapter IV, three firms, each with its own set of preferences. The firm desiring the highest rate of expansion dominates the setting of the rate of investment because other firms cannot maintain a lower rate of expansion without a declining market share. (This is analogous to the followership of the firm with the lowest price preferences.)

The rate of investment then depends upon the rate set by the investment leader. Generally, this would be higher than that under monopoly, partly because an oligopoly is likely to have at least one firm more expansion-prone than a monopolist. Furthermore, oligoply adds still another dimension to investment decisions, for any postponed expansion may be pre-empted by a rival.

[3] The relation between risk and trading on the equity is discussed in more general terms in Michael Kalecki, *Essays in Economic Fluctuations* (New York: Farrar and Rhinehart, 1939), chap. IV.

[4] See the discussion and sources in Chapter IV.

As in other forms of oligopolistic rivalry, each firm may accept the status quo upon the assumption that the others will do likewise. Obviously, stepping up the rate of investment beyond that dictated by the "normal" investment behavior involves a high degree of risks by all the participants. Still, the oligopolistic rationale for investment behavior may be less effective than for prices, because the time lag in the competitor's response as well as the absence of an immediate compulsion to match the rivals' actions means one firm can achieve a differential advantage over its rivals.

Price leadership itself may serve to limit investment rivalry, particularly if the new capacity has a higher cost than existing capacity and the price leader is not the investment leader. Yet, if the investment leader maintains a high pace of investment, the price leader may increase his investment in order to maintain his market share. Thus, the increase in costs of new capacity will also affect the price leader, and in turn may lead to a price increase. As a result there is a complex interaction between the veto power of the two kinds of leadership. The capital market may constitute still another veto on investment rivalry if the most expansion-prone firm faces capital rationing. Yet, as shown subsequently, these vetos seem to have little effect upon investment, at least for the rate of investment occurring in the aluminum industry since 1954.

The Postwar Expansion of Aluminum Capacity

As noted above, the postwar history of the aluminum industry cannot be used to verify the foregoing statements. From 1945 to 1948 there was little expansion of reduction capacity. In 1945, there was a 1,500,000-ton inventory of scrap and virgin aluminum, which as the Surplus Property Board stated, might "hang over the market for a number of years." [5] In that year there was also general pessimism concerning postwar economic prospects. It was this general climate of business opinion and these special circumstances which made the disposal of the government's aluminum so difficult.

These pessimistic expectations were not realized. Rather, the postwar decade proved one of the most prosperous in the history of the American economy. The government inventories were not dumped on the market, but instead this primary aluminum was

[5] Surplus Property Board, *Report to the Congress, Aluminum Plants and Facilities,* September 21, 1945, p. 4.

released to Reynolds and Kaiser to supplement their own production. By 1948 it was clear that excess demand for aluminum had developed and that additional capacity would be required in the near future. Yet, in response to a Bonneville Power Authority query, Kaiser and Reynolds indicated that they planned no expansion of reduction plants other than to bid on the still unsold government plant in Riverbank, Califorina. Alcoa anticipated adding 100,000 tons of annual capacity in the Northwest if cheap power were available.[6] Alcoa also had the only actual construction in this period, the Port Comfort, Texas, plant, the first reduction plant with natural gas as the power source.

This lag in investment is explained at least in part by the newness of Kaiser and Reynolds and the uncertainties of the pending antitrust action. Furthermore, few low-cost hydropower sites were available, which necessitated transition to other power sources and all the uncertainties that entailed. The Korean War cut short this period before a pattern of peacetime investment emerged.

Instead, the actual expansion of the aluminum industry occurred in the abnormal context of a defense economy. A memorandum submitted by the Department of the Interior to the National Resources Board in 1948 estimated annual mobilization requirements for aluminum as between 1,560,000 tons and 3,400,000 tons.[7] Since the 1948 capacity was only 726,000 tons, the gap between potential defense requirements as then visualized and current capacity was obviously substantial. Even though this study was completed in 1948, only with the Korean War did the concern about an industrial base for mobilization acquire sufficient urgency for action.

In the fall of 1950, the Office of Defense Mobilization initiated an expansion program to be accomplished in several successive

---

[6] *Record,* government exhibit 283, pp. 3120, 3423, and defendant's exhibits 209 and 210, pp. 2872–2874, United States v. Aluminum Company of America, 91 F. Supp. 333 (S.D.N.Y., 1950). Henceforth cited as *Remedy Record.*

[7] Department of the Interior, *Aluminum and Federal Power Policy,* Staff Paper, July 6, 1948, submitted to the National Security Resources Board, Reprinted in House Select Committee on Small Business, Subcommittee No. 3, *Hearings, Aluminum Industry,* 84th Cong., 1st Sess., 1955, pp. 615–640. Henceforth cited as *Small Business Hearings, 1955.* The general policy of the Munitions Board was to increase the material requirements of World War II by one-third in planning full-mobilization goals. This computation produced the minimum goal. Maximum mobilization demand assumes no metal available from Canada, plus an allowance for additional aluminum which was not used in military equipment during World War II because of the shortage of the metal. Civilian consumption is based on the 1948 use. The maximum total requirement is the sum of civilian consumption plus maximum defense demand, the minium total is the minimum defense demand.

"rounds." In the first, announced in December 1950, new reduction capacity was distributed as follows.[8]

	Annual capacity (thousands of tons)
Alcoa	120
Reynolds	100
Kaiser	100
Harvey Machine Company	72
Apex Smelting	54
Total	446

Each company received an accelerated five-year amortization certificate for 85 percent of the cost of the facilities, a provision generally available to defense-supporting investment. The unique provision was that each company received in addition a contract requiring the government to purchase all primary aluminum output from the new plants which could not be sold commercially. The purchases were to be at the published price, and this provision applied for the first five years of the operation of the new capacity. Thus a primary producer was guaranteed a market until the new capacity would be nearly fully depreciated. The government also had the option to buy any or all of the output from the new facilities at the primary producer's list price.[9]

With the second round, it was apparent that neither Apex Smelting nor Harvey Machine Company would construct the capacity originally assigned to them. The new program called for the following allotments of capacity.[10] (These figures include capacity of the first expansion plan.)

	Capacity (thousands of tons)
Alcoa	205
Reynolds	180
Kaiser	228
Harvey (later Anaconda)	50
Total	663

[8] In addition to the expansion of capacity, high-cost plants in Badin, N.C., and Massena, N.Y., were reactivated with the government paying all power costs in excess of 5 mills. Department of Commerce, Business and Defense Services Administration, *Materials Survey: Aluminum,* November, 1956, p. VII–13. Henceforth cited as *Materials Survey: Aluminum.*

[9] *Materials Survey: Aluminum,* p. VII–14. The complete text of these contracts is reprinted in *Small Business Hearings, 1955,* pp. 68off.

[10] *Materials Survey: Aluminum,* p. VI–14.

The third round of expansion was announced in October 1952 and called for the following additional allocations of capacity.[11]

	Capacity (thousands of tons)
Harvey	54
Olin Industries	110
Wheeland Company	50
Total	214

None of this latter capacity was under construction when the expansion program was closed in September 1955. Harvey and Olin continued to hold the certificates of accelerated amortization.

For the model of investment behavior expounded earlier in this chapter, the implications of this historical period are perhaps obvious. The post-Korean period involved a 91-percent increase in reduction capacity to serve defense demand. This expansion could not be financed from internal funds, and this high-risk situation required some special device to minimize risk. However, the primary producers insisted on and were able to obtain a risk protection unique in American industrial history, a guaranteed government market for almost one-half of the industry's output for a five-year period.

The Financial Effects of the Government Contracts

In addition there was the financial assistance from accelerated amortization. This allowed the overstatement of depreciation and so reduced corporate income taxes for the first few years of an investment, thus providing a substantial flow of funds to the corporation during these early years. Once the property was fully depreciated, there was no further depreciation expense and income taxes increased. The effect was to postpone the payment of corporate income taxes, and thus to provide interest-free financing.

The funds provided by accelerated amortization were sufficient to permit internal financing of over one-half of the post-Korean expansion. (See Table 20.) This result was exactly that intended by accelerated amortization. It is, however, a striking demonstration of the impact of accelerated depreciation that aluminum, one of the most capital-intensive industries, could finance internally one-half of such a substantial expansion.

The external financing was largely through borrowing. Such a reliance on debt throughout a large expansion program demon-

[11] *Ibid.*

TABLE 18. Capital structures of major aluminum companies

	Alcoa		Reynolds		Kaiser[a]	
	millions of dollars	per-cent	millions of dollars	per-cent	millions of dollars	per-cent
December 31, 1950						
Funded debt	146.3	30.0	99.6	60.1	56.3	51.6
Preferred stock	66.0	13.5	4.4	2.7	0	—
Common stock and surplus	275.0	56.5	61.6	37.2	52.8	48.4
Total	487.3	100.0	165.6	100.0	109.1	100.0
December 31, 1954						
Funded debt	336.4	42.5	226.0	64.0	150.8	53.8
Preferred stock	66.0	8.4	0	—	7.9	2.8
Common stock and surplus	388.8	49.1	126.9	36.0	121.6	43.4
Total	791.2	100.0	352.9	100.0	280.3	100.0

[a] Years ended May 31, 1951 and May 31, 1955.

Source: Annual Reports, 1950–1954 inclusive, as computed in William L. Nichols, "The North American Aluminum Industry: Its Evolution and Present Status" (unpublished thesis, The Graduate School of Banking conducted by the American Bankers Association, Rutgers University, 1956), p. 70.

strates the high financial standing of the aluminum companies, but it may also indicate that the capital market has made allowance for security provided by government purchase contracts.

Yet there remained important differences in the financing of the three companies. Alcoa's interest costs were significantly lower than those of either Kaiser or Reynolds. As of September 30, 1955, the weighted average effective rate of interest to maturity for Alcoa's debt was 3.03 percent compared to 4.335 percent for Reynolds and 3.776 percent for Kaiser.[12] The other loan provisions such as the limitations on dividends were generally more restrictive for Kaiser and Reynolds than for Alcoa.[13] Hence, despite the same general

[12] United States v. Aluminum Company of America, 153 F. Supp. 132 at 152.

[13] For example, for Kaiser, the following provisions of a $115,000,000 loan were: (a) The company must maintain consolidated net current assets of $15,000,000 from Feb. 9, 1951 until Dec. 31, 1952; $20,000,000 for the following year; and $25,000,000 thereafter as long as any indebtedness under the bank loan agreement is outstanding. (b) The earned surplus of $27,732,798 which existed on the date of the loan was restricted as to the payment of cash dividends or redemption or other acquisition of the Corporation's capital stock. (c) No new bonds or additional borrowing can be contracted as long as the bonds and loan covered by the agreement are more than 66⅔ percent of the total debt of the corporation. This provision meant that Kaiser could not borrow again until $30,000,000 of its $115,000,000 was repaid. See *Annual Report of the Kaiser Aluminum and Chemical Corporation*, 1950–1951, Notes to the Financial Statement, and *Prospectus Issued by the First Boston Corporation and Dean Witter and Company*, January 9, 1952, p. 16.

security of government purchase agreements, the capital market distinguished between the companies.

The reasons for this distinction are fairly obvious. Reynolds and Kaiser initially started with a smaller equity buffer to protect the debt than Alcoa, and they continued to have a relatively high proportion of debt (see Table 18). Both Kaiser and Reynolds had a higher rate of expansion than Alcoa (see Table 19). As a result Alcoa was able to finance a greater share of its expansion internally. Reynolds financed all of its expansion through debt while Kaiser issued new common and preferred stock (see Table 20). This may explain why Reynolds paid a higher rate of interest than Kaiser.

TABLE 19. Expansion of aluminum capacity since 1950

	Alcoa	Reynolds	Kaiser
Primary capacity, 1950 (tons)	448,750[a]	225,000	170,000
Additions to capacity, 1951–1955 (tons)	205,000	189,500	238,200
Total capacity, end of 1955 (tons)	653,750	414,500	408,200
Percent increase, 1950–1955	46.0	84.2	140.1

[a]Includes 79,000 tons of standby capacity.

Sources: William L. Nichols, "The North American Aluminum Industry: Its Evolution and Present Status" (unpublished thesis, The Graduate School of Banking conducted by the American Banking Association, Rutgers University, 1956), p. 67.

TABLE 20. Capital expenditures and working capital, 1951–1954

	Alcoa		Reynolds		Kaiser[a]	
	millions of dollars	per-cent	millions of dollars	per-cent	millions of dollars	per-cent
Capital expenditures	465.0		219.6		241.7	
Increase in working capital	56.3		41.6		32.0	
Total	521.3		261.2		273.7	
Supplied from:						
Net increase in debt	190.0	36.4	126.4	48.4	94.5	34.5
Net increase in preferred stock	0.0		–4.4	–1.7	7.9	2.9
Sale of common stock	0.0		0.0		34.0	12.4
Depreciation and retained earnings	331.3	63.5	139.2	53.3	137.3	50.2
	521.3	100.0	261.2	100.0	273.7	100.0

[a] Fiscal periods May 31, 1951 to May 31, 1955.

Source: William L. Nichols, "The North American Aluminum Industry: Its Evolution and Present Status" (unpublished thesis, The Graduate School of Banking conducted by the American Bankers Association, Rutgers University, 1956), p. 70.

Financing, however, cannot be viewed apart from the rate of profits in the industry. It is the rate of return on investment relative to that prevailing elsewhere in the economy that largely determines the ability to raise funds externally. There are wide variations in the relative use of debt and equity financing so that the most meaningful measure of the rate of return on investment is the net income plus long-term interest as a percentage of the net worth plus the long-term debt.

Profits rates so computed are shown in Table 21. Industry aver-

TABLE 21. Return on investment for selected firms in various industries (measured as net income plus interest as a percent of capitalization, average 1950–1955)

Industry	Percent
Motor cars	22.7
Chemicals	19.8
Drugs	16.8
Aluminum	*14.8*
Petroleum, integrated	13.7
Cement	13.1
Steel	10.0
Baking	9.3
Tobacco	8.9
Distilling	7.1
Sugar refining	6.5
Meat packing	5.5

Source: For other than aluminum: CAB General Fare Investigation (Docket No. 8008), Bureau Counsel Exhibit BC 113.8 (Revised); for aluminum: Computations from data from Moody's Investors Service, *Moody's Industrials* (New York: By the Company).

ages are the unweighted average of the three or four largest firms in the industry so that the universe is composed of large well-established firms. Furthermore, these comparisons are based upon historical accounting data and so reflect the varying accounting practices inherent in such data.

Despite its limitations, the fact that the aluminum industry ranks fourth suggests that, in spite of the government aid and whatever market power may exist, the primary aluminum producers have realized approximately the same return as other large firms in primarily oligopolistic industries. Furthermore, because of the transfers of government plants at less than cost and the accelerated amortization of World War II, the investment base of the aluminum industry is understated and hence the profit rate is overstated. Only a relatively small part of these profits accrued immediately to the stockholders, for most of the earnings were retained (see Table 22.)

TABLE 22. Cash dividends as percent of net earnings

Year	Alcoa	Reynolds	Kaiser[a]
1954	27.1	13.8	23.2
1953	27.1	15.9	38.5
1952	32.7	10.6	42.9
1951	45.1	9.8	36.0
1950	22.1	11.8	25.7

[a]Fiscal year ended May 31 of following calendar year.
Source: William L. Nichols, "The North American Aluminum Industry: Its Evolution and Present Status" (unpublished thesis, The Graduate School of Banking conducted by the American Bankers Association, Rutgers University, 1956), p. 70.

In sum, this history demonstrates that government aid permitted the private financing of an extremely high rate of expansion. At the same time, the industry in this period was able to earn a rate of profits comparable to that of large firms in other primarily oligopolistic industries. Clearly the original objective — a doubling of capacity — was achieved, and perhaps equally obviously, some sort of government assistance was required.

The Record of Government Purchases

The history of purchases by the government under these contracts must be understood in terms of Limited's role in the post-Korean expansion program. In August 1950, Limited made an offer to the Munitions Board of 37,000 tons to be delivered in 1951, 72,000 in 1952, and 110,000 in 1953. The current American market price would be charged, but since sales to the government were duty free, Limited's net realization would be 2 cents per pound more than in its sales to private customers. The higher return was justified by Limited's management as necessary to meet the higher costs of purchased power required to provide the additional output.[14] The National Security Resources Board rejected the offer because it

[14] Mr. Davis, president of Limited, testified: ". . . in order to fulfill this contract, it was necessary for us to expand our facilities and reactivate old facilities and purchase power from outside sources. Purchased power in Canada costs us about 3 mills. We are spoiled, but we consider 3-mill power to be high-cost power. That alone would account for an increase in cost, in making that aluminum, of 2 cents per pound." *Monopoly Power Hearings, 1951*, p. 528.

provided relatively little metal in 1951 and 1952, and after that date, the Canadian supply would be competitive with the expansion of domestic production.[15]

In December 1950, another proposal of Limited was transmitted by Mr. C. P. Howe, Canadian minister of trade and commerce, to Mr. Sawyer, then secretary of commerce. Early in 1951, the National Production Authority reopened negotiations with Limited for aluminum for immediate delivery, but by this time most Canadian output was under contract to the United Kingdom and so unavailable for immediate delivery. Limited's final proposal in 1952 differed markedly in substance from the two earlier ones.[16] The plan called for Limited to guarantee the annual export of 100,000 tons to the United States from 1952 to 1958, in return for which the government would guarantee to purchase up to 450,000 tons at the current market price if no commercial buyers could be found. Essentially then, this was a government guarantee of a market rather than a direct purchase of metal. Such a purchase guarantee was comparable to that which the government provided to the domestic producers.

This proposal was under consideration in the National Production Authority throughout 1952, but considerable Congressional opposition developed. Various Congressmen preferred to help American firms, and furthermore, past American government purchases of aluminum from Limited left a Congressional suspicion of any dealings with the Canadian firm.[17] The Defense Production Administration favored the proposal primarily because the alternative was further expansion by Alcoa, Kaiser, and Reynolds.[18]

[15] Joint Committee on Defense Production, *Defense Production Act Progress Report No. 20, The Aluminum Program,* 82d Cong., 2d Sess., S.R. No. 1987, 1952, p. 2.

[16] *Ibid.,* pp. 3–4.

[17] In 1941, the United States government made a contract with Limited for the delivery of 6,820,000 tons of aluminum with $68,500,000 to be paid in advance and the balance on delivery. At that time, Limited did not actually have the facilities but rather constructed them in part from funds involved in the advance payment. This practice plus a price of 2 cents above the American market price was severely criticized by the Truman Investigating Committee. (Limited later reduced its price voluntarily). In fairness to Limited it should be pointed out that the net cost to the Government was undoubtedly lower than the domestic wartime plants, dismantled because of their high operating costs. (See *Monopoly Power Hearings, 1951,* pp. 454–457.)

[18] Testimony of Mr. Samuel W. Anderson, deputy administrator for Aluminum, Defense Production Administration. Joint Committee on Defense Production, *Defense Production Act Progress Report No. 19, Hearings on Canadian Aluminum Proposals,* 82d Cong., 2d Sess., 1952, pp. 982–985. Cited henceforth as *Defense Production Act Progress Report No. 19.*

The independent fabricators were increasingly concerned about a supply of ingot, and these purchases represented an increase in the supply of ingot that would be available to them. Congressional opposition, however, was apparently such that Limited's offer was not accepted.

During these months, Limited shifted its effort to obtaining long-term sales contracts directly from the primary producers. Limited first concluded a 600,000-ton contract with Alcoa with delivery from 1953 to 1958 at the current price for ingot. A contract was then signed with Kaiser for 181,000 tons with the same terms and delivery dates.[19]

These contracts were signed at a time when aluminum was still in short supply. But the important point here was that the long-term sales contracts were risk-free for the American buyers, because they held government purchase contracts. Hence, if demand were insufficient to absorb their current output plus the purchases from Limited, these firms could sell the output from their new plants to the government and continue their purchases from Limited without expense to themselves. Alcoa, for example, constructed 205,000 tons of capacity which were covered by the purchase contracts, so that any demand downturn of less than 205,000 tons could be met by selling the government that amount. The purchases from Limited increased the government's risk in that Alcoa was still guaranteed a market for 205,000 tons of sales, and with an additional 200,000 tons annually from Limited, the probability that Alcoa could not find a market for all its aluminum increased.[20]

The results of these arrangements were demonstrated in the first half of 1957 when the commercial demand for aluminum began to decline. During this period, Alcoa sold 175,500 tons to the government while it purchased 49,000 tons from Limited.[21] Similarly in the first half of 1957, Kaiser purchased 14,600 tons of aluminum from Limited and sold 63,750 tons to the government.[22]

---

[19] These contracts are described in Petition of the United States in United States v. Aluminum Company of America, *et al.*, reprinted in Joint Committee on *Defense Production, Defense Production Act Progress Report No. 41, Hearings*, 85th Cong., 1st Sess., 1957, pp. 21ff. Henceforth cited as *Defense Production Act Progress Report No. 41*.

[20] The contract between the government and Kaiser provides: "Contractor may first dispose of the production from such other facilities or utilize for its own purpose the production of such other facilities before disposing of or utilizing aluminum from the additional facilities." *Defense Production Act Progress Report No. 41*, p. 31.

[21] *Ibid.*, pp. 2, 14.

[22] *Ibid.*

Considerable Congressional criticism of this practice developed. Subsequently, the General Service Administration negotiated an amendment to the contract reducing the 1957 tender or sales rights of Alcoa and Kaiser by roughly the amount of primary aluminum they purchased from Limited.[23] For the future sales, rights to sell to the government were to be reduced by the total amount of

TABLE 23. Potential savings to the government under aluminum supply contract amendments (as compared in September 1957)

Reduction	Quantity (pounds)	Value (dollars)
Alcoa		43,950,000
in tender for production period ended Mar. 31, 1957	40,000,000	10,000,000
in tender rights for production period Apr. 1, 1957 to completion	132,000,000	33,750,000
under price protection provision	20,000,000	200,000
Kaiser		42,930,000
in tenders for production period ended Mar. 31, 1957	7,000,000	1,750,000
in tender rights for production periods Apr. 1, 1957 to completion	158,000,000	41,080,000
under price protection provision	10,000,000	100,000
Reynolds		11,280,000
in tender right for production period Apr. 1, 1957 to completion (estimated primary purchases)	500,000	130,000
in tender rights for production period Apr. 1, 1957 to completion (estimated pro-rata share military set-asides)	37,000,000	9,500,000
by reason of inventory freeze, Mar. 31, 1957	6,400,000	1,600,000
under price protection provision	5,000,000	50,000
Total potential savings		98,160,000

Source: Compiled by the General Service Administration. Reproduced in House Select Committee on Small Business, Subcommittee No. 3., *Hearings, Aluminum Industry*, 85th Cong., 1st and 2d Sess., 1958, p. 371.

primary ingot and pig purchased. (In addition, as noted earlier, the "reserved share" of independents was increased from 25 to 35 percent of the output from the new facilities. Prices of government purchases were to be based on the lower of either the price prevailing on the delivery date or that prevailing during the month prior to filing of a claim for tender rights. The savings to the govern-

[23] See the testimony of Franklin G. Floete, administrator, General Services Administration, in House Select Committee on Small Business, Subcommittee No. 3, *Hearings, Aluminum Industry*, 85th Cong., 1st and 2d Sess., 1958, p. 367–397. Henceforth cited as *Small Business Hearings, 1958*.

ment, as estimated by the General Service Administration, are shown in Table 23.) Notably, the primary producers received no offsetting concession in return, perhaps a concrete demonstration of the bargaining power given to the G.S.A. by the avowed Congressional disapproval of the contracts.

TABLE 24. Past and present purchases under the stockpiling program, by calendar years (short tons)

	Alcoa	Kaiser	Reynolds	Harvey	Total
Total Purchased as of Dec. 31, 1957	248,325	253,221	200,266	0	701,812
Purchases — Calls					
1953	5,971	0	10,631	0	16,602
1954	131,539[a]	94,976	90,837	0	317,352
1955	38,834	54,120	57,428	0	150,382
1956	3,983	3,978	1,371	0	9,332
Puts, 1957	67,998	100,147	39,999	0	208,144
Total remaining put rights (estimated)	134,500	111,147	240,882	270,000	757,110
1958	110,125	97,012	137,367	0	344,504
1959	24,375	14,716	103,515	54,000	196,606
1960	0	0	0	54,000	54,000
1961	0	0	0	54,000	54,000
1962	0	0	0	54,000	54,000
1963	0	0	0	54,000	54,000
Total calls, puts, and remaining puts	382,825	264,949	441,148	270,000	1,458,992

[a] An additional 7,397 short tons was purchased under the excess power cost program.

Source: House Select Committee on Small Business, Subcommittee No. 3. Hearings, Aluminum Industry, 85th Cong., 1st and 2d Sess., 1958, p. 364.

The total government program under these purchase provisions is shown in Table 24. Calls are purchases at the initiative of the government, largely to build up its strategic stockpile, whereas the puts are government purchases at the request of the producers. The right to request such purchases expires five years after the new facilities are in operation. Except for Harvey, these put rights expired in 1959.

The exact cost of this program is difficult to estimate, since the prices at which purchases were made were constantly changing. A rough order of magnitude would be somewhere around $300,000,-000. This is probably a small price for the government to pay for the doubling of capacity in what was then considered a strategic industry. In terms of national defense requirements as viewed in the 1960's aluminum may not be essential, but hindsight is not a fair basis for criticism. In any case this kind of expansion served the civilian economy, although as the extensive investment subsequent to this program suggests, such expansion might have been forthcoming without government aid. Yet, upon a pragmatic basis of achieving the expansion of the aluminum industry at a minimum cost, the program might be considered a success. (In the ancillary objectives of increasing the supply of ingot to the independents surely the expansion program was a very limited success, as the discussion in Chapter VII indicates.)

The original wording that allowed the primary producers to make almost riskless purchase agreements with Limited, however, seems to have been overly generous. These provisions may have postponed Limited's efforts to establish itself as a supplier to the independent fabricators. Yet, it can be argued that without the long-term sales contracts Limited might not have built the additional capacity that now serves the independent fabricators.

The Expansion of Capacity After 1954

The expansion of reduction capacity did not end with the closing of the government program. During 1955 and 1956, all three companies initiated further construction scheduled for completion in 1958 and 1959 (see Table 25). If completed, these projects will create a reduction capacity of 2,600,000 tons compared to 727,000

TABLE 25. Expansion of aluminum capacity
since the end of the government expansion program

	Ton	Current status, June 1958
Alcoa	187,500	
Warrick, Indiana	150,000	Construction suspended
Massena, New York	37,500	Completed
Reynolds	223,000	
Listerhill, Alabama	123,000	Completed
Massena, New York	100,000	Completion planned for summer 1959
Kaiser		
Ravenswood, West Virginia (originally planned as 220,000 tons)	145,000	Completed
Total	555,500	

tons in 1948. This nearly fourfold expansion in one decade is unique for a major and established industry. Some of this expansion has now been postponed, and Kaiser's Ravenswood plant, originally announced for 220,000 tons, is now planned for 145,000 tons. These changes were largely a result of the 1957–58 recession which severely reduced aluminum sales.

Apart from the recession, it may also be that aluminum capacity has been over-expanded relative to the demand of the next few years. This is not solely because of the government-sponsored program, for the construction of one-half million tons of capacity has been initiated since the closing of the program. Rather there are several factors that explain the high rate of investment since 1954. First, there was excess demand for aluminum products for a good part of 1955 and 1956 despite the doubling of output since 1954. Such a record of increasing demand may have led to a "growth industry" climate of opinion. At least the speeches of industry spokesmen reiterate "the unlimited growth potential" and "great growth potential" of aluminum. In such an atmosphere, the possibility of over-expansion is unlikely to be carefully considered.

This growth optimism was formalized in the use of trend lines to make projections of aluminum consumption that were mentioned in the speeches of officers of aluminum companies.[24] Assuming such forecasts were the basis of the investment decision, they were subject to four errors.

Trend-line forecasting, that is, extrapolating the past rate of growth, assumes a constancy in the rate of growth, whereas in fact the increase in aluminum consumption has been highly irregular. The postwar reduction in the price of aluminum relative to that of copper and steel, as shown in Fig. 8, prompted a marked increase in the use of aluminum. The substitution of one metal for another in response to these marked relative price changes would occur only gradually, given the inertia in the learning process for a new application. At some point the adjustment to these relative price changes would be complete, for as Fig. 8 indicates, relative metal prices have changed very little since 1949. This is not to say that

[24] See the public forecasts of aluminum demand and supply as made by Mr. Rhoades, vice president of Kaiser, "Producers Answer Extruders' Questions," *Modern Metals*, Vol. 11, No. 12 (January, 1956), p. 60; Donald Wilmot, vice president of Alcoa, *Ibid.*, p. 56; Mr. Bergman, "Diecasters Debate: Aluminum Shortages and Zinc Prices" *Modern Metals*, Vol. 11, No. 9 (October 1955), p. 90.

aluminum is a mature industry whose growth phase is finished. Continuous technological change has created new uses for aluminum, and the relative price of aluminum, particularly after allowance for the cost of manufacture, may continue to decline. Yet the sharp downward shift in relative price, combined with the high rate of

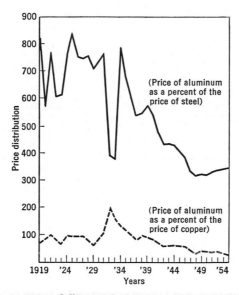

Fig. 8. Price differentials between aluminum, copper, and steel, 1919–1954. Relative price is stated in volume rather than weight because volume is a better approximation of the equivalent metals for the same function.

Source: James E. Rosensweig, *The Demand for Aluminum: A Case Study in Long Range Forecasting* (Urbana: Bureau of Economic and Business Research, College of Commerce and Business Administration, University of Illinois, Business Study no. 10, 1957).

expansion of the economy that characterized the postwar decade, is no longer present. As a result, the rate of growth in aluminum consumption of these years seems unlikely to continue.

Second, as of 1954, 16 percent of the aluminum output was estimated to be consumed in aircraft construction, of which a large percentage was military.[25] The transition to missiles, unforeseen in

[25] Estimate in *Modern Metals*, Vol. 10, No. 5 (June, 1954), p. 94.

1956, has reduced this market. Even though missiles use aluminum, the volume of aluminum required with a comparable defense effort is much less. This, then, is a source of demand that may have declined permanently.

Third, the decisions to expand may have been made upon the current government stockpiling program for aluminum. In 1951 the aluminum stockpile objective was set at two and one-half million tons, more than one year's current output.[26] By the end of 1956, the government had stockpiled only one-half million tons, so that there remained a substantial stockpile deficit.[27] According to the Office of Defense Mobilization policy memorandum, stockpile purchases were to be made "when the markets are soft and supplies are readily available."[28] Such a countercyclical timing of purchases together with the large absolute volumes involved seemed to insure any expansion against demand downturns.

By 1957, however, the government had abandoned its original stockpiling program. Further purchases were to be limited to those required by the put rights. The stockpile goal was reduced so markedly that the new minimum stockpile goal was already achieved. In 1958 an advisory committee considered lowering the stockpile objective to less than that already accumulated.[29] The shift in stockpiling policy reflected the view that in the next war economic capability would be a negligible factor, presumably because after a few days the main problem would be one of human survival.

Finally, by 1955 accelerated amortization was creating high rates of depreciation, and earnings were at record highs. The combined effect was to more than double the primary producers' volume of investible funds (see Table 26). This may have further precipitated expansion.

Thus the business setting of 1955 and 1956 was optimism about future demand and a substantial volume of investible funds. The catalyst was apparently an investment "race" between the primary producers. Shortly after the closing of the government expansion program, Kaiser announced the construction of a 220,000-ton plant

[26] *Defense Production Progress Report No. 19*, p. 948.
[27] *Small Business Hearings, 1958*, p. 364.
[28] *Defense Production Act Progress Report No. 19*, p. 948.
[29] See testimony of Gordon Gray, director, Office of Defense Mobilization, *Small Business Hearings, 1958*, pp. 339–382.

TABLE 26. Availability of internal funds for the primary
aluminum producers (millions of dollars)

	1950	1951	1952	1953	1954	1955	1956
Alcoa	66.4	62.1	77.6	107.1	102.6	132.7	140.4
Depreciation	19.5	22.8	34.1	58.2	40.7	45.1	50.8
Net income	46.9	39.3	43.5	48.9	61.9	87.6	89.6
Reynolds	19.3	23.4	25.3	32.4	37.3	52.4	60.6
Depreciation	6.7	7.6	10.6	14.1	17.0	18.1	19.4
Net income	12.6	15.8	14.7	18.3	20.3	34.3	41.2
Kaiser	20.5	18.1	21.8	28.8	46.1	62.9	60.2
Depreciation	4.7	5.3	9.6	14.8	17.5	19.6	17.9
Net income	15.8	12.8	11.8	14.0	28.6	43.3	42.3

Source: Oppenheimer and Co., *A Realistic Report on Aluminum* (New York: By
the Company, 1957).

TABLE 27. Distribution of domestic primary aluminum capacity, 1949, 1955,
and 1958 (includes capacity under construction).

	1949		1955		1958	
	Tons	Percent	Tons	Percent	Tons	Percent
Alcoa	369,750	51	706,500	44	1,000,000	38
Reynolds	224,950	31	414,500	26	701,000	27
Kaiser	132,375	18	408,200	26	609,500	24
Anaconda	0	0	60,000	4	60,000	2
Harvey	0	0	0	0	54,000	2
Ormet	0	0	0	0	180,000	7
Total	727,075	100	1,589,200	100	2,604,500	100

Source: 1949: U. S. v. Aluminum Company of America, 91 F. Supp. 333 at
366–368; 1955: United States v. Aluminum Company of America, 153 F. Supp.
132 at 140; 1958: Computed from data in [The United States Aluminum Producers]
World Trade and the Aluminum Industry (New York: [The United States Aluminum
Producers], 1958), pp. 42–43.

in the Ohio Valley.[30] Kaiser had consistently taken a disproportionate
share of the government expansion program so that its share of the
capacity existing and under construction increased from 18 percent
in 1949 to 26 percent in 1955 (see Table 27). At about that time
both Alcoa and Reynolds initiated several new plants so that by
1958 Kaiser's share had declined from 26 to 24 percent. The other

[30] W. B. Griffin, "Kaiser Aluminum: More Metal for More Products for More
People," *Modern Metals*, Vol. 11, No. 12 (January, 1956), p. 101.

producers then may have expanded in response to Kaiser's expansion, which is, after all, the behavior implied in an investment rivalry.

Such a high rate of expansion required a substantial volume of external financing in addition to the funds generated by accelerated depreciation (see Table 28). Kaiser, as the firm with the highest

TABLE 28. New issues of the three major primary producers, 1954–1958.

Issue date	Maturity date	Type	Amount (millions of dollars)	Interest rate (percent)
Alcoa				
June 1954	1979	Sinking fund debenture	87	3
Jan. 1957	1982	Sinking fund debenture	125	4⅛
April 1958	1983	Sinking fund debenture	125	3⅞
Kaiser				
Oct. 1956	1981	First mortgage bond	120	4¼
May 1956		Cumulative preferred	30	4⅛
June 1957	1987	First mortgage bond	50	5½
June 1957		Cumulative convertible preferred	30	4¾
Reynolds				
July 1955	1980	First sinking fund	155	4⅜
Feb. 1956		Cumulative preferred	38.8	4⅜
Dec. 1956	1981	First sinking fund	60	4¼

Source: Moody's Investors Service, *Moody's Industrial Manual 1958* (New York: By the Company, 1958).

rate of expansion, paid a slightly higher rate of interest than the others, but this seemed to have little effect on its investment behavior. Nor did the rationing of capital appear to restrain the rate of investment in these years.

The tendency for investment rivalry to create a closer margin between capacity and demand may explain the increasing use of long-term sales contracts. In this way, of course, some of the risks of excess capacity are shifted to the purchasers as explained in the preceding chapters. At the same time more capacity increased the eagerness of the primary producers to sell ingot to the independent fabricators. Even though the excess capacity may be in large part a temporary recession phenomenon, the existence of closer balance between demand and supply seems likely to alter substantially the future pattern of market behavior.

ENTRY INTO ALUMINUM REDUCTION

T<small>HE</small> entry of new firms into an industry is generally conceded to have major impact upon competition. In conventional economic analysis, entry occurs in response to the long-run rate of profit; the higher the rate of profit presumably the greater the likelihood of entry.[1] This entry-profit function has varying shapes. In some industries only a very high rate of profit will induce entry. This can be stated alternatively as a situation with high barriers to entry.

To say whether a barrier to entry is high or low in a specific industry requires measurement. Ideally, this should be the measurement of the response of potential entrants to various levels of profits. Since this information is unavailable, a feasible substitute is a comparison of the barriers to entry in any one industry with those prevailing elsewhere in the economy. If aluminum reduction is high in such a ranking, then the entry barriers can be said to be high enough to preclude entry except at very high profit levels.

Barriers to Entry into Aluminum Reduction

The specific sample for such a comparison is a study of twenty manufacturing industries by Professor Bain.[2] (These industries are listed in Table 29). Since manufacturing has higher barriers to entry than any other sector in the economy except mining, the sample represents the sector with generally substantial barriers to entry. Hence, if the aluminum industry ranks high in this group, its

---

[1] There is, of course, the complication of the time lag in the response of entrants to profit rates.

[2] For a complete description of this sample, see Joe S. Bain, *Barriers to New Competition* (Cambridge: Harvard University Press, 1956), p. 9.

barriers to entry are truly substantial. On the other hand, if the aluminum industry ranks low in comparison with this group, it does not indicate entry is easy in the sense of the theoretical model of pure competition, or as compared to such sectors as retailing or farming. It may, however, indicate that there is sufficient ease of entry to alter substantially market behavior.

Professor Bain evaluated the barrier to entry through an examination of the market and the technology of an industry. This approach is followed here. The sources of barriers to entry are classified by Professor Bain under four categories: scale economies, capital requirements, product differentiation, and an absolute cost barrier. The scale-economy barrier is a direct function of the proportion of the industry capacity required for a minimum-sized efficient plant. If a new entrant must have a high percentage of industry capacity to be an efficient competitor, entry with such capacity will create excess capacity in the industry and, in turn, either increase costs or generate a price war. In either case, profits are reduced and so entry is discouraged. Alternatively, the entry at less than optimum scale increases the entrant's costs and so reduces the profits of a new firm, again discouraging entry.[3]

Aluminum reduction is carried out in numerous discrete production units, and the difference between large and small plants is largely in the number of such units. There are certain economies of scale in material-handling facilities, but these are relatively minor. The new Anaconda plant in Montana is reported to be an extremely efficient plant, although it has only 3 percent of the industry's capacity.[4] In seven wartime plants of 20,000- to 120,000-tons capacity, the variation in the amount of investment required per unit of output was found to be principally a function of geography rather than of size.[5] Hence it can be concluded that 3 or so percent of the industry capacity suffices to realize fully the technological economies of scale of an individual plant.

Eleven of the twenty manufacturing industries in Bain's study have less than 2.5 percent of the national industry capacity in the

[3] This argument is fully developed in Bain, *Barriers to New Competition*, pp. 53–56.

[4] House Select Committee on Small Business, Subcommittee No. 3, *Hearings, Aluminum Industry*, 84th Cong., 1st Sess., 1955, p. 18.

[5] Pierre Crosson, Gregory C. Zec, and Francis J. Kelley, "Capital Coefficients in the Aluminum Industry," Department of the Interior, Bureau of Mines, Office of Chief Economist, Inter-Industry Analysis Branch Item No. 43 (mimeographed material), 1953.

most efficient size plant.[6] Furthermore aluminum has a national market, whereas transportation cost creates regional markets for many of these industries. This evidence, then, suggests that aluminum reduction ranks low in this barrier to entry compared to the sample of manufacturing industries.

This conclusion no longer holds if entry is possible only as a firm integrated into alumina production, bauxite mining, and electric power generation and fabrication. Alumina plants do involve substantial economies of scale. As of 1956, there were but six alumina plants in existence, with three more under construction. The six then in existence had from 24.4 to 9 percent of the industry's capacity.[7] The largest size plant is not necessary for the lowest costs, since the largest plant is laid out with three separate operating units sharing only material-handling facilities.[8] Still, the smallest has nearly 10 percent of the capacity of the industry and this appears to be a rough approximation of the minimum size necessary for efficiency. The shift from 2 percent to 10 percent changes the relative ranking of aluminum, for only four of the twenty industries required such a large proportion of capacity.[9]

Economies of scale appear even greater at stages further back in the productive process. Bauxite is largely produced by open-strip mining, in which a relatively small operation can realize the economies of scale in the process itself. However, since most available bauxite deposits are now in underdeveloped countries, the opening up of such deposits requires the construction of port facilities and railroads. Such expenditures are feasible only for large-scale projects.

Even greater economies of scale exist for hydropower generation. A complete hydropower system such as Bonneville, the TVA, or the Canadian Kitimat development could serve one-third or one-fourth of the present domestic aluminum reduction capacity, and the full efficiency of hydropower production requires the construction of several dams to be operated as a system. In the United States such projects have been constructed by the government, so that a hydro-

---

[6] Bain, *Barriers to New Competition*, pp. 76–77.

[7] Department of Commerce, Business and Defense Services Administration, *Materials Survey: Aluminum*, November, 1956, p. III–1. Henceforth cited as *Materials Survey: Aluminum*.

[8] *Record*, p. 1086, United States v. Aluminum Company of America, 91 F. Supp. 333 (S.D.N.Y., 1950), henceforth cited as *Remedy Record*.

[9] Bain, *Barriers to New Competition*, pp. 76–77.

power project serves several firms. If entry should require the construction of a hydropower system, barriers to entry are obviously greatly increased. In the last two or three years, however, power has been supplied largely by steam plants, and a single steam plant can supply efficiently a single reduction plant.

Economies of scale for the firm, as opposed to the single plant, are much more nebulous for their source is organizational rather than technological. Administrative economies of scale involve the question of whether large firms are more efficient decision-making organizations than small firms, a subject about which much has been said and little concluded. The research and marketing advantages of the large firm in the aluminum industry are discussed elsewhere, and in each the economies of the very large firm are not overwhelming. Finally, the analysis of vertical integration of Chapter VII shows that the vertical integration may minimize uncertainty.

Despite the lack of evidence, it is concluded that the multiplant or multifirm economies of scale are not substantial. According to Professor Bain, the economies of a multiplant firm are either nonexistent (this is the case for six industries) or relatively small (the case for six industries). The most substantial multiplant economies are in industries like steel, cement, and gypsum where a multiplant firm can minimize the high freight costs through the existence of several points of shipment.[10] Freight costs are insignificant in aluminum as compared to these industries.

In sum, then, the size of the barriers to entry attributable to economies of scale depend upon whether new entrants must be as vertically integrated as the existing three primary producers. If such vertical integration is required, then the aluminum industry ranks near the top quarter in Bain's sample on the economies of scale barrier. Without vertical integration, aluminum ranks in the lower half.

Economies of scale also create another type of entry barrier, the necessity of raising large amounts of capital to construct an efficient-sized plant. This is separate and distinct from the percentage effect described above, since it is a function of capital intensity of the technology and is independent of the size of the market. High capital requirements create a barrier to entry simply because the number of individuals and institutions with fifty, one hundred, or more mil-

[10] *Ibid.*, pp. 86-89.

lion dollars to invest in a new enterprise are few, and the holders of large blocs of capital may prefer to minimize their risks by distributing investment among several industries.

Capital requirements in the aluminum industry again depend upon the necessity of vertical integration. A fully integrated aluminum firm complete with bauxite deposits, alumina, and reduction and fabricating plants of an optimum size was estimated to cost at least $400,000,000 in 1949, which would be $600,000,000 to $800,000,000 in 1958 prices.[11] In contrast, an efficient-sized reduction plant would cost about $63,000,000.[12] If aluminum reduction alone is considered, then aluminum is placed in the middle group of Bain's sample. If, on the other hand, entry requires a full range of vertically integrated facilities, then aluminum has capital requirements comparable to steel and automobiles, the two industries with the highest capital requirements in Bain's sample.[13]

A high degree of product differentiation is a barrier to entry because the new entrant must spend large sums to gain consumer acceptance for his product. This factor does not create a significant barrier to entry in the aluminum industry. To be sure, there is some product differentiation in aluminum ingot through service, reliability, and so forth, but the typical independent fabricator buys from several sources of supply and in the shortages of the past few years, purchases were made from any available source. Product differentiation is greater in fabricated products, but still well below that in such products as cigarettes, for which Bain ranked this barrier as substantial.

The final barrier to entry is an absolute cost advantage held by the existing producers. If a new firm must operate at a cost disadvantage, entry will obviously be discouraged. One source of such a cost advantage in the aluminum industry is the difference between old and new capacity, arising in part from the inflation of construction costs and in part from the availability of cheap hydropower for the older capacity. A further factor is that Reynolds and Kaiser obtained considerable capacity from the government on the bargain terms as described in Chapter II, while accelerated amorti-

[11] Industry source.
[12] Apex, a potential entrant, planned a 125,000-ton alumina plant and a 54,000-ton reduction plant at an estimated cost of $85,000,000. (United States v. Aluminum Company of America, 153 F. Supp. 132 at 144.) The approximate cost of the Anaconda plant is $63,000,000, and it is considered an efficient size.
[13] Bain, Barriers to New Competition, pp. 158–159.

zation of World War II enabled Alcoa to depreciate fully much of its capacity. Similarly, the recent expansion was aided by accelerated amortization, which creates another cost differential between old and new firms.

There are no data for estimating the absolute cost advantage of established firms although a relative comparison indicates their significance. Bain divides his twenty industries into two categories of absolute cost advantage: sixteen for which it is "slight," and four for which it is substantial.[14] Alminum appears to fall between these two groups. "Slight" is hardly the correct adjective for a recurring factor in the history of recent attempts to enter aluminum reduction. On the other hand, absolute cost barriers are not so substantial as almost to preclude entry, which is the case for Bain's four industries classified as having substantial barriers to entry. The process is unpatented and sufficient know-how is publicly available, unlike Bain's example of gypsum. There are no scarce essential resources completely controlled by existing firms, unlike Bain's example of copper, although some sources of bauxite might require a considerable capital investment in transportation.

Professor Bain assigns ordinal rankings to each of these factors as follows: III for very important, II for medium, and I for low. (In case of absolute capital requirements, there are four ratings with ϕ to designate the smallest.) A similar classification of the aluminum industry as shown in Table 29 is based upon two alternative assumptions; that vertical integration is or is not required for entry. In each case aluminum is assigned a roman numeral upon the basis of its correspondence to the industries already so classified by Bain. Bain's judgment of the over-all extent of the barriers to entry is not based upon a simple addition of the numerical values of each factor. Rather, it reflects an intuitive weighing of the total pattern of barrier to entry in the industry.[15] The same kind of judgment was used to rank aluminum in this sample, although considerable weight was attached to the correspondence of the pattern of Roman numerals for aluminum with those industries classified by Bain.

In this comparison, aluminum ranks as an industry with high barriers to entry. Any other result in an industry without a single entrant until 1940 would be surprising. The important point is the

[14] *Ibid.*, pp. 147–156.
[15] *Ibid.*, pp. 167–172.

TABLE 29. Ranking of aluminum reduction with twenty manufacturing industries according to the estimated height of the aggregate barrier to entry and a summary of the relative heights of specific barriers (higher numbers denote higher entry barriers; within each group the listing is alphabetical)

	Scale economy barrier	Product dif- ferentiation barrier[a]	Absolute cost barrier	Capital requirement barrier
A. Industries with very high barriers to entry				
Automobiles	III	III	I	III
Aluminum Reduction with Vertical Integration	III	I	II	III
Alumina and Bauxite Mining	III	I	II	II
Cigarettes	I	III	I	III
Fountain pens (quality grade)	—	III	I	I
Liquor	I	III	I	II
Tractors	III	III	I	III
Typewriters	III	III	I	—
B. Industries with substantial entry barriers				
Aluminum Reduction without Vertical Integration	II	I	II	II
Copper	—	I	III	—
Farm Machinery	II	I–III	I	—
Petroleum Refining	II	II	I	III
Shoes (high priced men's)	II	I–II	I	φ
Soap	II	II	I	II
Steel	II	I	III	III
C. Industries with moderate to low barriers to entry				
Canned Fruits and Vegetables[b]	I	I–II	I	I
Cement	II	I	I	II
Farm Machinery (small sample)	II	I–III	I	—
Flour[b]	I	I–II	I	φ
Fountain pens (low priced)	—	I–III	I	I
Gypsum Products[c, d]	—	I	III	I
Meat Packing[b]	I	I	I	φ or I
Metal Containers[c, d]	—	II	I	I
Rayon	II	I	I	II
Shoes (women's and low- priced men's)	II	I–II	I	φ
Tires and tubes	I	II	I	II

[a] Alternative ratings refer generally to different product lines within an industry.
[b] The barriers to entry for meat packing generally, and for major segments of the flour and canned-goods industries, lie at the "low" extreme.
[c] Refers to period subsequent to 1950. Classification under Group B is indicated for earlier periods.
[d] Product-differentiation rating refers to the period subsequent to 1950. A rating of III is probably indicated for earlier periods.
Source: Joe S. Bain, *Barriers to New Competition* (Cambridge: Harvard University Press, 1956), pp. 169–170.

significance of vertical integration in determining the conditions of entry. With vertical integration, aluminum reduction shifts its classification of the barriers to entry from "substantial" to "very high."

The History of Entry into Aluminum Reduction

From 1940 to 1946, there were, of course, two new producers of primary aluminum and from 1950 to 1955 there were three additional new producers. This record of entry does not contradict the existence of the substantial barriers to entry, for in all cases there was considerable government assistance. Chapter II describes the assistance extended to Kaiser and Reynolds.

The entry of the Harvey Aluminum Company best demonstrates the importance of government aid during the post-Korean years. This firm was a successful producer of metal aluminum parts in Los Angeles. Yet, compared to Alcoa, Reynolds, and Kaiser, it was a relatively small firm. At the close of the war, the Harvey Company bought a Defense Plant Corporation extrusion plant and initiated inquiries regarding the purchase of the government-owned aluminum-reduction plant at Riverside, California. The high power costs made this plant commercially uneconomical and the plant was eventually dismantled.[16] Harvey continued to maintain an engineering group specializing in aluminum reduction.[17]

In the second round of expansion, Harvey was allocated 50,000 tons, receiving the 85-percent accelerated amortization and the five-year government purchase contract granted to the other producers.[18] In addition Harvey received a long-term power contract from the Bonneville Power Authority for power from the new Hungry Horse Dam in Montana, an asset of considerable value because of the general unavailability of cheap hydropower.[19] At the same time, Harvey signed a contract with Reynolds Metals for a supply of alumina.[20] Since Harvey already possessed fabricating facilities, these two contracts would allow Harvey to bypass the barriers to entry created by vertical integration.

The project foundered on the inability of Harvey to raise the

[16] See Mr. Harvey's testimony in *Remedy Record*, pp. 239–244.

[17] House Select Committee on Small Business, Subcommittee No. 3, *Hearings, Aluminum Industry*, 85th Cong., 1st and 2d Sess., 1958, p. 277. Henceforth cited as *Small Business Hearings, 1958*.

[18] *Materials Survey: Aluminum*, p. VII–14.

[19] *Ibid.*, p. III–4.

[20] *Ibid.*

$50,000,000 or more required. In 1953 Harvey sold 95 percent of its stock in its newly-created aluminum subsidiary, Harvey Machine Company of Montana, to Anaconda.[21] This company held the power and alumina contracts for aluminum production, while the certificate of original accelerated amortization was reissued to the Montana company.[22] The name of the company was changed to the Anaconda Aluminum Company shortly thereafter, and in April 1957, Anaconda bought the remaining 5 percent interest of Harvey.[23]

This outcome did not deter Harvey's receiving another supply contract and certificate of accelerated amortization in the third round of expansion in 1953. This was for a 54,000-ton reduction plant in Oregon.[24] Harvey also obtained a second power contract, this time from the Bonneville Power Authority.[25] The following year Congress deleted the monies for the construction of transmission lines to the Harvey plant from the appropriation of the Bonneville Power Authority, and so precluded the Authority from fulfilling its contractual commitment to deliver power. Thereupon Harvey sued the Authority for $70,000,000 damages for breach of contract. In an out-of-court settlement, Harvey constructed its own transmission lines and in return became eligible for a special on-site power rate.[26] Furthermore, the General Services Administration agreed to make advance payments to Harvey for its sales to the stockpile, and these payments together with a $44,000,000 bank loan solved the company's financing problem.[27]

Harvey then negotiated a five-year contract with two Japanese companies for the processing into alumina of bauxite that Harvey planned to buy in Malaya.[28] Prior to that agreement, Kaiser, Reynolds, Limited, and Alcoa refused to sell Harvey alumina on the grounds that their own needs required the full utilization of

[21] *Small Business Hearings, 1958*, p. 243. Harvey retained the right to purchase up to 25 percent of the output.

[22] The certificate of accelerated amortization was not "sold" in this transfer of assets; rather, the original certificate was canceled at Harvey's request and then a new certificate was applied for and issued to the new Montana Company. *Ibid.*, p. 279.

[23] *Ibid.*, p. 237.

[24] *Modern Metals*, Vol. 9, No. 5 (June 1953), p. 90.

[25] *Modern Metals*, Vol. II, No. 8 (September, 1955), p. 101.

[26] *Ibid.* Also United States v. Aluminum Company of America, 153 F. Supp. 132 at 142.

[27] *Modern Metals*, Vol. 11, No. 9 (October, 1955), p. 110.

[28] *Small Business Hearings, 1958*, p. 294.

their alumina capacity.[29] Harvey considered the production of alumina, but at that time the company regarded constructing an alumina plant as requiring excessively large capital expenditures for an initial entry into primary aluminum production.[30] As a longer-run solution to its alumina supply, Harvey bought an abandoned government experimental alumina plant for research on the problem of obtaining alumina from clays of the Columbia River basin.[31] As of 1958, Harvey's reduction plant was not yet in operation. It will, of course, begin production at a time when there is an over-supply of aluminum, but the government purchase contracts assure a market for all its output for the first five years.

Anaconda's assumption of Harvey's original place in the expansion program provided a valuable power contract, as well as a source of alumina. Anaconda also received accelerated amortization, but it declined a government purchase contract. The loss of the government guarantee, however, meant there was no requirement to sell to the independent fabricators or to the government stockpile. Financing the $63,000,000 plant was apparently no problem for a large, established company with a net worth of $701,000,-000.[32]

The Anaconda plant began production in August 1955.[33] The rate of production was at full capacity until the summer of 1957, when output was reduced to 75 percent of capacity. In January 1958, output was increased to 88 percent of capacity.[34] Considering that Anaconda had no government purchase contracts, this cutback in production was relatively modest for the 1957–58 recession. Two-thirds of sales were made to outside customers and the remainder was consumed by other Anaconda subsidiaries.[35] The company, already a major fabricator, has built considerable new fabricating facilities for wire and cable, sheet, and rod and bar, and it has purchased a foil company.[36] Some of these new facilities were not in operation in 1957 and 1958, which may explain in part the high proportion of ingot sold to outside customers.

[29] Ibid.
[30] Ibid., p. 295.
[31] Modern Metals, Vol. 9, No. 4 (May 1953), p. 88.
[32] Materials Survey: Aluminum, p. VII–14, and United States v. Aluminum Company of America, 153 F. Supp. 132 at 139.
[33] Materials Survey: Aluminum, p. VII–14.
[34] Small Business Hearings, 1958, p. 238–239.
[35] Ibid.
[36] Ibid., p. 238.

Anaconda's major problem appears to be the supply of alumina. The mill costs of the new plant are currently estimated as 6 percent higher than the other producers' because of the purchase of alumina.[37] The original alumina contract with Reynolds made by Harvey expires in 1960.[38] After that date, Anaconda will obtain alumina from Kaiser under a twelve-year requirements contract. Anaconda's general counsel described the new contract as one with more favorable terms than the agreement with Reynolds.[39] As part of the over-all transaction, Anaconda advanced Kaiser $17,000,-000 for the expansion of its alumina facilities.[40] According to Anaconda's general counsel, ". . . the only way we could get alumina for our plant at the termination of the Reynolds agreement was to supply money to somebody in the alumina business to increase the planned capacity of their plant. . . ."[41]

The company is also carrying on research into the production of alumina from domestic clays. This is a large-scale research effort carried out in a million-dollar pilot plant at Anaconda, Montana.[42] Anaconda has no plans to construct its own alumina plant because the construction of an alumina plant to serve only a 60,000-ton reduction plant is considered uneconomical.[43]

The third successful entrant was Ormet, a joint venture of Olin Mathieson and Revere Copper and Brass.[44] Initially both Revere

---

[37] Letter of the General Counsel, which states, "It is our belief that in 1956 our mill costs are comparable with those of Kaiser with the possible exception that Columbia Falls total operating costs, before depreciation, interest, and other charges, are approximately 6 percent higher due to our purchase of alumina from outside sources." *Ibid.*, p. 441.

[38] *Ibid.*, p. 237.

[39] *Ibid.*

[40] *Ibid.*

[41] *Ibid.*, p. 249.

[42] *Ibid.*, p. 236.

[43] *Ibid.*, p. 248.

[44] In addition to the American entry, there have been "rumors" and apparently actual entry in Canada which may have some significance for the American market. The "confirmed" entry is that of British Aluminium Company Ltd. This is an old and sole producer of ingot in the United Kingdom whose expansion has been blocked by the shortage of hydropower. In 1955, this company began the construction of a 160,000-ton reduction plant in Quebec. The power is to be supplied by an expansion of the power plants owned by the Quebec North Shore Paper Company, a wholly owned subsidiary of the *Chicago Tribune*. In July 1956 the plans were for a formation of the Canadian British Aluminum Company, jointly owned by the *Tribune's* subsidiary and the British, which in turn will own an interest in the Manicouagan Power Company, the power subsidiary of the paper company. (*Modern Metals*, Vol. 11, No. 12 (January, 1956), p. 113; Vol. 12, No. 6 (July, 1956), p. 88).

Kaiser is rumored to have plans to construct a reduction plant in Seven Islands, and Olin planned to produce primary aluminum individually. Revere was a long-time aluminum fabricator, although its principal prewar business was copper fabrication.[45] According to its president, the shortages of ingot during the Korean War convinced the company that it would eventually have to own its own reduction facilities.[46]

On August 2, 1955, Revere filed an application for accelerated amortization certificates for a reduction plant of 60,000-ton capacity and for an alumina plant of 120,000-ton capacity.[47] On September 22, the Office of Defense Mobilization announced the closing of the expansion program for aluminum capacity.[48] Shortly thereafter, Revere's application was returned, with the explanation that existing commitments for new capacity would meet the current expansion objective. Revere protested this decision, arguing that without accelerated amortization it could not compete with the recipients of both purchase contracts and accelerated amortization. According to Revere, the filing of the application had been delayed until plans were sufficiently final to proceed with the project. This was in accord with government regulation, yet if the application had been filed earlier, the chairman of the board of Revere said, ". . . we would have been given favorable treatment regardless of the fact that we might not have proceeded for several years. We are now paying the penalty for having handled our application in strict accordance with our understanding of the Government's wishes." [49]

The Revere correspondence also stressed the position of Harvey. In September 1955, the same month Revere's application was rejected, Harvey was awarded a supply contract as well as advanced

Quebec, as well as one in Castlegar, British Columbia. Reynolds has bought Aluminum Rolling Mills, Limited, a Canadian independent fabricator which is considered as a possible springboard into aluminum reduction in Canada. (*Modern Metals*, Vol. 11, No. 8 (September, 1955), p. 16 and Vol. 12, No. 1 (February, 1956), p. 18).

[45] *Small Business Hearings, 1958*, p. 323.

[46] The president's complete statement is: "Beginning in the early 1950's and continuing through 1955, when aluminum was in extremely short supply, Revere was required to enter into a series of large, firm, long-term contracts with the aluminum producers in order to assure to Revere and its customers the essential supplies. These contracts have not involved any price concession to Revere. When we made the last contract, there appeared to be no possibility of our getting into primary production for several years. It became clear, however, that Revere would ultimately have to secure its own source of primary aluminum." *Ibid.*, p. 325.

[47] *Ibid.*, p. 453–454.

[48] *Ibid.*, p. 455.

[49] Letters to Arthur S. Fleming, director, Office of Defense Mobilization, December 15, 1955, and February 21, 1956. *Ibid.*, pp. 456–458, 460–461.

payments on government purchases, more aid than Revere requested. Furthermore, this company had been in the program for several years without beginning the construction of a plant. The Office of Defense Mobilization replied that defense requirements had been met and the legislation did not authorize the granting of certificates for nondefense purposes. As for Harvey, the contracts reflected in part earlier commitments and "the balance was in consideration for the settlement of an anticipatory breach of contract suit which the Harvey Company proposed to bring against the government." [50]

Shortly thereafter, Revere entered into a joint venture with Olin. (Olin, which managed one of the government plants during World War II, had been certified for 120,000 tons of primary capacity in 1952, but the construction was delayed by financing difficulties.) Ormet, a joint venture formed in the fall of 1955, was capitalized at $231,000,000. Of this sum, $200,000,000 was a loan from insurance companies, and the remainder was contributed equally by Revere and Olin.[51] Ormet was to construct a 180,000-ton reduction plant, 60,000 tons more than originally planned by Olin, and a 345,000-ton alumina smelter at Burnside, Louisiana, instead of the much smaller Ohio Valley alumina plant. Construction was scheduled for completion in 1958.[52]

Olin and Revere signed a 25-year agreement to take the ingot produced by Ormet at its full cost of manufacture and these companies will sell the metal in either ingot or fabricated form. Olin will have 64 percent and Revere 36 percent of the production.[53] This joint venture, then, adds one more producer but two more sellers of primary aluminum.

Ormet is only one aspect of Olin's entry into aluminum. The company constructed a rolling mill in Ohio and bought three ocean-going ore carriers. It is expanding its fabricating facilities in extrusions, wire and cable, and sheet and strip.[54] The total expenditure for these ventures plus Olin's contribution to Ormet totals $475,000,000.[55] This complex, however, will have but 3 or 4 percent of the total capacity of the industry.

[50] Letter from Arthur S. Fleming to J. M. Kennedy, February 15, 1956. *Ibid.*, pp. 461–462.
[51] *Ibid.*, p. 335.
[52] *Ibid.*, pp. 325–326.
[53] *Ibid.*, p. 335.
[54] *Ibid.*, p. 257.
[55] *Ibid.*, p. 261. This includes all expenditures on Ormet.

Included in this $475,000,000 is a venture that deserves special note. Olin owns a $109,000,000, 53-percent interest in Fria, Compagnie Internationale pour la Production de l'Alumine, which is constructing an alumina plant in French Guinea, West Africa for processing native bauxite. The other owners are two French, one Swiss, and one British primary producer. The alumina will be distributed to these companies in proportion to their ownership interest rather than sold in the open market.[56] In this connection, an Olin vice president stated, ". . . alumina does not sell on the open market in the same sense that aluminum does, or any other commodity does." [57]

The history of unsuccessful entrants is equally instructive for the problems of entry into the aluminum industry. Three firms made extended efforts to enter the aluminum industry. One, St. Joseph's Lead Company, was a large company ($69,000,000 in assets) and, like Anaconda and Revere, important in the copper industry as well as in lead. The company was not a fabricator nor did it intend to fabricate aluminum.[58] The large power plant that was to be constructed would serve both an aluminum reduction plant and a zinc smelter. These power facilities were to be constructed jointly with the Pittsburgh Consolidation Coal Company ($194,800,000 in assets), which later became part of the Ormet plan. St. Joseph canceled its plans because of the unavailability of accelerated amortization.[59]

Wheeland, a producer of oil-drilling equipment, and Apex Smelting Company, a secondary smelter, were certified in the third round of expansion. As very small companies (net worths of $3,000,000 and $4,000,000), these two had difficulties in raising capital. Apex proposed that the government provide sufficient financial assistance to keep Apex's over-all cost of capital to a 4 percent interest charge, and to purchase ingot at Apex's cost of production plus a fair profit, rather than at the market price. When these terms were rejected, Apex withdrew from the program. Wheeland also withdrew because of inability to obtain financing. Neither company had begun construction of reduction plants.[60]

[56] Ibid., p. 262.
[57] Ibid.
[58] House Select Committee on Small Business, Subcommittee No. 3 on Minerals and Raw Materials, Report, Small Business and the Aluminum Industry, 84th Cong., 2d Sess., H.R. 2954, 1956, p. 39.
[59] Ibid., p. 39.
[60] Based on material in United States v. Aluminum Company of America, 153 F. Supp. 132 at 144–145.

This history indicates certain generalizations about conditions of entry into the aluminum industry. Successful entry is restricted to large firms, a point implicit in previous discussion of the capital requirements. But recent history underlines that the term "large" is primarily restricted to the five hundred largest industrials. Not only is Olin the 59th largest industrial company and Revere the 217th in the *Fortune* list of the five hundred largest American industrial companies, but their entry as Ormet involved the cooperation of the Consolidation Coal Company (the 145th largest industrial company) as a supplier of steam-generated power. Anaconda is the 72nd largest industrial company. Thus the parent firms of the new aluminum producers are comparable in size to Kaiser (the 95th largest industrial) and Reynolds (the 87th largest) and only slightly smaller than Alcoa (the 46th).[61]

Harvey's entry does not refute the importance of large size as a condition for entry. Rather, this instance would seem to be a triumph of persistence over economic logic. Without discounting Harvey's pluck, the firm also received unique assistance in power contracts and advance government payments over and above the accelerated amortization and government purchase contracts. Furthermore, the entry was fraught with difficulty — it took over five years, and the first effort was finally transferred to Anaconda. The other two small firms, Wheeland and Apex, never successfully entered the industry.

All the entrants were established aluminum fabricators, so that a market for the product presented no problem. Rather an assured ingot supply, particularly in the case of Revere, created an added incentive for such firms. These two factors, size and an established position in light metals, create a group of what might be termed a likely entry category. But this category is necessarily small; size of the order involved here limits the group to the five hundred largest industrials, and of these, only a few are in light metals.

Even for these firms significant barriers to entry remain. Most obvious is the availability of alumina. Alumina is not freely purchasable, and at the same time the economies of scale are sufficiently sizable so that only the largest new entrant constructed an alumina plant. Government assistance, now no longer available, was clearly

[61] These rankings are based upon *Fortune's* Directory of the 500 largest U. S. Industrial Corporations in 1958. *Fortune*, Vol. 60, No. 1 (August 1959) pp. 125ff. The ranking is by reported sales. Obviously, this is only a rough ranking of relative size.

important in overcoming the barriers to entry. Once such assistance was no longer available, a competitive differential between those with government benefits and additional newcomers was created. From the correspondence of Revere, this was apparently a factor of considerable importance.

Finally, as noted in a preceding chapter, profits in aluminum reduction are lower than in fabricating, and over-all profits are comparable only to those of other oligopolistic industries. Four out of the five firms initially interested in the aluminum industry told the staff of the Joint Committee on Defense Production that "the probable profit did not warrant the heavy capital investment required." [62]

Given the combination of relatively low profit rates and very high barriers to entry, it is not surprising that only three firms have entered the industry despite the availability of government aid.

Entry and Market Behavior

The value of policy measures to facilitate entry depends upon the relation of entry to competition. Theories of competition assign two differing roles to entry in modifying market performance; the effects of potential entry (whether or not such entry occurs) and the effects of actual entry. The weight assigned to these roles differs among economists. Profesor Bain argues that the market behavior of a wide class of oligopolistic industries is largely determined by the efforts of existing firms to forestall potential entry, and more specifically that prices are set at some entry-forestalling level.[63] The more limited view of entry stresses its importance simply because actual entry rearranges the market structure in the direction of less concentration. Then and only then will market behavior be altered.

In the aluminum industry it appears that potential entry has had little discernible effect on market behavior. It may well be that the lower profit rate in the ingot stage can be explained in part by efforts to forestall entry. But the strongest empirical test of the effects of potential entry on market behavior in Bain's hypothesis that the prices are set at the point which produces a rate of profits that will not attract a considerable new entry. The higher the barriers to entry, the higher this profit rate would be. Aluminum,

---

[62] Joint Committee on Defense Production, Defense Production Act Progress Report, No. 24, *Aluminum Expansion Program and Competition*, 83d Cong., 1st Sess., 1953, p. 12.

[63] Bain, *Barriers to New Competition*, chap. I.

as an industry with substantial barriers to entry, should have a high profit rate. A comparison of Tables 21 and 29 shows aluminum does have comparable rates of profits with industries having substantial and very high barriers to entry. Yet within this group there is a significant variation in profit rates, and to the extent the industry classifications in the two tables are comparable, the differences between substantial and very high barriers to entry are not positively correlated with the differences in profit rates. This suggests that, once the barriers to entry are substantial, other factors, such as interindustry competition, oligopolistic rivalry, the effects of the small business fringe, and foreign competition, are more decisive than potential entry in determining the level of prices and the rates of profit. This seems the case in the aluminum industry.

It is to early to determine the effects of actual entry of three new firms on market behavior. The investment rivalry described in Chapter IX coincided with the new entry, but new entry was only one of several factors that may have precipitated the expansion of capacity. The general value of more firms in an oligopolistic industry is that adding more centers of decision-making leads to a wider spectrum of views on the proper pricing, the pace of investment, and the nature and extent of sales efforts. Since the firm with the lowest price, the most successful sales efforts, and the highest rate of investment dominates in setting of the market variables, increasing the spectrum of possible policies increases the likelihood of a lower price, a greater marketing effort, and a higher rate of investment.

Still, adding three new relatively small firms with 10 to 12 percent of capacity is likely to have less effect on market behavior than the extent of the tariff on imports, the activities of the independents, and so forth. Since entry, like everything else, has its price, public policy in these other areas may deserve higher priority than extensive direct government intervention to encourage further entry. This may be particularly so when such measures can no longer be an ancillary objective of a mobilization program as they were until 1955.

XI

INVENTIONS IN THE
ALUMINUM INDUSTRY[1]

ONE of the critical questions in industrial organization is the
effect of market structure upon the rate of invention. In approaching this problem for the aluminum industry it is useful to divide
inventions into two categories. The first is new alloys, new processes
in manufacturing products from aluminum, and new techniques for
fabricating aluminum ingot that permit new commercial uses of
aluminum. The second is new techniques that have reduced the
cost of aluminum ingot.[2]

This distinction is based upon the roster of potential inventors.
For the first group of inventions, the firms that could profit from
and have the technical knowledge for inventions include independent fabricators, manufacturers of end-products made from aluminum, and makers of fabricating and manufacturing equipment, as
well as producers of aluminum ingot. These different types of
firms realize the profits from invention in varying ways, so that
comparing the nature of the profits of invention for each class
of firms with the actual record of invention tests the effects of various
incentives and opportunities for invention. For the second group of
inventions, the primary aluminum producers are the sole likely
source of invention, for these firms alone have access to the

---

[1] A substantial part of the material in this chapter was presented as a paper
to the Conference on the Economic and Social Factors Determining the Rate and
Direction of Inventive Activities (sponsored by the National Bureau of Economic
Research at the University of Minnesota, May 12–14, 1960). A volume of papers
from this conference is scheduled for publication by the National Bureau of Economic Research.

[2] Cost-reducing inventions, through their effects upon price, obviously increase
demand just as the so-called demand-increasing inventions may reduce the cost of
fabricating.

technology and can profit directly from introducing inventions into their own operations.

The postwar changes in market structure have altered the relative positions of these various groups. To determine what difference these changes have made requires an examination of the importance of each group as a source of invention. This examination covers the years 1946 to 1957.[3]

The Sources of the Data

Invention is defined here as the introduction of a new product or production technique. It suffices if an invention is described as an advance in the state of the art in either the trade paper of the industry, *Modern Metals*, or another trade publication.[4] This is not only a low standard of novelty but it may be influenced by the public relations and advertising efforts of the inventor as well as the editorial judgment concerning reader interest. These sources do impose a minimum level of prospective economic significance, as viewed by trade press editors.

The inventions so recorded will vary widely in terms of their novelty and economic significance. An attempt has been made to distinguish between major and minor inventions according to their discussion in the trade press. Evaluating inventions, however, is a difficult problem even for those with more technical qualifications and with more reliable sources than the author's. All that is reported here is an interpretation of the contemporary trade press discussion rather than the ex post facto analysis of the economic significance of various inventions.

Even though *Modern Metals* and other trade publications have an impressive record of accuracy and coverage, the preceding discussion indicates the limitations of these sources. The records and calculations of the firms involved were unavailable, which further restricts the reliability of this study and makes the discussion unduly speculative. Therefore the conclusions should be regarded as tentative, though perhaps no more so than with other histories of invention.

[3] For the early history of inventions in the aluminum industry, see Donald Wallace, *Market Control in the Aluminum Industry* (Cambridge: Harvard University Press, 1937), Appendix A.

[4] *Modern Metals* (Chicago, Modern Metals Publishing Company). Another standard source is the U. S. Department of Interior, Bureau of Mines, *Minerals Yearbook* (Washington).

Hypotheses about the Origin of Inventions in Manufacturing Techniques for Aluminum

The increased consumption of aluminum is in part dependent upon advances in the manufacturing techniques for aluminum as well as inventions in the aluminum industry narrowly defined. This is particularly so because aluminum is less workable by some of the common production methods than steel or copper. Although these inventions might be considered outside the boundaries of the aluminum industry, the primary aluminum producers obviously profit from advances in the state of the manufacturing art that expand significantly their one and one-half billion dollar market for aluminum.[5]

Indeed, this situation is highly conducive to invention beyond the narrow bounds of an industry. The primary producers manufacture end-products, so they are not lacking in direct experience with the technical problems involved. Their sales engineers are in continuing contact with the end-product manufacturers so that the primary producers can facilitate the adoption of inventions in manufacturing processes. Kaiser, Reynolds, and Alcoa are among the one hundred largest American manufacturing companies in *Fortune*'s list,[6] and each has the extensive research organization that typifies the large corporation.[7] Primary aluminum reduction is one of the most concentrated of American industries. Hence, if as is sometimes argued, size and fewness are conducive to invention, the primary producers should be the major contributors to the technical progress of their customers.

In contrast, the manufacturing processes for aluminum are only one of many technical problems confronting the end-product manufacturer. An end-product manufacturer would profit directly only from the incorporation of the invention in his own aluminum-manufacturing process. Such profits would be relatively modest compared to the gains accruing to the primary producers from an

---

[5] For a description of the range of end products involved, see *Record*, United States v. Aluminum Company of America, 91 F. Supp. 333 (S.D.N.Y., 1950) p. 1091, henceforth cited as *Remedy Record*. Nevertheless, only about 10 percent to 15 percent of aluminum ingot output is used by the primary producers for their own end products.

[6] "The Fortune Directory," *Fortune*, Vol. 58, No. 1 (July, 1958), p. 131–150.

[7] The research organizations have been described in various articles in the trade press and they generally appear to have about the character typical of a large heavy manufacturer.

invention resulting in even a small increase in the consumption of aluminum. Yet the end-product manufacturers, numbering some 24,000,[8] have the law of large numbers in their favor. Given the accidental character of invention, this factor might offset the differences in expected profits and make the end-product manufacturers a major source of inventions.

Aircraft manufacturers are a special category among the end-product manufacturers. Aluminum manufacturing techniques represent an important technical problem for such firms. Furthermore, these firms have large engineering staffs and can charge a share of their research expenses to defense contracts.

Inventions in manufacturing techniques are often incorporated in new machinery so that the makers of equipment for aluminum manufacturing constitute a third source of inventions. An equipment maker profits from these inventions, both from a larger share of the equipment market and from an expansion of the total sales of equipment that accompanies the acceleration in the rate of obsolescence of existing machinery and the increased use of aluminum. Compared to the end-product manufacturers who can utilize new manufacturing technique directly only in their own operation, the equipment makers can capitalize upon the adoption of an invention by end-product manufacturers generally. This is offset by the smaller size of equipment makers relative to such end-product manufacturers as the aircraft companies and by their fewer numbers (several hundred equipment firms compared to 24,000 end-product manufacturers).

The comparison of the expected profits from invention for the equipment makers and for the primary producers is even more difficult and nebulous. In general, the total profits from the sum of advances in manufacturing techniques are much greater for the primary producers than the equipment makers simply because the sales of aluminum are so much greater than the sales of equipment. Yet the profits of invention for the equipment makers are more certain, immediate, and greater in proportion to the size of the firm. The equipment makers' profits are more certain since some inventions displace existing machinery rather than facilitate new applications for aluminum. The effects of invention cannot be fore-

[8] House Select Committee on Small Business, Subcommittee No. 3 on Minerals and Raw Materials, *Small Business and the Aluminum Industry*, 84th Cong., 2d Sess., H.R. 2954, 1956, p. 7. Henceforth cited as *Small Business Report, 1956.*

seen with sufficient accuracy for the primary producers to discriminate according to the results of inventions, whereas the equipment maker benefits in either case. The equipment makers' profits are more immediate because the sale of new machinery takes place over a relatively short time, whereas the increase in aluminum consumption from a new use made possible by the machinery occurs over a long time span. Finally, a single invention may change markedly an equipment maker's market share and so create a large percentage change in the firm's profits. Since aluminum has a wide variety of uses, any one invention is unlikely to increase markedly the profits of the primary producers.

In addition, the equipment makers are under more competitive pressures to invent. Relative technical merits are an important element in the sale of equipment so that a firm that does not invent may suffer a loss of market share. Since a loss of market share is said to be a greater stimulus to business effort than an equivalent gain, the existence of these competitive pressures would further favor the equipment makers as a source of inventions. In contrast, an increase in the demand for aluminum from an improvement in manufacturing techniques might be distributed among all the primary producers.

Up to this point only the profits directly realizable from the inventing firm's own operation have been considered. Clearly an end-product manufacturer could sell patent rights for a new machine to an equipment manufacturer and such transferability makes the economic position of the inventor less decisive. It is assumed here, however, that the market for inventions is sufficiently imperfect that the sale of inventions does not alter substantially the relative profitability of invention for these three groups. This assumption is further strengthened by the nonpatentability of a minority of these inventions.

These views on the marketability of inventions imply that individual inventors and commercial research organizations will be a relatively minor source of inventions since their profits from inventions are realized solely through the sale of patent rights. Universities, government laboratories, and foreign sources are considered as sources of invention outside the scope of market incentives and pressures.

Two other types of firms, the secondary smelters and the independent fabricators, are unlikely sources of inventions in manufacturing techniques. Both these types of firms are individually small compared to the primary producers, so that they neither realize the profits accruing to primary producers from an increased demand for aluminum nor possess the research funds of a large corporation.

From this analysis of the nature of the expected profits from invention and the resources for research of the primary producers, the end-product manufacturers, and the equipment makers, it is possible to argue a priori that each will be the major source of inventions. Admittedly, this is a highly qualitative argument based upon the nature of expected profits, rather than a quantitative examination of the net historical profits from past inventions for each group. Data are lacking for such a study.

Inventions in the Joining of Aluminum

To discover which of these three groups, the primary producers, the end-product manufacturers, or the equipment makers, are the major source of inventions in manufacturing techniques for aluminum requires the selection of a technical area that is important for an increase in the total demand for aluminum, of significance to a wide class of end-product manufacturers, and with a substantial group of equipment makers. The joining of aluminum fulfills these specifications.

Not only is joining metal components common to the manufacturing of most end-products, but aluminum cannot be joined by conventional welding as easily as other metals.[9] Joining is a widespread technical problem among the end-product manufacturers so that one of the principal deterrents to the more extensive use of aluminum is the difficulty in joining.[10] Finally, there is a well-established group of manufacturers of welding equipment for use with other metals. Since 1940 some of these companies have supplied specialized welding equipment for use with aluminum.

The sources of inventions in joining from 1946 to 1957 are summarized in Table 30. The blanks and near-blanks drawn for secondary aluminum producers and independent fabricators was to be expected, while the applied character of these inventions rules out

[9] Aluminum has a much lower melting temperature than steel. A tendency for oxidation and the diffusion of heat throughout the metal creates heat reactions. For a discussion, see Reynolds Metals Company, *Reynolds Aluminum Alloys and Mill Products* (Louisville: By the Company, 1948), p. 18.

[10] *Modern Metals*, Vol. 9, No. 3 (April 1953), p. 46.

the universities. The absence of any contribution by an individual inventor appears surprising in view of Professor Jewkes' recent study which emphasized the contributions of individuals relative to those of corporate laboratories.[11] What might be termed "individual inventors" have sometimes joined one of the companies within the industry for the final stages in the development of their invention. Furthermore, many of the equipment makers have small engineering organizations that provide the institutional environment of the individual inventor. Even so, independent inventors appear to be an unimportant source of invention.

TABLE 30. Sources of inventions in the joining of aluminum

Source	Number
Primary aluminum producers	6
Independent fabricators	0
Secondary aluminum producers	1
End-product manufacturers	9
Aircraft 6	
Others 3	
Equipment makers	26
Commercial research and development companies	3
Individual inventors	0
Universities	0
Government laboratories	1
Foreign sources	6
Total	52

Note: The number of inventors exceeds the number of inventions because of 4 joint inventions.

Source: A survey of inventions reported in the trade press and compiled by the author. A listing of these inventions, brief descriptions, and the citations in the trade press may be obtained from the author.

The relatively low contribution of the primary producers and the relatively high contribution of the equipment makers is more striking. According to the preceding discussion, this would indicate that the competitive pressures and the immediate, more certain, and larger relative change of profits for the equipment makers more than offsets the greater potential long-run profits and the greater resources of the primary producers. The end-product manufacturers as a group are not an important source of invention despite their large numbers. Among the end-product manufacturers, the aircraft

[11] John Jewkes, David Sawers, and Richard Stillerman, *The Sources of Invention* (London: Macmillan, 1958), p. 821.

companies predominate, which can be explained by the factors discussed previously.

Four of these inventions have been mentioned repeatedly. Of these, the Koldweld process appears to be the most significant. The idea originated with an RAF officer, Sowter, who observed that when two sheets of copper were cut with dull shears a weld sometimes occurred on the sheared edge. This phenomenon was well known, but Sowter attempted to establish the conditions under which a weld would result. Upon demobilization, Sowter joined General Electric Ltd., a British welding-equipment manufacturer. A research program conducted by the company developed the Koldweld process for aluminum. Even though the original idea was conceived by an individual inventor, it was within a large corporation that the invention was converted into a commercially feasible process.[12]

The Koldweld Corporation was organized to license the process in the United States.[13] Under argreements with this corporation, the Utica Drop Forge and Tool Corporation developed and marketed a line of tools for the Koldweld process.[14] This process, the first departure from conventional heat welding, is particularly important for those uses of aluminum in which the molecular structure of aluminum must be preserved. (Heat welding changes the physical characteristics of aluminum.) The use of Koldwelding is spreading, although it is by no means in general use.

At present, the most common method of welding aluminum is the heilarc process. Heilarc welding was developed by the Northrop Aviation Corporation in 1940 and is considered a "tremendous boon to the light metals industry."[15] In the postwar decade the Air Reduction Company, a welding-equipment manufacturer, made significant improvements in this process.[16]

The last two inventions accorded special mention are methods of brazing. Brazing joins metals through the flow of molten metal between joints without melting the metals to be joined and hence

[12] W. A. Barnes, "Connecting Aluminum Conductors by the Koldweld Process" *Modern Metals,* Vol. II, No. 9 (October 1955), pp. 62ff. A Swiss aluminum fabricator is reported to have developed independently a similar process at about the same time.

[13] "Fast Process Welds Aluminum without Heating," *Modern Metals,* Vol. 5, No. 11 (December 1949), p. 28.

[14] W. S. Barnes, "Now Available: Tools for Koldwelding Wire and Sheet," *Modern Metals,* Vol. 10, No. 3 (April 1954), p. 57. Alcoa was reported as developing methods which extend the range of alloys that can be Koldwelded.

[15] "Welding Aluminum," *Modern Metals,* Vol. 7, No. 6 (July 1951), p. 26.

[16] *Ibid.*

changing their physical properties. It is used primarily in air conditioning, automobile, and aircraft components for which preserving the original heat-transfer properties of aluminum is important.[17] The Trane Company, a maker of aluminum components for aircraft and air conditioning, has developed a brazing process described as "the most significant aluminum fabricating development in a quarter of a century." [18] The dip-brazing process, invented jointly by United Aircraft Products and Alcoa is said "to increase production rates, cut costs, and give a more efficient product design." [19]

The origin of these apparently major inventions corresponds roughly with the results from the counting of inventions, with one each from a British equipment maker, a domestic equipment maker, and an end-product manufacturer, and the joint effort of an end-product manufacturer and a primary producer.

Inventions in the Finishing of Aluminum

Although aluminum does not rust, it is subject to corrosion and water staining. This has restricted the use of aluminum generally, although it is particularly crucial for aircraft components where aluminum aircraft gears, impeller blades, and so forth are subject to heat erosion and abrasion.[20] Because the incidence of this technical problem is concentrated in the aircraft industry, it is a less valid test of the relative role of different classes of inventors. Rather, the aircraft companies could be expected to be major sources of invention.

The computations in Table 31 indicate this is the case. Otherwise the results are similar to those for inventions in joining aluminum; namely, equipment makers are a major source of inventions and the primary producers are a relatively unimportant source. None of these inventions has been discussed extensively in the trade press.

Inventions in Fabricating Techniques

The reporting of fabricating inventions in the trade press is incomplete for products such as aluminum sheet in which the

[17] The Aluminum Company of America, *Aluminum and Its Alloys* (Pittsburgh: By the Company, 1950), p. 92.

[18] "Brazed Aluminum Heat Exchangers," *Modern Metals*, Vol. 7, No. 9 (October 1951), p. 25.

[19] "Dip Brazing Cuts Costs," *Modern Metals*, Vol. 9, No. 3 (April 1953), p. 40.

[20] *Modern Metals*, Vol. 8, No. 1 (February 1952), p. 72.

TABLE 31. Sources of inventions in aluminum finishing

Source	Number
Primary aluminum producers	1
Independent fabricators	0
Secondary aluminum producers	0
End-product manufacturers	9
Aircraft 7	
Others 2	
Equipment manufacturers	13
Commercial research and development corporations	3
Individual inventors	1
Universities	0
Government laboratories	0
Foreign sources	0
Total	27

Source: A survey of inventions reported in the trade press. A listing of these inventions, brief descriptions, and the citations in the trade press may be obtained from the author.

primary producers account for over 90 percent of the production, apparently because such inventions are of interest only to the few independent sheet mills that carry out the complete rolling process. Consequently, the inventions in fabricating techniques reported here are largely limited to the fabricating carried on by both the independents and the primary producers. As noted earlier, the primary producers account for about 40 percent of the production fabricated by both independents and primary producers, with their share of individual products varying from 10 percent in casting to 75 percent in cable. The independents are, of course, particularly significant in extruding and casting.

The primary producers realize the gains from inventions in fabricating techniques through the increased demand for aluminum. For example, extrusion output expanded at about three times the rate of all fabricating output from 1950 to 1955,[21] in large part because the newer extrusion presses reduced the cost of this type of fabrication. Yet, as with the inventions in manufacturing techniques, the gains of the primary producers are deferred and uncertain compared to that of the equipment makers. This is partially offset by the primary producers' direct gains through the utilization of fabricating techniques in their own operations, for these gains are more the immediate reduction in costs rather than the longer-run profits from an increase in demand for aluminum.

[21] See data in *Small Business Report, 1956.*

The equipment makers occupy the same position with respect to the realization of profits as with manufacturing techniques. The independent fabricators here are comparable to the end-product manufacturers in that they use the inventions directly in their own operations. The end-product manufacturers as the consumers of fabrications would profit from improvements in their supply.

TABLE 32. Sources of inventions in fabricating techniques

Source	Number
Primary aluminum producers	10
Independent fabricators	13
Secondary aluminum producers	0
End-product manufacturers	6
Aircraft 5	
Others 1	
Equipment manufacturers	37
Individual inventors	1
Commercial research and development companies	0
Universities	0
Government laboratories	2
Foreign sources	7
Total	76

Source: A survey of inventions reported in the trade press. The listing of these inventions, their brief description, and citations in the trade press may be obtained from the author.

As Table 32 indicates, the equipment makers are the major source of fabricating inventions. Again, the more immediate and certain profits from invention for such firms appear to be the more effective stimulus for invention. Fabricating machinery, however, is often custom-made for a specific fabricator with engineers from both the fabricator and the equipment maker working together on its design. Consequently, many inventions are the joint work of a fabricator and equipment maker.

The three major inventions in fabricating technique originated abroad. Shell molding, the most frequently discussed of the three inventions, utilizes a plastic shell as a mold rather than a more expensive metal die. Johannes Croning, a German engineer, invented the process in connection with wartime aircraft production. After the war, Croning joined the Polygram Casting Co., Ltd., an English foundry, to further improve the process.[22] Polygram holds

[22] F. L. Church, "The Shell Molding Process," *Modern Metals,* Vol. 8, No. 3 (April 1952), pp. 28–33.

the English patent and has applied for an American patent. As of 1953 the patent situation was described as "confused." [23]

Three companies outside the aluminum industry were instrumental in the introduction of the Croning process in the United States. The Bakelite Division of Union Carbide and Chemical and Monsanto Chemical Company promoted the process, which required the plastics they manufacture.[24] Professor Shallenberger of the Stanford Business School and some of his former students developed new machinery for shell casting.[25] About 100 foundries had adopted the process by 1953,[26] and its reception was such that one metallurgist cautioned, "the Croning process, though promising is no panacea." [27]

The Properzi continuous-casting process was invented by an Italian engineer, again for wartime aircraft production. Properzi made further improvements after the war and the Nichols Wire and Aluminum Company, an American independent fabricator, introduced the process into the United States. Continuous casting permits a single machine to convert aluminum ingot directly into redrawn rod, thus eliminating several intermediate steps of the conventional production process. According to Mr. Properzi, "When contrasted to the multi-million dollar plants and large labor forces needed for conventional production of rod, it becomes obvious that continuous casting processes are revolutionary in their economic impact." [28] To date, however, the economic impact of the process has been limited, despite the considerable discussion of the Properzi process. Adoption has been discouraged by the initial cost of the machine ($175,000) and by the radical changes required in existing operating techniques. There are now seven installations in the United States.[29]

[23] Polygram claims, ". . . it would be a serious mistake to assume that in its commercially practicable form (the Croning process) is open to free exploitation and that no Polygram license is necessary." *Modern Metals*, Vol. 9, No. 2 (March 1953), p. 30. Another group, Crown Casting Associates, has applied for an American patent. *Modern Metals* reports, "It has since been contended by some influential foundrymen that the patent claims are not valid and that an unlicensed foundry can, without fear, adapt the process in its own operations." (F. L. Church, "The Shell Molding Process," p. 28).

[24] *Ibid.*, p. 29.

[25] *Modern Metals*, Vol. 9, No. 7 (August 1953), p. 26.

[26] *Modern Metals*, Vol. 9, No. 3 (April 1953), p. 29.

[27] E. Elliott, "Aluminum and Its Alloys in 1953 — Some Aspects of Research and Technical Progress Reported," *Metallurgia*, Vol. 49, No. 2 (February, 1954), pp. 82–90.

[28] *Modern Metals*, Vol. 9, No. 11 (December 1953), p. 92.

[29] Modern Metals, Vol. 9, No. 10 (November 1953), p. 30.

The last major invention in fabricating technique is the large forging press. During the war, German aircraft firms built four extremely large presses that could form entire aircraft subassemblies, thus reducing the number of aircraft parts and so simplifying assembly and increasing the structural strength.[30] In 1948 the United States Air Force shipped two of these presses to the United States for installation in fabricating plants owned by Alcoa and the Bridgeport Brass Company. (The Russians took the other two presses.)[31] In 1950 the Air Force commissioned the building of even larger presses to be operated by Wyman Gordon, Alcoa, Kaiser, Harvey, and Curtiss Wright.[32] These presses are considered a major engineering advance, but their commercial value has yet to be established.

None of these inventions was introduced into the United States by the primary producers, which is consistent with the relatively limited role of these firms in the invention of fabricating techniques.

Inventions in the End-Product Applications of Aluminum

The new product uses of aluminum since 1946 are so numerous as to preclude their listings.[33] Examples would be such diverse products as: tubing for irrigation purposes; shelving and refrigeration units for refrigerators; lifeboats, davits, and ship superstructures; mine props and beams; low-tension electrical wire; building products such as store fronts, lighting fixtures, window frames, and wall panels. Most of these inventions involved less of an advance in the state of the arts than those in the preceding sections, although some new applications involved difficult technical problems. The end-product manufacturers are the major source of these inventions. In view of their numbers and direct economic interest, any other result would be surprising. But the primary producers are also important contributors to this kind of technical change, both through assisting end-product manufacturers and through devising new end-products.

Elsewhere the primary producers have been given low marks as sources of demand-increasing inventions. New end-product appli-

[30] "The aircraft designer has long been attracted to the idea of abandoning many of his substructures at present fabricated from sheer and extrusion and using forgings." E. Elliott, "Aluminum and Its Alloys," p. 82.

[31] *Modern Metals*, Vol. 12, No. 8 (September 1956), p. 94.

[32] *Ibid.*, p. 96.

[33] For a discussion of new application, see the testimony of Mr. Wilson, president of Alcoa, in *Remedy Record*, pp. 953–970.

cations, however, have a much more immediate payoff than other types of inventions. Consider a shipyard deciding the relative merits of steel and aluminum lifeboats. A primary producer assisting in the development of a new aluminum lifeboat can expect an immediate increase in its sales of aluminum. In contrast, a new method of welding or new fabricating techniques will increase the demand for aluminum only as these new techniques become widely diffused and permit new applications.

The concentration of the primary producers upon end-product applications is reflected in the limited public descriptions of the sales and research organizations of the primary producers.[34] The sales staff as described in Chapter VIII is in part organized into groups for each major end-product industry such as building materials or automobiles. These sales groups discover various technical problems that are then passed on to the research organization for solution. Notably, there is apparently no comparable sales group to promote invention in fabricating techniques or general manufacturing processes for aluminum.

Inventions in Aluminum Alloys

The inventors of new alloys from 1946 to 1957 are listed in Table 33. As this table indicates, the primary producers are the predominant source of inventions. This is to be expected for there are no groups comparable to equipment makers and the end-product manufacturers have no access to the technology and only the remote interest of improving their source of supply.

The primary producers have apparently concentrated their inventive efforts in alloys.[35] This may be because new alloys can be directly incorporated into the product line of the inventor so that the profits are relatively immediate compared to the profits from the inventions in fabricating and manufacturing techniques. But, perhaps of more significance, an alloy more than other inventions can increase the primary producer's market share. (Alloys are usually patentable, whereas most new end-product applications

---

[34] See W. B. Griffin, "Kaiser Aluminum: More Metal for More Products for More People," *Modern Metals*, Vol. 11, No. 12 (January 1956), E. A. Farrell, "Selling Aluminum," *Modern Metals*, Vol. 12, No. 6 (July), and No. 7 (August 1956), and F. L. Church, "Man of the Year: David P. Reynolds," *Modern Metals*, Vol. 10, No. 12 (January 1955).

[35] No data on the allocation of research expenditures was available to the author. This statement is based upon the qualitative descriptions of the research programs.

TABLE 33. Sources of inventions of aluminum alloys

Source		Number
Primary aluminum producers		30
Alcoa	11	
Kaiser	10	
Reynolds	6	
Harvey	2	
Limited	1	
Independent fabricators		2
Secondary aluminum producers		1
End-product manufacturers		1
Equipment manufacturers		0
Commercial research and development companies		0
Individual inventors		0
Universities		0
Government laboratories		1
Foreign sources		4
Total		39

Source: A survey of inventions in the trade press. The listing of these inventions, their brief description, and the citations in the trade press may be obtained from the author.

are not.) Furthermore, a new alloy yields a profit for a primary producer even when it displaces an existing alloy as long as the inventor's market share increases, while a new manufacturing or fabricating technique adds to a primary producer's profits only to the extent that it creates new uses for aluminum. Since the economic effect of an invention cannot be foreseen at the outset of the research, the twofold possibility increases the certainty of profits from a new alloy.

But if immediacy and certainty characterize the profits from inventions in alloys, it does not follow that new alloys have been the most effective inventions in increasing the over-all demand for aluminum. New alloys account for only a small fraction of the total sales of aluminum ingot, and so, even without deducting those displacing other sales of aluminum ingot, these inventions have apparently played a minor role in the increase in aluminum demand.[36] In contrast, extrusions sales, a product with significant changes in fabricating techniques, have grown from a few percent of the prewar total fabricated output to nearly a quarter of the 1958 output.[37]

[36] In 1948, patented alloys accounted for 9 percent of Alcoa's sales. This company at that time held the most alloy patents.

[37] See data in *Small Business Report, 1956*, p. 20.

Vertical Integration and Demand-Increasing Inventions

Primary producers were the important source of inventions of the new product applications and alloys while they contributed relatively little towards the advances in welding, finishing, and fabricating. Yet it is the inventions in these last three categories that account for substantial increases in the demand for aluminum.

This is consistent with the proposition that the primary producers direct their inventive efforts towards those sectors in which their profits are likely to be the highest, if profits are discounted for time and uncertainty. The significant finding is that the discounts required to explain the primary producers' behavior are of substantial magnitude and more than offset the greater resources of the large firms.

An alternative explanation is that the primary producers could count upon inventions by others to exploit technical opportunities in fabricating and manufacturing techniques. Hence the primary producers have concentrated their resources on the invention of alloys where there were no other sources of invention and so their own contribution had a high marginal value in increasing the demand for aluminum. Yet this view is inconsistent with the fact that the primary producers were active in the development of new end-product applications, for here the end-product manufacturers were an effective alternative source of inventions. The difference between end-products applications and manufacturing and fabricating techniques was apparently the greater immediacy and certainty of the profits from inventions in the end-product applications.

Thus, the determinants of the direction of primary producers' inventive activity are the immediacy and certainty of the profits from invention. Vertical integration has an obvious bearing upon these factors. Without their fabricating facilities, the primary producers' efforts to create new end-product applications would have the same generalized character as their efforts to expand the use of aluminum through new manufacturing and fabricating techniques. A new end-product application would result in the first instance in greater sales for an independent fabricator. This would increase the demand for aluminum ingot but because most fabricators buy from several primary producers, the inventor would receive only a share of the increased demand. Such indirect and generalized gains from invention have not led the primary producers to contribute greatly to the advances in manufacturing and fabricating technology. Therefore, vertical dissolution would tend to reduce this kind of inventive activity by the primary producers.

The effects of vertical dissolution would be most marked in its impact upon marketing activity. As noted above, marketing effort to establish new applications is an integral part of the process of invention. The marketing organization not only discovers the technical problems, but provides the organizational requirements for the technical efforts. Without the possibility of an immediate gain in sales, much of this organizational impetus might be lost. Notably, there has not been the same specific marketing requirement for inventions in either fabricating techniques or general manufacturing techniques and here the primary producers were less active inventors.

Vertical dissolution might also reduce the invention of new alloys in that many of these inventions are intended to solve technical problems in a new end-product application. Without direct contact with the manufacturers, the marketing requirement for such inventions might be less urgent and specific. Furthermore, the primary producer would have to obtain the cooperation of independent fabricators in order for the product to reach the consumer.

There are, of course, the activities of other inventors that might offset the loss of inventive activity by the primary producers. Indeed, the rate of invention in joining, finishing, and fabricating techniques was comparable to that in sectors where the primary producers were the dominant source of inventions. Among these other inventors, the equipment makers were clearly the most important.

Yet, with a vertical dissolution of the primary producers, the equipment makers would not assume an increased role in the invention of either alloys or new product applications, for here their interest is relatively remote. The primary producers would still be the major source of invention for alloys, but vertical dissolution, by cutting the connection between immediate sales and invention, might diminish the rate of such inventions. The independent fabricators, a possible alternative source of new product applications, have a poor record as a source of inventions, which makes it unlikely that the activities of these firms would offset the reduction in inventive effort by the primary producers. The end-product manufacturers have created a number of new applications, yet the primary producers are still a major source of this type of invention.

In sum, then, a vertical dissolution of the primary producers would reduce the rate of invention and this must be counted as one of the costs of vertical dissolution. This is the same conclusion as that reached in Chapter VIII for the marketing efforts of the primary producers. Because marketing and inventive effort are so intertwined, vertical dissolution is likely to affect both in the same way.

At the same time, the degree of vertical dissolution that has occurred with the expansion of the share of the independent fabricator has favored inventions in fabricating techniques. The independent fabricators provided an expanding market for the equipment makers that was probably more conducive to invention than the prewar market in which Alcoa was the dominant fabricator. The sheer increase in size of the market, of course, may account for the greater rate of invention. Yet, if the same expansion had followed the prewar pattern, the three primary producers as customers might not have provided the same impetus to the inventive activities of the equipment makers. But to insure this result vertical dissolution is not necessary. It is only necessary that the independent fabricators continue to survive as a substantial market for fabricating equipment in such products as extrusions and castings.

The tentative character of the preceding paragraph might be removed if information were available for a comparison of the technical progress in sheet, in which the primary producers continue to be the dominant fabricators, with the progress in extrusion and castings. Technical change in sheet rolling, however, is not reported in detail in the trade press. It is only apparent that technical progress has been greater in extrusions and casting than it was in the immediate postwar period. For the same reasons, no answer can be given whether some degree of vertical dissolution in sheet would bring forth a higher rate of technical change.

Oligopoly, Monopoly, and Demand Increasing Inventions

Oligopoly is often considered a priori more conducive to invention simply because of the greater number of independent decisions and technical approaches to problems. It is possible, of course, to have parallel efforts within a single research unit, but the cost of duplication makes this unlikely. Truly independent decisions with a single hierarchial organization are even more difficult. Further, an oligopolist may sponsor more research for fear a rival may exploit the technical possibilities to achieve a gain in market share. The simple case for monopoly is its ability to realize more fully the economies of scale in research as well as a higher profit rate that may provide more funds for research.

A historical comparison between the prewar and postwar periods indicates that inventions have occurred at a higher rate in the postwar oligopolistic era. Some of the new applications represent the culmination of Alcoa's prewar technical pioneering. An industry nearly eight times its prewar size should be expected to have a larger absolute research effort and hence more inventions. Still, at least some part of this increased activity is assignable to the introduction of oligopoly. Notably, within a relatively short time Kaiser and Reynolds have generated inventions at about the same rate as Alcoa even though Alcoa is the largest firm of the three. In alloys, Alcoa has only one more invention to its credit than Kaiser, and in the new product applications, Reynolds appears to be the leader. This hardly suggests that, if Alcoa were the only seller and so twice its present size, the total rate of inventions would be greater.

The transportation of bauxite, a related process, provides an illustration of the value of independent and competing units in promoting technical change.[38] After the war, there was discussion of the value of specialized ore vessels for the carriage of bauxite ore. At the *Remedy* proceedings in 1949, Mr. Reynolds, president of Reynolds Metals, spoke highly of these specialized ore carriers.[39] A few days later, the president of Alcoa testified: "We have made a continued and constant study as to the type of ship and type of service which will result in the lowest transportation costs and have figured ore carriers, which I heard Mr. Reynolds testify to, . . . we have examined the possibility of an ore carrier, one or more ore carriers — and to date we do not believe there will be any economy in utilizing an ore carrier. They are very expensive pieces of equipment and as such cannot be used for any other purpose than just the hauling of ore." [40]

Shortly thereafter Reynolds commissioned an English firm to construct the *S. S. Carl Schmedeman*, the first self-loading bauxite carrier. The ship went into service and received "good reviews" in *Iron Age, The Engineer,* and *The Shipbuilding and Shipping*

[38] I am indebted to Mr. Alan Strout of the Harvard Economic Research Project for this example. The interpretation here is my own.
[39] Testimony of R. S. Reynolds, *Remedy Record*, p. 188.
[40] Testimony of I. W. Wilson, *Ibid.*, p. 726.

Record.[41] All these sources claimed a reduction in cost with such a ship, and one estimated the cost savings to be as much as one-third of the shipping costs with conventional equipment. Alcoa has since ordered two specialized ore carriers, which may be more conclusive proof of their economic value.[42]

The ore carrier is typical of the technical changes since the war — fairly prosaic and originating in the general advances in technology. Alan Strout, of the Harvard Economic Research Project, describes the technical changes in aluminum reduction "as a procession of nonrevolutionary though significant factor saving innovations."[43] He lists the changes in the location of production facilities, the use of new fuel sources, the increases in the size of reduction pots, the greater amperage, the introduction of a continuous process for alumina digestion and electrode formation, the improvement in electrical generation and transmission, the mechanization of material handling, and the improvement in the electronic control system.

The prewar pattern of technical change was quite similar except that there were several more major inventions to enliven the record.[44] The best known is the Soderberg process, which utilizes an anode self-baked in the reduction pot and continuously restored by additions of a carbon mixture. This process is considerably cheaper than using a prebaked anode.[45] The continuous-digestion, the lime-and-soda, and the starch processes were significant modifications of the Bayer process for converting bauxite into alumina. The Soderberg process was invented by a Norwegian producer and the Bayer process modifications by Alcoa.

[41] *Shipbuilding and Shipping Record,* Vol. 80, No. 23 (December 4, 1952), pp. 739–742; *The Engineer,* Vol. 193, No. 3 (January 16, 1953), p. 98; and *Iron Age,* Vol. 170, No. 3 (December 4, 1952), p. 209.

[42] *Shipbuilding and Shipping Record,* Vol. 85, No. 19 (May 12, 1955), p. 606. Such specialized ore carriers are now used in hauling other ores and are ranked "As one of the most important changes which has marked shipbuilding in recent years." *Merchant Ships,* 1954 (New York: Macmillan, 1955), p. 64. Even without Reynold's leadership, Alcoa would have probably eventually adopted this general shipping practice.

[43] Alan M. Strout, "The Aluminum Industry," Harvard Economic Research Project Report on Research for 1956 (Cambridge, hectographed, 1957), p. 71.

[44] Professor Wallace, writing in 1937, stated, "With a few exceptions, which will be noted in due course, no fundamental alterations of process or apparatus have occurred since the birth of the industry." *Market Control,* p. 7. Similarly, speaking about the Bayer process since 1928, Mr. Wilson, president of Alcoa, testified, "[Since 1928 the Bayer process has had] only such changes as result in material handling and general processing equipment." *Remedy Record,* p. 975.

[45] Department of Commerce, Business and Defense Services Administration, *Materials Survey: Aluminum,* November 1956, pp. VI 8–10.

Aluminum is still produced by the Hall process discovered in 1887, and alumina by the Bayer process discovered in 1920. There have been rumors of revolutionary discoveries in the offing. For example, Reynolds has patented a process to extract aluminum directly from bauxite, thus by-passing the production of alumina.[46] The British Columbia Aluminum Company has announced the reduction of aluminum by long-wave electrical energy.[47] The Bureau of Mines, Alcoa, Harvey, and Anaconda have large research programs directed at the production of alumina from domestic clays.[48] Yet, except for brief press announcements of "promising" results, this research has been to no apparent avail, and the Hall and Bayer processes are likely to be used for years to come.

Continuous minor improvements have made these two processes highly efficient. For example, the Bayer process recovered on the average 95 percent of the alumina in the bauxite ores even before the war and today the recovery is 97 percent.[49] Similarly, the electrical input per pound of aluminum was 12 kilowatt hours in 1926, 10 kilowatt hours in 1940, and 7.8 kilowatt hours in a plant constructed in 1954.[50] At the same time, the Hall and Bayer processes appear to have exploited fully the electrochemical knowledge that accumulated at the turn of the century. Processes that have had continuous minor improvements and that were initially major advances in the state of the art are difficult to surpass.

What is required for major inventions is another major increase in scientific knowledge comparable to that which made possible the Hall invention. Professor Wallace traces the Hall invention back to "scientific research and formulation of general principles governing the relations of electric currents to chemical changes. . . ."[51] Such advances in scientific knowledge are the culmination of a series of scientific discoveries and are relatively rare events. For

[46] *Modern Metals*, Vol. 4, No. 8 (September 1948), p. 48.

[47] *Modern Metals*, Vol. 8, No. 2 (March 1952), p. 18.

[48] For a history of the early efforts, see John V. Krutilla, *The Structure of Costs and Regional Advantage in Primary Aluminum* (Cambridge, Mass.: Harvard University dissertation, 1952), and for more recent discussion see *Modern Metals*, Vol. 9, No. 9 (October 1953), p. 28; Vol. 9, No. 4 (May 1953), p. 88; and December 1955, p. 92.

[49] T. G. Pearson, "The Chemical Background of the Aluminum Industry," Royal Institute of Chemistry, *Lectures, Monographs and Reports*, No. 5 (London: By the Society, 1956), p. 34.

[50] The last figure is for the Anaconda plant, built in 1954. Edwin O. Wooster, "A Description of the Anaconda Aluminum Plant at Columbia Falls, Montana," Address at the Colorado Mining Association, February 7, 1956.

[51] Wallace, *Market Control*, p. 4.

this kind of technical change, economics, at least the kind involved in the study of markets, is irrelevant.

A Concluding Comment

The conclusions, as stated in each section, are not particularly novel. Most economists would agree that oligopoly is more conducive to invention than monopoly. The evidence here supports this proposition, although at the reduction stage the changes in market structure made no observable difference in the rate and nature of invention. The finding that even large firms focus their inventive activities in areas where the profits are relatively immediate and certain is not surprising, although there are a few statements about the limits of inventive activity of a firm, largely because few have posed the question.

The role of the equipment makers demonstrates that a substantial part of the technical change in one industry is likely to originate from the progress of another industry. The importance of growth industries for particular historical periods, such as automobiles and rayon in the 1920's, are a common theme in economic history. There may well be less obvious industries that are the major carriers of technical change not only for a single historical period, but more or less continuously by virtue of their position in the economy.

XII

ECONOMIC THEORY AND
PUBLIC POLICY

As stated in Chapter I, this study is intended as an examination of economic analysis and public policy in the field of industrial organization. This chapter attempts to fulfill this commitment, recognizing, of course, the tentative nature of conclusions based upon a study of one industry.

Oligopolistic Indeterminacy and Market Leadership

Theoretical models of oligopoly have proliferated because of the inherent complexity of the problem of mutual interdependence; what A does depends on what B will do in response to A's actions, and yet what B will do depends on B's estimate of A's response and so forth. This situation can be a theoretical delight, particularly when elements of bluff and randomized strategy are introduced. Such models contain important elements of reality, otherwise poker would not be so popular in business circles.

Yet, reversing the usual dictum, the reality here may be simpler than the theory. The existence of a well-established price leader reduces the oligopolistic uncertainty to the rare instances when one firm decides to depart from the established pattern. In the aluminum industry, departures from the leadership of Alcoa were infrequent and were usually explainable by the special position of Limited.

Such leadership can be based upon custom alone. But it has been argued that the role of price leadership in the aluminum industry is assigned to the firm with the preference for the lowest market price. As a result, the leadership can count upon followership for price increases because the rivals prefer a higher price and followership for price reductions because the rivals must protect their share of the market.

Such an interpretation minimizes the collusive character of oligopoly. Leadership as expounded here does not imply a contract curve solution, but rather the simple selection by the leader of his preferred market price subject to the loss of leadership if this price exceeds the preferred market price of one of the followers. The followers are aware of the restraints on their price policies imposed by the price leaders, and the price leader in turn recognizes the possibility of the assumption of leadership by one of the followers. Yet this is essentially a conventional view of oligopoly for there is still the mutual awareness that rivals will react immediately to a firm's actions. Consequently, a firm's pricing actions are directed toward changing the market price rather than toward obtaining a differential advantage over its rivals.

Conceptually then, pricing decisions are like those of a monopolist in that both are concerned with the industry price. In the aluminum industry, prices are not set to achieve short-run profit maximization. Rather, the behavior of the price leader, namely Alcoa, is consistent only with long-run profit maximization. Given a long-run demand function that is elastic, relatively low prices increase the rate of growth in demand so that long-run profit maximization requires "low" prices. As a result, aluminum prices (or at least the profits resulting from the prices) were relatively modest when Alcoa was the sole producer of primary aluminum.[1] Alcoa has apparently continued the same policies under the postwar oligopoly, with the deviation from prices maximizing short-run profits even more observable through the existence of excess demand.

The high long-run price elasticity, in turn, is explained by the nature of the product. Aluminum is a newer metal displacing established applications of steel and copper, and for this initial substitution the price sensitivity is high, although the character of the consumers and the existence of close substitutes in other metals insures a relatively high degree of price elasticity as a permanent feature of the aluminum market.

In this situation, long-run profit maximization is based upon

---

[1] See Judge Hand's statement, "A profit of ten percent (by Alcoa) could hardly be considered extortionate." United States v. Aluminum Company of America, 148 F. 2d 416 (2d cir., 1945) at p. 426.

the preference between present and future profits. A simple price policy is evidently the behavior corresponding to this complex theoretical problem. Alcoa sets prices to realize a 10-percent return on investment, and the additional short-run gains possible from higher prices are foregone in order to increase the rate of growth of demand. This kind of profit standard appears to be highly institutionalized and a product of market experience, the expectations of the financial community, and the mores of an ill-defined community of professional managers. Finally, vague political pressures from both the government and the unions may play a role in setting profit standards.

This picture of market behavior is little different from that of the monopolist, albeit of the more "dynamic" kind. The point then becomes how does a three-firm oligopoly of the postwar aluminum industry limit market power of the individual firm and improve market performance over that with a single monopolist?

First, the price leadership is in the "right" direction in the sense that the firm setting the lowest price, the highest rate of investment, and the greatest marketing effort becomes the leader. Still, with only two other firms, at least until recently, it is possible for the leader's market behavior to be little different from that of a monopolist. And, since the leader, Alcoa, is the former monopolist and continues to pursue the same business policies, there is no obvious difference here between oligopoly and monopoly. Such a history undermines the sharp distinction assigned to monopoly in law and economics. Indeed, one Henry Ford could introduce a new price policy, whereas fifteen sellers with conservative styles of business might produce results akin to the most "static" of monopolies. As a result, the difference in outcome between oligopoly and monopoly depends in large part on the particular participants in the market. This is disappointing in a discipline that attempts to abstract from history, but it seems nevertheless a characteristic of oligopoly and monopoly.

Yet there remains an important long-run distinction even between one and two sellers. Competitors, however few, limit the market power of a single firm, for they provide other firms that could take over as leader. Since the "aggressiveness" of a firm is often an historical accident of a particular management it is well that another firm can assume this role should the leader's zeal slacken. As a general rule, the greater the number of firms the greater the probability that there will be at all times an "aggressive" seller. In the aluminum industry, then, the addition of more sellers serves as a long-run insurance that leadership will continue to be in the "right" direction.

Oligopoly also adds a second factor not existent in monopoly: uncertainty over the rival's response and his future actions in such areas as marketing effort, the rate of expansion of capacity, and the extent of research. A firm would experience a declining market share if other firms moved forward more rapidly in these areas. And here the subsequent matching of rivals' behavior cannot be achieved immediately as it can in pricing. Since what will offset the rivals' efforts can never be known with certainty, prudence dictates over-insurance by maintaining a slightly greater effort than the apparent programs of the rivals'. For example, there has apparently been an investment race in the aluminum industry that is explainable by these kinds of factors. Less dramatically, there seems to be an accelerated pace of marketing effort compared to the immediate postwar period. Nothing like this has happened in pricing, for here the immediacy of the rivals' response eliminates the uncertainty.

Although uncertainty about rivals' behavior, as well as the possibility of a gain in market share, has meant greater nonprice competition, several practices of the primary producers minimize the consequences of the uncertainties about the future level of demand as well as preclude sudden shifts of customers from one primary producer to another. Indeed, the minimization of such uncertainties explains a good deal of the behavior of the primary producers — the long-term sales contracts, the structure of vertical integration, the buying of scrap and secondary aluminum, and in part, the molten-aluminum contracts. The priority attached to the minimization of uncertainty is explained by the importance of fixed costs in aluminum reduction.

Reduction in uncertainty may be desirable, but here it has been achieved largely at the   cost of increasing the uncertainty borne by other firms. The molten-metal contracts best illustrate how a contract between a large buyer and a large seller can be mutually advantageous by throwing the burden of demand fluctuations on a host of small suppliers. Elsewhere, leadership toward lower prices, marketing innovation, and expansion in capacity seem to be reasonably effective in producing desirable market behavior.

These forms of market leadership promise either a bigger market or an enlarged market share. But, for a firm to forego long-term contracts offers no such benefits, particularly when aluminum is in such short supply that customers can be selected. Rather, as one firm takes the lead in securing its market share through long-term contracts, others may match this behavior in self-defense. Hence, leadership is in the "wrong" direction.

This result merely reflects the basic fact that competition between the three firms permits the existence of considerable jointly held market power. For this reason a third difference between the current oligopoly and the predecessor monopoly is crucial: namely, the existence of Limited and the independent fabricators. Both are outsiders vis-à-vis the primary producers and so have a quite different pattern of market behavior. As a result, they are sources of competitive pressure upon the oligopolists. Specifically, the independent fabricators are so numerous that they are outside the mutual awareness of the oligopolists. When demand slackens, it is these small firms that cut prices. This introduces an element of price flexibility and limits the level of prices for certain fabrications.

Limited serves as a restraint upon the market power of the domestic primary producers for different reasons. It is the one major primary producer without fabricating facilities and it plays a major role in West European markets. This means Limited may have a different view of the desired price structure and level of prices. For example, though until 1957 Limited followed the United States price (barring the special events in 1948), it was as a consequence of Limited's actions that the ingot price was reduced during the 1957 recession. This 8-percent reduction in list price was notable compared to the price increases in other oligopolistic industries. In crucial periods, then, Limited's presence in the American market is decisive.

The three new primary producers constitute still another possible group of outsiders, although to date they have largely followed the prices and practices of the established producers. At some future date they may deviate from this pattern, although their market position is not as different from the other three primary producers as that of Limited or the independent fabricators. Consequently they are not as promising candidates for the role of outsiders.

In sum, this is an industry that functions as it would with a "dynamic" monopolist, with the important modifications introduced by the uncertainty of the rivals' behavior, the basis of leadership, and the presence of outsiders. All these create some competitive pressures toward lower prices, expansion, and product improvement — but it is still an open question whether this is sufficient for the purposes of public policy.

The Antitrust Remedy Reconsidered

It is clear that Judge Knox has not created an excessive remedy. There has been no observable dampening of Alcoa's aggressiveness. The two new firms, as well as Alcoa, were large enough to realize the economies of scale of production and to support research programs. Antitrust action is often alleged to lower the rate of technical progress through reducing the monopoly power that provides the funds and the incentive for invention. From the evidence in Chapter XI, the antitrust action has, if anything, increased the rate of invention, although a direct comparison with the prewar period is extremely difficult. Perhaps the important point is that a great deal of technical progress originates outside the aluminum industry, narrowly defined, and so would be unaffected by antitrust action.

The more interesting question is whether the remedy was sufficiently extensive to meet the requirements of an antitrust policy. Certainly, the horizontal divestiture of Alcoa properties involved practical difficulties. Alcoa had only two alumina plants, one of which, the St. Louis plant, was obsolete and on the verge of abandonment.[2] As a result, a new firm, an Alcoa B, would have had a marked cost handicap. Similarly, it was difficult to assemble a collection of diversified fabricating plants for two companies. Finally, the central management and research laboratories could be apportioned between firms only with great difficulty. Faced with these problems the government, having concentrated in the *Remedy Hearings* on the inadequacies of the present market structure, came up with only a hasty plan for further relief.[3] It is not

---

[2] Aluminum Company of America, *Reply to the Supplemental Brief of the United States*, United States v. Aluminum Company of America, 91 F. Supp. 333 (S.D.N.Y., 1950) at p. 7, henceforth cited as *Remedy Record*.

[3] The government did not offer a plan for divestiture until requested by the Court. Then it stated, "Nothing like a definite plan could be stated without the assistance of specific findings of fact by the Courts." It offered two suggested plans, each requiring the new company to build a replacement of the East St. Louis Aluminum Plant. *Supplement to the Brief of the United States, Remedy Record.*

surprising, then, that the Court rejected the government's plea for dissolution.

Yet it may well be that the Court underestimated the benefits of further dissolution. Since 1949, Alcoa's market share has declined and three new producers have been added to the industry, largely as a result of the government's expansion program. Creating an Alcoa B would have achieved the same results, that is, a reduction in Alcoa's market position and the addition of another seller. The probability that a new firm would not be a viable economic unit may have been overestimated, for three new firms have now been established. Still, the expansion program provided subsidization and market guarantees to new firms outside the powers of the Court. The rate of expansion of the aluminum demand could hardly have been foreseen, and the costs and complexities of dissolution could have been substantial. Consequently, the Court's failure to create a new firm through dissolution appears eminently reasonable.

Government aid to create more primary aluminum producers may now encounter diminishing returns. The aluminum industry has substantial economies of scale, so the technology requires an oligopoly. More sellers might well be desirable, but now that the industry has become much less concentrated with three established and three new producers, the case for subsidization of entry into the aluminum industry becomes no more valid than for other equally concentrated industries. Dissolution is an even more costly way of creating more sellers, involving as it does the division of a going firm, while the differences in market power between Alcoa, Reynolds, and Kaiser are now sufficiently small that there is no reason to single out Alcoa. As the industry expands there may well be some additional entry, although from the evidence in Chapter IX, this will not be frequent enough to have a marked impact on market behavior. Finally, the moderation of postwar inflation and the catching up of reduction capacity with demand will add to the competitiveness of the industry. At least in the 1958 recession, aluminum ingot was plentiful enough to eliminate the supply restrictions on the expansion of the independent fabricators.

Vertical dissolution is a much less easily resolved issue. Most of the indications of insufficient competition — the problems of the independent fabricators, the excess fabricating capacity, and the peculiarities of the price structure — originate largely from the vertical integration of the ingot producers into fabricating. Similarly, the barriers to entry are greater because of vertical integration. In view of its importance, it is puzzling that vertical integration was never examined in the proceedings before Judge Knox. Rather, the sequence of events by which the remedy developed seems to have precluded its consideration. The Surplus Property Board assumed that no further dissolution of Alcoa could be counted upon, so that any new firm must be as vertically integrated as Alcoa.[4] By 1949, in the hearings before Judge Knox, the government had already established vertical integration for the newer firms so that any proposal for the vertical dissolution of Alcoa would place Alcoa at a disadvantage relative to Reynolds and Kaiser, as well as reverse the previous government policy. Furthermore, the record itself was devoted entirely to the ingot market rather than to the entire industry, since the remedy was for monopolization in the ingot market.

All this is most unfortunate, since vertical dissolution is the action that matters — one that would produce quite a different aluminum industry. But how much better would such an industry be?

At the fabrication level, there are markedly differing economies of scale for various products. At the one extreme, aluminum sheet, the primary producers had but two plants apiece so that at the most only eight or nine hot-rolled-sheet firms could be created. Just how such a bilateral oligopoly would function becomes highly speculative.

The relation between tin can manufacturers and the tin plate producers represents an approximation to the new market structure that would be created in aluminum sheet. The price of tin plate is

[4] See the comment, "Vertical Integration in the Aluminum Industry: A Bar to Effective Competition," *Yale Law Journal*, 60:294–310 (February 1951). In 1945 the Attorney General stated, "Newcomers, to be able to compete with Alcoa, must enter the industry on an integrated basis. . . ." Quoted in Joint Committee on Defense Production, *Defense Production Report, No. 24, Aluminum Expansion and Competition*, 82d Cong., 2d Sess., 1953, p. 15. Likewise, the War Asset Administration stated in a 1947 report, ". . . surplus plants disposals have strengthened Alcoa's competitors by enabling them more fully to integrate their operations." Quoted in *Ibid.*, p. 16. Similarly, the Senate Small Business Committee in a 1946 report stated, ". . . only strong integrated corporations can survive if they are to be truly competitive with Alcoa." *Ibid.*, p. 17. The stress on vertically integrated firms was predicated upon the existence of vertically integrated Alcoa, but by the time of the Remedy proceedings, it provided an impressive record in favor of vertical integration in general. This same record was used in the 1953 report of the Joint Committee on Defense Production to support vertical integration. (*Ibid.*, pp. 16–22.)

set annually by a key bargain between American Can and U. S. Steel and the sales are largely under annual contracts.[5] Similarly, a key bargain between Alcoa and a leading sheet roller might be expected to occur. Likewise, some kind of contractual arangements are likely to develop, for the volumes of ingot involved for each buyer and seller require some kind of long-run relation between them.

This would have the substance if not the form of vertical integration with one important difference. The individual buyers of sheet are so few that they have more bargaining power vis-à-vis the primary producers than the extruders. Hence, they might be able to exert a downward pressure on ingot prices particularly during periods of slack demand. Such is the pattern in the tin plate market. These price reductions, in turn, might be passed on to the buyer of sheet, although the oligopolistic character of this market means such price reductions are likely to be considerably less than those for products with flexible price histories. But for most of the years there would be a pattern of price leadership in both markets that might be little different from that now prevailing with vertical integration.

The principal changes with vertical disintegration would be of this nature and confined to these products. In what has been termed the small business sector, extrusions, castings, and perhaps cable, vertical dissolution would make little difference. In these sectors the primary producers' market share has declined, and they are more price followers than leaders. These sectors are already sufficiently competitive so that the complete withdrawal of the primary producers would add little to effective competition.

According to the analysis in Chapter VIII, these possible gains would be bought only by sacrificing at least some of the marketing effort carried on by the primary producers. Similarly, it was concluded in Chapter XI that the rate of invention would be reduced by a vertical dissolution. As pointed out in these two chapters, these are benefits of high value to the economy. Finally, neither complete nor partial dissolution would solve the problem of allocation of ingot supply during a shortage. The marked difference in size would make the sheet customers more valuable than the ex-

[5] In recent years, shorter-term contracts have been used, and a substantial volume of purchases are made on a spot basis. For a discussion of this market see James W. McKie, *Tin Cans and Tin Plate* (Cambridge: Harvard University Press, 1959), chap. IV.

truders. As a result the sheet mills as big buyers might be favored in the distribution of ingot. At least as parts of vertically integrated firms, sheet operations can be more easily denied ingot whenever a primary producer deems it expedient to preserve a position in the ingot market. Therefore, even though most of the important problem areas of market behavior are connected with vertical integration into fabricating, dissolution does not seem worth its cost.

Another bilateral oligopoly would be created by the vertical dissolution of aluminum reduction and alumina production. The number of producers of alumina would be unchanged, for the marked economies of scale on alumina manufacture preclude any radical increase in the numbers of producers without a loss in efficiency.

The major gain of such a dissolution would be to lower the barriers to entry. Even though the unavailability of alumina has discouraged entry, the integrated producers, perhaps through fear of the antitrust laws, have apparently offered to sell alumina whenever their capacity permitted. Yet the capital-intensive character of the technology and the "lumpiness" occasioned by the economies of scale have precluded small increases in capacity to serve new customers. Old customers are unlikely to be displaced to serve new ones. This would occur under any form of ownership, so that the difficulties of a company like Harvey in obtaining alumina would not be changed by vertical dissolution.

This is particularly so because, with both the buyer and seller having capital-intensive facilities, with each critically dependent upon the other, and with a large volume of sales between individual buyers and sellers, long-run contractual devices of informal understandings are likely to recreate the substance of vertical integration. The only apparent gains would be that each producer would be on a strict price parity for alumina and there would be perhaps a greater willingness to create capacity for newcomers. Even with the vertical dissolution of the alumina facilities, the barriers to entry would remain substantial. The entry of one or two more primary producers promises only a small change in market behavior, as the preceding discussion of horizontal dissolution indicates.

At the same time, such vertical dissolution would greatly complicate the planning of investment. Reduction and alumina capacity must expand simultaneously. Given the lumpiness and capital-intensive character of both types of investment, some joint understanding between an alumina and an aluminum producer would be necessary. Such agreement would be more difficult between two independent organizations than between two divisions of the same company. Hence vertical dissolution might slow down the rate of investment. The risk does not seem worth the small change in market behavior.

This leaves us in a position of ratifying the present market structure of the aluminum industry, not because it is workably competitive, but only because the alternatives do not promise benefits worth their costs.

Some Recommendations for Public Policy

This does not mean that we are without public policy recommendations. There is the fairly obvious step of assuring that Limited remains an important seller in the ingot market by continuing the present low tariffs on ingot.[6] (The high tariff on fabricated products, however, discourages vertical integration of Limited and so insures the company's continuance as a supplier to the independent fabricators.) It is clear that Limited contributes to effective competition in the American market. On the other hand, Limited has not in the past indulged in any practices that can be fairly described as dumping or price warfare, nor does it appear likely in the future that it will do so. Yet, as the discussion in Chapter IV indicates, these terms are likely to cloak efforts to circumscribe Limited's role as a competitor.

Similarly the present low tariff upon alumina should be maintained. Two of the newcomers, Harvey and Ormet were able to solve their alumina supply problems through joint ventures and contracts with foreign firms. Maintaining the low tariffs here is less of a political problem, since some of the other American primary producers are reputed to be planning future alumina plants near their Caribbean bauxite. Such locations reduce markedly the cost of transportation.

---

[6] The tariff on ingot was 3 cents per pound in 1946. It was lowered to 2 cents in 1948 and 1.5 cents in 1951. Reynolds and Kaiser argued unsuccessfully for a tariff increase in 1948, and all three producers successfully argued against further reductions in 1955. All these changes and proposals were made as part of the Reciprocal Trade Agreements. Select Committee on Small Business, Subcommittee No. 3, *Hearings, Aluminum Industry, Part II*, 84th Cong., 1st Sess., 1955, p. 604.

The more complex problem is the protection and encouragement of the small business groups in the aluminum industry: the fabricators, and to a lesser extent the distributors. These firms have contributed greatly to competition, yet their growth has been limited by certain practices of the primary producers. More specifically, the primary producers' marketing policies preclude the distributors from handling large orders; the primary producers' purchases of secondary aluminum to meet peak ingot requirements increase the fluctuations in the price of secondary aluminum, a hardship for the regular buyers of secondary metal; the primary producers' maintenance of stable prices on ingot, combined with the flexible prices on some fabricated products, has narrowed the margin for some fabrications; and finally, the rationing system of the primary producers has made the entry of new fabricators difficult. The first three practices are not easily remedied for they are inherent manifestations of the imperfections of the market structure, while the last is no longer a problem because of the recent expansion of aluminum capacity. Furthermore, changes here would require special legislation to single out the aluminum industry.

With three other practices — price discrimination; long-term contracts for the sale of aluminum to end-product manufacturers, such as those with the automobile companies; and long-term contracts for the sale of ingot by Limited to the American primary producers — more positive recommendations seem justified. The first two are intertwined, for price discrimination is most likely to occur as an inducement to the signing of a long-term sales contract by a big buyer of aluminum. Indeed, the case of economic price discrimination is the molten aluminum contracts, where this was part of a ten-year contract.

In general, such contracts, at least of the duration and size of those with the automobile companies, foreclose both the primary producer from a segment of the ingot market and the independent fabricator from a segment of the casting market. These contracts reduce the uncertainty of both the parties involved only at the expense of larger fluctuations in demand for the independent fabricators. Consequently, there is little net reduction in uncertainty. The cost-saving which might be accomplished through such contracts means that a *per se* prohibition is unwarranted. But in view of their potential anticompetitive effect, the interpretation of cost justification should be limited to direct production costs. This interpretation would restrict the use of such contracts, while still permitting their use in cases of significant production cost savings.

For another class of long-term contracts, that between Limited and the American primary producers for the sale of ingot, a stronger position seems justified. Limited has truly emerged as a fourth competitor, thus fulfilling Judge Knox's hopes, largely through supplying the independent fabricators. Contracts like those of 1947 and 1952 jeopardize the supply of ingot to the independents, although defense requirements at that time may have justified these particular contracts. Such contracts may give Limited an influence over the prices of the other primary producers, as the events in the summer of 1948 indicate. Therefore, these contracts should be prohibited.

These two types of long-term contracts are a form of quasi-vertical integration. As such they present the same issues as in earlier discussions of vertical integration. Yet we have reached different conclusions here. We have accepted vertical integration for the primary producers and, in contrast, we have argued against these two types of long-term sales contracts. We distinguish between these two situations because of differences in the market structure and in the probability of real cost savings from vertical integration. Alumina reduction, for example, has a technology that creates economics of scale so that the number of firms will be few in any case. In contrast, die casting does not involve such large economies of scale and, indeed, there is a thriving group of independent fabricators. The long-term contracts between Limited and the American primary producers jeopardize both Limited's role as the "fourth" competitor envisaged in Judge Knox's remedy and Limited's role as an ingot supplier to the independent fabricators. And here the economies of scale, if any, are limited to the highly nebulous reductions in business risk. In both cases, striking down or limiting the use of these contracts serves to maintain the "outsiders" that serve as a check on the market power of the big three.

On the other hand, a third class of long-term contracts, that for the sale of ingot to independent fabricators, is not an immediate problem. Such contracts make the sale of ingot more attractive to the primary producers and serve to reduce inventory speculation. Longer-term contracts, exclusive requirements, and a larger coverage of the ingot market than now appears to exist would substantially lessen the mobility of sellers required for competition without creating off-setting gains in economic efficiency. Present practices probably do not transgress these limits, for there remains a substantial fraction of ingot output available for spot sales. If they should do so in the future, it would require little extension of the existing doctrine to find that such practices substantially injure competition.

The limitation on the business practices cited above appears to be well tailored to the kind of problems presented by the aluminum industry. The general argument against government action directed at business practices is that, if competition is present, the action is redundant — for competition itself polices business practice. On the other hand, if competition does not exist, then antitrust action is required to change the market structure to create competition. This argument ignores the possibility of a situation in which further changes in market structure might create additional competition only at a great cost in efficiency, and yet the existing level of competition does not sufficiently protect the small business sector. This is more than a question of equity, for it is the competition from the small business sector that may create the competitive pressures upon the large firms.

The other general objection to such policies is that their administration tends to turn them into a device for the protection of competitors rather than competition and so insures the continued existence of the inefficient. This presumes that small business, usually the beneficiary of such laws, is less efficient than big business. This generalization is based largely upon studies of distributive trades where a pattern of small wholesalers, jobbers, and retailers has been challenged by the growth of large, vertically integrated firms. These large firms have been generally more efficient than the distributive network they have displaced.

In the aluminum industry the historical sequence is reversed. The large, vertically integrated firms represent the established order that has been displaced in certain sectors by small firms. This historical sequence, as well as the technology of these fabrications, suggests that small independent fabricators are at least as efficient as the primary producers in certain product lines. Hence, prohibition practices would not protect a group of inefficient competitors. Furthermore, the competition between these small firms would eliminate any individual inefficient fabricator.

Some Reflections on Disorderly Antitrust

As the preceding account makes clear, the structural changes in the aluminum industry have been more the work of administrative agencies and Congressional pressure than of the decisions of courts. This is true of the original 1950 decision in which Judge Knox largely ratified the disposal plans of the War Assets Administration and the Surplus Property Board. Similarly, actions of the General Services Administration and the Defense Production Administration during the Korean War account for the subsequent changes in market structure.

This study has not questioned the existence of such programs. In retrospect, they may read as if they represented the businessman's version of the welfare state. But hindsight is not the proper basis for the criticism of policies induced by the mobilization requirements of 1950. We can not forego, however, the observation that these programs seem to have been almost carbon copies of those of World War II, even though by 1950 it should have been clear that atomic weapons require a different kind of economic mobilization. Economic mobilizers are perhaps as prone as generals to prepare for the last war.

These programs did expand aluminum capacity, which was the stated primary objective, so that in their own terms they were a success. The program facilitated the entry of three new producers and the relative expansion of the independents and Kaiser and Reynolds. In terms of the secondary objective of protecting the independents' supply of ingot, the program did not live up to its promises. Furthermore, the market protection for new capacity was indirectly extended to imports of primary aluminum.

The aluminum industry in the years 1950 to 1956, of course, offered a singular justification for this kind of government intervention. Yet the role of the federal government is now so all-embracing that administrative agencies are inevitably making decisions on industrial organization for a wide range of the so-called unregulated industries. The mixed record of this kind of intervention suggests that the activities of administrative agencies in promoting competition deserve some of the scholarly attention now lavished on the antitrust decisions of the courts.

As far as the aluminum industry itself is concerned, it is highly probable that there may be new government programs of procurement or hydropower development that afford administrative agencies an opportunity to promote competition by giving preference to the three new primary producers and to the independent fabricators. Such actions need not result in increased costs to the government, for the terms offered by different firms are likely to be similar. (For example, all the various firms now sell to the stockpile on identical terms.) A policy favoring new entrants and the independents has done much to change the market structure in the past, and its continuation might well serve to further reduce the market power of the primary producers at much less cost than judicial action. Even though any one action might have a limited effect, in the long run the cumulative effect of such policies could further alter substantially the market structure of the industry.

Carrying out the promotion of competition through a diverse group of executive agencies has its limitation, as the history in Chapter VIII shows. Government administrators are under considerable pressure to be "fair," that is, to divide a government program proportionally among all the established firms rather than to give preference to one type of firm in order to promote competition. Likewise, these programs have a primary objective other than promoting competition. The most expedient way of disposing of government power, procuring aluminum, or obtaining more primary aluminum capacity may be to rely on Alcoa, Reynolds, and Kaiser.

Even though the Antitrust Division of the Justice Department could insure some consistency and coordination by insisting on the clearance of actions affecting market organization, the Courts and Congress play a special role in providing a sanction for such policies. For example, various officials repeatedly quoted Judge Knox's dictum that competition was not fully established in the aluminum industry as a justification for their actions. Without further litigation, Congress must be the source of pressures to promote competition and provide the justifications for the actions of officials. Certainly it was Congressional pressure in large part that insured efforts by executive agencies to protect the independent fabricators and to encourage new entrants into primary aluminum production.

The more intriguing role of Congress is in its direct pressure upon large firms. The independent fabricators were probably treated differently by primary producers as a result of Congressional interest. Similarly, there may be some connection between the ingot price reduction in the spring of 1958 and earlier Congressional questioning about why the price did not decline in a recession, for this may have demonstrated to Limited that it need not fear a tariff increase if it reduced prices. The repeated necessity of justifying other aspects of business policy in a Congressional forum probably changed to a substantial degree the practices of the primary producers.

Still, Congressional wisdom is dependent on the happenstance of the committee seniority system. Congressmen are perhaps more interested in the fate of particular competitors than in the process of competition. Congressional investigations are likely to contain as much political rhetoric as thoughtful inquiry, and the choice of subjects and the scope of investigation may be highly capricious. At times there may be an element of political blackmail of the large firms that violates the most elementary notions of equity and due process. Even so, to date, Congressional investigations of the aluminum industry appear to be on balance a positive element in regulating the exercise of market power. Whether they will be so in the future is, of course, problematical.

As imprecise and inconsistent as it is, such informal antitrust action may still be vastly superior to the rigidities of formal government regulation.

A Concluding Comment

This is to say that we have no satisfactory solution to the dilemma posed in Chapter I. The aluminum industry seems to be justly placed in that limbo category of industries in which antitrust action has reached diminishing returns, and yet the competition remains insufficient. The regulation of various practices, the action of various government agencies, and the pressures from Congress, though to date promising, may not be worth the political risks. Such an evaluation obviously depends on a judgment of the effectiveness of the various political processes.

The dilemma, however, may be artificially created by imposing an excessively high standard for the level of acceptable competition. If effective competition is defined as that prevailing in other highly concentrated industries in the American economy, such as automobiles and steel, then the aluminum industry no longer represents a public policy problem. Certainly this level of competition has the pragmatic justification that the economy of which it is an important part has created a unique standard of well-being. Consequently, the proper function of antitrust policy may be only to alter the most extreme situations of market power to conform to the general level of competition prevailing in a wider sector of the economy.

By this ultra-conservative standard, the various government efforts to promote competition in the aluminum industry are a success, for competition here seems as effective as in other oligopolistic industries. As to which is the valid position, one can only say it depends on a total view of society encompassing such issues as the relative evils of government and private power and the politically tolerable levels of protection for small business. Perhaps to insist upon more rigorous standards for competition is to overlook the achievements of current antitrust policy and to insist upon an unrealistic degree of perfectionism.

INDEX

INDEX

P
P
K   P
P

51
52
53

60
90